Cultures of Forgery

CultureWork
A book series from the Humanities Center
in the Faculty of Arts and Sciences at Harvard University
Marjorie Garber, editor
Rebecca L. Walkowitz, associate editor

Also published in the series:

Media Spectacles
Marjorie Garber, Jann Matlock,
and Rebecca L. Walkowitz, editors

Secret Agents
Marjorie Garber and Rebecca L. Walkowitz, editors

The Seductions of Biography
Mary Rhiel and David Suchoff, editors

Field Work
Marjorie Garber, Paul B. Franklin,
and Rebecca L. Walkowitz, editors

One Nation Under God?
Marjorie Garber and Rebecca L. Walkowitz, editors

The Turn to Ethics
Marjorie Garber, Beatrice Hanssen,
and Rebecca L. Walkowitz, editors

Historicism, Psychoanalysis and Early Modern Culture
Carla Mazzio and Douglas Trevor, editors

Cultures of Forgery
Making Nations, Making Selves

Edited by
**Judith Ryan
and Alfred Thomas**

ROUTLEDGE
NEW YORK AND LONDON

Published in 2003 by
Routledge
29 West 35th Street
New York, NY 10001
www.routledge-ny.com

Published in Great Britain by
Routledge
11 New Fetter Lane
London EC4P 4EE
www.routledge.co.uk

Printed in the United States of America on acid-free paper.

10 9 8 7 6 5 4 3 2 1

Library of Congress Cataloging-in-Publication Data

Cultures of forgery : making nations, making selves / edited by Judith
Ryan and Alfred Thomas.
    p. cm. — (Culture work)
Includes bibliographical references and index.
  ISBN 0-415-96831-3 (hard : alk. paper)—ISBN 0-415-96832-1 (pbk. :
alk. paper)
  1. Arts—Forgeries.   I. Ryan, Judith, 1943–   II. Thomas, Alfred, 1958–
III. Series.
  NX636.C85   2003
364.16'3—dc21

    2003004077

Contents

PART 2: Forging Selves

Figures

Preface

In Dante's vision of hell, "falsifiers" were relegated to the eighth circle, where they lay helplessly on the ground, afflicted with loathsome diseases. In early New South Wales, convicts who had served their time for forgery were given jobs in the colony's newly established banks. Today, forgery is still a crime, but in the public imagination there is also something appealing about what have been called the "great forgers." We are drawn in not just by the large amounts of money that are sometimes involved, but also by the sensational nature of the scandals exposed and the astonishing degree of skill that permits certain forgers to carry off their schemes successfully, at least for a time. Accounts of their exploits are among the great real-life adventure stories of the present day. This ambivalence about forgery is a telling symptom of modern culture.

A recent book by a curator at the Metropolitan Museum of Art, Oscar Muscarella (*The Lie Became Great: The Forgery of Ancient Near Eastern Cultures* [2000]), claims that the contemporary period is marked by a "culture of forgery." A combination of several factors has led to the forgery culture: the proliferation of individual collectors, ambitious scholars' desire to win fame by making an important discovery, and the extraordinary sums of money that art objects now command at auction. The public hungers less for the objects themselves, perhaps, than for the extravagant stories that surround their emergence and ultimate exposure. It is perennially amusing to hear of fakes that fool the experts, since we have always suspected that specialists are not what they have been cracked up to be. But just as we live in a "forgery culture," so it is also true that our culture is forged.

Conversations about the double meaning of the word "forge" initiated the project that has become this volume. We were struck by the number of instances in which the two meanings—to create or form, on the one hand, and to make falsely, on the other—are intertwined in the shaping of a nation, an individual, or an artifact. Indeed, the foundational legends of many cultures, the way they "forge" their identity, involve creating false narratives, objects, or documents. By the same token, many forgers, while creating false artifacts, also forge a persona for themselves that, however despicable, will not rapidly be forgotten. We were fascinated by the interplay of these two principles: the one suggesting creation from the ground up, as it were, and the other suggesting a parasitical fabrication through imitation. Were there more examples of this sort of interplay? It was time to forge ahead and get colleagues involved with the project.

This collection of essays does not lay any claim to system or completeness. Rather, it is intended as a set of case studies from a variety of humanities disciplines: literature, music, the fine arts, and film. Since forgery is often contrasted with originality, we knew we would find numerous examples between 1800—the initiation of the Romantic notion of original genius—and the present—dominated at once by a persistent belief in originality and a profound skepticism about this concept. But we also wanted to reach back into earlier periods, such as classical antiquity and the Middle Ages, to take a fresh look at the relation of forging and forgery in pre-modern times. We also wanted to work with very recent cases, in which the critical wisdom has not yet formed a consensus. Instead of revisiting the famous cases, such as Macpherson, Chatterton, van Meegeren, and so forth, we focus on lesser-known examples that may shed new light on the fundamental issues involved in forgery. In particular, we wanted to explore the ways in which different cultures—and culture itself—are shaped by a variety of fabricating practices that can be seen as false, to some degree or another.

The volume is divided into two parts that separate the essays into those that focus, on the one hand, on the forging of nations, communities, and histories, and on the other, on forgery of selves through works of creative art. Given our guiding vision, however, that forging and forgery are frequently engaged in a complicated sort of interplay and entanglement, the book's central divide should not be understood as in any sense a clean cut. Each of the essays teases the boundaries between the invention of foundational stories and the spurious creation of fictions. For certain essays, a good case could be made for shifting it over the line. This is precisely the point of the collection. We did not solicit the contributions with reference to the rubrics under which they now appear. Nor did we ask the authors to consider specific aspects of the forgery perplex, though we did encourage them to write on what they knew best. We were delighted to find that, quite unprompted by us, connections emerged among entries that promised, at first blush, to remain quite remote from one another. The idea behind the volume is not to propose a new, all-encompassing theory of forging and forgery, but to permit a set of deliberately differing perspectives to illuminate one another in unexpected ways.

The first section takes its starting point in the recognition that forging national identity inevitably involves an element of fabrication. The foundational myths of a given culture are often created in song, art objects, and sacred or legal documents, and the myths these works create call forth other cultural productions in their turn. The opening essay, by Derek Pearsall, argues for a new way of thinking about textual forgeries in medieval England, where a desire for a sense of national origins, a continuous historical record, and "proof" of the founding of abbeys and monasteries led to the creation of false documents whose purpose was to fill a patent gap.

The other essays in this section look at the ways cultures have attempted to consolidate their imagined identities through the fabrication of texts, images, and even works of architecture. The cultural and national communities they explore range from ancient Rome to the eighteenth- and nineteenth-century Bohemian Lands, nineteenth-century Russia, and twentieth-century Catalonia. Sarolta Takács shows the role played by the Sybilline Books, with their unauthenticated provenience and chequered history, in establishing a sense of community and continuity in early Rome. Alfred Thomas examines the Bohemian National Revival and its re-invention of older cultural myths in newly fabricated texts that had the ring of authenticity and provided the Bohemian Lands with the cultural pedigree they desired. Julie Buckler's study of the imitative, anachronistic, and partially phantasmatic city of St. Petersburg re-reads this apparent counterfeit as an attempt to create a meta-city that contains all cities and cultures within itself. Brad Epps reads Salvador Dalí's art as an attempt to forge a Catalan culture in which the national idea, still not a politically recognized reality, can achieve its apotheosis. In contrast to an artist like Antoní Tàpies, who takes the national idea very seriously, Dalí's ambivalent international fame inflects his ambivalent national function. Just as the international community has trouble deciding whether Dalí is a genius or a fraud, so the Catalans are uncertain whether to celebrate or shun his playful, ironic attitude toward Catalonian tradition.

The second section of the volume focuses largely on the artistic fabrication of individual selves through a set of case studies that also involve either forgery or imposture. To open this section, Reinhold Brinkmann's *rondo burlesco* takes us on a rollicking tour of different kinds of musical fraud and forgery. His contribution covers an entire range of possible deceptions—spurious composers, stolen compositions, forged manuscripts of lost pieces, practical jokes—resonating in provocative ways with essays that follow. Many of Brinkmann's examples, notably the breathtaking episode of the six lost Haydn symphonies, derive from the realm of German musical scholarship. Here, the reader will be amused to discover, all is not permeated with traditional Germanic seriousness.

The next two essays in this section return to the visual arts. Ewa Lajer-Burcharth studies the eighteenth-century Swiss painter Jean-Etienne Liotard, who took on a "Turkish" identity as a way not only of creating an exotic self, but also of exploring the relation between the foreign and the familiar. Adopting a flat technique that privileged the surface of his paintings, he appropriated aspects of Ottoman miniatures as a way of questioning the facile distinction between self and other, Western and Eastern forms of representation. John Malmstad's contribution studies the paradoxical nature of self-representation in the Russian avant-garde. Starting from the observation that the "self" in "self-portrait" is a fabrication of the self rather than its actuality, Malmstad shows how the Russian avant-garde painters diverged from the traditional genre of self-portraiture, demolishing the opposition between aesthete and athlete that had predominated in art of the preceding period. These paintings forge an image of the artist as a person who can determine even the shape of his body, as an athlete pumps iron to create muscle and body mass.

The last group of essays in this section looks at works concerned with the Third Reich and the Holocaust. Two examine books written by impostors, and one deals with an actual forged manuscript about a figure who in many respects was a media creation. Judith Ryan studies a novel about Ukrainian collaboration with Nazism written by a young woman who presented herself as a first-generation descendant of Ukrainian emigrants to Australia. Ryan situates the novel in the tradition of literary hoaxes, showing how it enacts the theoretical tenet postulated by Roland Barthes that biographical facts about the author of a work are irrelevant to the reader's understanding of it. In so doing, she opens a number of contemporary beliefs about the relation between author and text to critical inquiry. Susan Suleiman casts her net more broadly, inquiring into problems of memoir-writing in the present day. At the center of her essay is Benjamin Wilkomirski's *Fragments*, a text that purported to be the memoir of a man who had survived the Nazi death camps during his childhood and subsequently been adopted into a Swiss family. Ultimately, Wilkomirski's status as a Holocaust survivor was questioned and his book exposed as a purely imaginative exercise by a writer with no first-hand experience of concentration camps at all. In contradistinction to those who regard this imposture as an offense against the memory of real survivors, Suleiman argues that *Fragments*, if regarded as a novel, can be seen as an attempt to get inside the consciousness of the victim and present the emotional devastation of the Holocaust from within the experiencing subject. Eric Rentschler, finally, recounts the story of the forged Hitler diaries and analyzes Helmut Dietl's film *Schtonk*, a satiric comedy of errors that narrates the afterlife of Hitler in modern consumer society, with its constant demand for Nazi artifacts. What is it about Hitler, he asks, that makes him such a sought-after figure more than fifty years after his death?

Unlike some other books on forgery, this volume does not play to the "romance of fraud" or the "pleasures of deception." Instead, it probes the difficult issues raised by today's more complex understanding of the relationship between fact and fiction. Above all, it asks questions about the position of forgery and fraudulence in cultural tradition. What purpose do these forms serve? On one level, forgeries can be seen as foils to original artifacts, helping us—at least in those cases where the distinction is visible on the surface of the work itself—to identify more clearly what it is we value in works we think of as authentic masterpieces. At the same time, forgeries alert us to changes taking place in cultural systems. What is indistinguishable from the original today frequently becomes quite blatantly dated—and thus exposed as a forgery—a generation or two later. The subtitle of Sándor Radnóti's book, *The Fake* (1999) is fittingly formulated as "Forgery and its Place in Art." The problem we confront consists not so much in identifying and exposing frauds and forgeries as understanding the function they fulfill for the cultural systems in which they emerge. Studying fraudulent cultural artifacts helps us perceive the limitations imposed by our own embeddedness in a particular cultural moment.

On another level, forgeries put our conceptions of scholarly expertise to the severest of tests, posing large questions about the nature of specialized knowledge and aesthetic discrimination as inculcated in contemporary cultural institutions. As K. K. Ruthven notes in *Faking Literature* (2001), "literary forgery is criticism by other means" (p. 171): In effect, it attacks those critics who claim to be able to identify originality and authenticity in literary texts, and unsettles our confidence in the ability of scholars to detect falsifications. Given these subversive aspects of literary forgery, Ruthven urges us to "start thinking more positively" (p. 3) about such texts, understanding them as part of our culture's reappraisal of our understanding of literature. Ruthven's argument, though couched in terms of literature, applies equally well to other forms of cultural production. Does this mean that we should cease to be outraged when we uncover yet another fake Rembrandt or forged Shakespearean drama? Not necessarily.

What it does mean, however, is that we need to use such occasions to reexamine the categories we use to evaluate creative works and remain alert to the sway exerted by contemporary interests and fashions.

Clusters of forgeries in a specific period can be seen as symptoms of a transition in which familiar categories of judgment are increasingly put into question. When we discover that ancient Rome or medieval England depended on fabricating a spurious past in order to establish a basis for cultural identity, we tend to think of them as remote from our own world and dependent on primitive ideas of truth. Yet their construction of a desired history is not essentially different from the spate of cultural fabrications that took place in the nineteenth century. Today, a new flurry of forgeries and impostures seems to strike at the heart of long-held values and traditions. Responding to our desire for authenticity by mirroring what we currently regard as the authentic, these recent acts of fraudulence in effect take the temperature of the contemporary world. If all culture is in some sense created by reinventing the past in order to resituate the present, what is the special nature of today's "forgery culture"? Probing acts of fraudulence at a wide range of historical moments, the case studies that follow are intended to help sharpen our understanding of the cultural functions of forgery.

Acknowledgments

The editors would like to express their gratitude to the Humanities Center of Harvard University for its generous sponsorship of a conference at which many of the contributions to this book were first tested in intellectual debate. We would like to give special thanks to Marjorie Garber, for her support and encouragement of the project, as well as to Aviva Briefel and Mary Halpenny-Killip, for their able administration of the conference. William Germano kindly encouraged us to collect these essays and provided significant impulses that helped give the volume its present shape. We are also grateful to Tenessa Gemelke, Mark Henderson, Richard Rothschild, and Lisa Vecchione for their able guidance of the volume through the production process. Alexandra Kirulcuk helped check several chapters of the copyedited manuscript, and Lawrence A. Joseph provided assistance with proofreading. Serena Vergano and Carme Fernandez-Mera Carcares stepped in at a critical juncture and enabled us to acquire images without which this book would have been sadly incomplete. We are grateful, finally, to the Simon Wiesenthal Annual for permission to reprint an essay by Susan Rubin Suleiman.

PART 1

Forging Nations

CHAPTER 1

Forging Truth in
Medieval England

DEREK PEARSALL

Evidence surrounding inauthentic documents and texts of the Middle Ages suggests a somewhat more flexible attitude toward truth, fiction, and falsehood than seems to be present in the common understanding of the modern English word "forgery." A symptom of this shift is the more recent word "fake," which first appeared (as a verb) in London underworld slang of the early nineteenth century with a range of meanings centering on "to 'do up,' for purposes of deception." "Forge," by contrast, was well established as a verb in English (from Old French *forgier*) from the mid-fourteenth century, both in its general sense, "to make or manufacture," and, in relation to stories, "to compose or fabricate."[1] It soon acquired, by the constant association of the composition of stories with the invention of falsehoods, a pejorative meaning in itself, and by the early fifteenth century, with the massive increase in the quantity of written legal instruments, it had come to have a specialized meaning referring to the counterfeiting of legal documents with intent to deceive and for purposes of gain. Here are two examples:[2]

> Which lettre, obligacion and sele were nevere made ne selyd by the same knyght but falsly contrefetid and forged by this same man that here stant. (1418)

> (They) havyn ymagened and by ther conspiracy forgyd oon obligacioun of a c mark in the name of the seide Thomas. (1439)

This is not of course to say that forgery was "invented" in England in the early fifteenth century, though it is true that the first civil remedy against forgery was given in a statute in the reign of Henry V.[3] The absence of a word does not prove that the practice or way of thinking to which it refers did not exist. Without entering into a rehearsal of a familiar linguistic-philosophical debate, one could point to the simple fact that in England there were two other languages available (Latin and Anglo-Norman French) with a more sophisticated range of vocabularies, including vocabularies of nefariousness, for which ample use had long been found in the condemnation of both documentary forgery and non-documentary forgery (of seals, coins, and relics, for instance). Nor is it necessary to argue that medieval people had a fundamentally different view of the relation between truth and falsehood from that commonly assumed to be held by people now. The argument here, more pragmatically, is that there is evidence from the Middle Ages, in relation to particular cases of what we would bluntly call "forgery," of a larger spectrum of possible views on that relationship (between truth and falsehood), in which fiction (making things up), distinct from lying (making things up that are known or thought by the speaker to be untrue), performed a mediating role between the frowning opposites.

My own particular interest in the matter began four years ago. In a chapter on "Language and Literature" that I contributed to the *Oxford Illustrated History of Medieval England*, edited by the historian Nigel Saul, I had been discussing the transition from Old English to Middle English and making the point that Old English in the eleventh century had established an extraordinary dominance in the writing down of texts and documents—in history, law, religion, and politics—that everywhere else in Europe were written down in Latin. But soon after the Conquest of 1066, Latin took over from Old English in these areas—most dramatically in the use of Latin for the exhaustive survey of English landholdings in the *Domesday Book* ("the book of the day of assessments") of 1086. I had used as an illustration (it was after all the Oxford *Illustrated History*) a photograph of a British Library charter with the great seal of William I, a confirmation in Latin of a grant of land to the Benedictine Abbey of St. Mary in Coventry made in about 1070. Only a few years after the Conquest, as the charter showed, Old English was giving way to Latin as the language of such legal instruments.

The book was published in 1997, and that was the end of the matter, as far as I was concerned, until the second edition of the *History* was being prepared two years later, when Professor Saul rang me up in some consternation to say that Professor J. C. Holt, the former Regius Professor of History at Cambridge, had written to tell him that the charter I had used in my illustration was a forgery and dated from no earlier than the first half of the twelfth century. What was I going to do about this? I found it difficult to work up any equivalent consternation: forty or fifty years doesn't seem such a long time to a literary scholar as it does to a historian, and I was not prepared to go digging around for more charters which might easily turn out to be forgeries too. So I suggested to Professor Saul that he might add a note to the picture-caption in the second edition to the effect that the charter was a forgery and demonstrated the skill with which monastic forgers were attentive to the linguistic shift I had spoken about in their desire to supplement the gap in their records.

As I thought about it afterward, it seemed to me that the answer I had arrived at as part of the general economy of effort (or, as one might say, through sheer idleness) had actually a lot to be said for it. This was not forgery in our sense, but the supply of a lack in the body of truth.

There is no doubt that in the twelfth century monks in major houses like Westminster, Canterbury and Winchester forged legal documents on a large scale. Half the extant charters drawn up in the name of Edward the Confessor date from after the Conquest.[4] Were their moral standards just very low? It does not appear so. It is clear that the monk-forgers thought that to fabricate charters on behalf of their house was a vindication of truth and justice. A forged charter is indeed sometimes no more than a repetition, from memory or tradition, of a genuine document lost or destroyed. Such charters usually claim privileges which had a consequence—rights to land, rights to exemption from episcopal visitation—but they rarely claim lands or rights which had never been granted. To edit history in this way was not perceived as a criminal act if the end were just and good. Such artificers of the word knew the difference between truth and falsehood but were less irritably exercised than we are about the difference between fact and "truthful fiction." They were more fully aware than we are, perhaps, that truth is a cultural artifact, or at least that a truth that is under the guarantee of a higher Truth does not have to answer petty questions about authenticity. If it was good that something be true, people believed it *was* true. "By this standard," as Giles Constable says in his careful and detailed discussion of the subject, "a forgery designed to promote truth and justice would not be considered a forgery, in the pejorative sense, at all."[5]

Written documents recording the lands and privileges granted to a monastery became a bureaucratic necessity in the developing documentary culture of the twelfth and thirteenth centuries and were produced, retrospectively, on a large scale throughout Europe. Of the eight earliest charters of the great imperial abbey of Reichenau on Lake Constance, seven are forged. They were done about 1150 by Odalrich the sacristan of the abbey, who also did many for other local abbeys. The charters laid claim, correctly, to an older foundation so that the abbeys would not be open to criticism from the newer reforming monasteries of the Cluniac persuasion.[6] In just the same way, English monasteries forged charters to prove in writing that their foundation went back to times before abbeys became subject to episcopal visitation. To settle a long-running visitation dispute between Evesham Abbey and the Bishop of Worcester, Thomas of Marlborough, Abbot of Evesham (1229–36), produced before the Roman curia papal bulls in the name of Pope Constantine I (708–15) granting exemption to Evesham. The bulls were put in the hands of Pope Innocent III who, after briefly handling them, pronounced them genuine.[7] They were undoubtedly "forgeries," though the claim they were brought forward to support was not in its essentials untrue.

Chertsey Abbey in Surrey had a whole series of thirteenth-century charters professedly dating from the seventh century, not necessarily inaccurate in the information they contain, but certainly "forgeries." They were probably first written down in the 1080s to prepare for the *Domesday Book*, and then re-edited in the thirteenth century.[8] Even the most cursory examination by a scholar trained in techniques of historical analysis would reveal the documents to be forgeries. They tend, for instance, to get the most obvious things wrong. The abbey is referred to as having been founded in 666 by Egbert, King of England, who reigned more than a century later. The putative founder was actually Egbert, King of Kent, but he was a much less famous person than his later namesake. Unexpected names appear: A boundary list for a charter has the name Sir Giffreus de la Croix, unlikely, to say the least, in the seventh century, but very likely and indeed actually the name of a real person in the thirteenth.[9] Yet "forgery," as Clanchy says, seems an inappropriate term to describe the attempts of an abbey to renew evidence in writing of titles to lands and rights long accepted in custom, practice, and oral memory.[10] The case here seems more than usually persuasive, since Chertsey Abbey had indeed been twice burnt down by the Danes (in 871 and 1010) and had lost whatever records it may have had.

Sometimes, the monastic document-maker, not content with manufacturing a plausible substitute for what had been lost or never written down, would construct richly imaginative narratives of recovery. One of these is reported by Matthew Paris, the famous thirteenth-century monk-historian of St. Albans. Sometime in the early eleventh century, it is alleged, while workmen were demolishing a building, they found a sixth-century cache of ancient books and rolls hidden in a cavity in the walls of the Roman foundations beneath the abbey. Most of the books were invocations to pagan deities such as Phoebus and Mercury, but one concerned the life of St. Albans and gave an account of the foundation of the abbey. It was hurriedly translated from the ancient British language into Latin by an old priest named Unwona (the Anglo-Saxon name means, appropriately enough, "strange" or "unusual"), whereupon the original exemplar "was suddenly and irretrievably reduced to dust and collapsed annihilated."[11] This, it must be admitted, is so much better than, "It got lost," or, "We just can't find it any more."

But of course there was a distinction, which the monastic artificers were well aware of, between "invented" truth and forgery, between the supplying of defects in the record and the manipulation of documents for personal profit. The latter practice, more unambiguously recognizable as forgery in the modern sense, became more common as the use of legal documents became more widespread. In 1469 an Irish clerk had papal letters forged by which he laid claim to the Cistercian Abbey of Kilshanny. He proceeded to add further support to the authenticity of his claim by persuading a local lord to take a band of armed men to the abbey, where they ransacked the buildings, killed one of the monastic servants, and beat up poor abbot Cormac Ykahyr.[12]

Richard Firth Green tells a story of a disputed inheritance in 1432 when a man called John Lydeyard claimed that a property held by Thomas Seyntcler was really his by right of inheritance from his wife.[13] Seyntcler knew that a document proving his claim drawn up in 1353 and bequeathing the property to his ancestor Peter St. John was in the Tower of London, but suspected that Lydeyard might try to tamper with it. His suspicions were well founded: Lydeyard bribed an exchequer clerk, William Broket, to get hold of the document and make some little alterations. Seyntcler's lawyer uncovered the forgery and the case collapsed. All that the clerk did, as he revealed in his confession, was that with his fingernail he erased the number XL and with fresh ink wrote again the said number and blotted it (*renovavit et blottavit*) so that at that point the document might appear especially suspect. The number was the age of Peter St. John at the time of the 1353 bequest and for there to be a question hanging over age and fitness to inherit would have severely compromised Seyntcler's defense. The record reveals how forgery was clearly understood to be forgery at this time—though there seems to be also some residual hesitation about the deliberate falsifying of official documents for personal advantage. As we see, Broket didn't actually change anything. Forgery of this kind was still a specially heinous crime, for the forger did not just alter legal texts, did not just betray the relationship between words and things, but the relationship between men that was secured in words as it was secured in an oath.[14]

The supply of defects in the record takes other forms, all simplified and degraded as forgery in modern structures of thinking. Archbishop Matthew Parker, a great collector of Anglo-Saxon manuscripts and benefactor of Corpus Christi College in Cambridge, kept skilled amanuenses in his household whom he employed to supply—whether from other manuscripts or from invention—any deficiencies or lacunae that were discovered in the old manuscripts he had collected. They did this so skillfully that they sometimes deceived the great codicologist and bibliographer M. R. James. Sometimes the act of repair is acknowledged: of a portion of text missing from Aelfric's *Colloquy*, it is said, "illam eleganter suppleri jussit reverendissimus Mattheus Parker."[15]

Medieval hagiographers also used invention on a large scale to supplement the gaps in the record. Again, "forgery" does not seem the right word to describe what they did. Writing the lives of the early saints was a problem. Often they had never existed, and even where they had existed there was no record of their lives. But since the function of the life of a saint is to bear witness to the truth of faith in God, it could be said that in some sense their lives are always already known even if they never lived them. A picture could provide the necessary inspiration, a picture of a generic saint, that is, like the members of the early house of Stuart whose generic portraits fill the gallery at Holyrood House. As the ninth-century compiler of saints' lives, Agnellus of Ravenna, explains:

> Where I could not uncover a story or determine what sort of life they led . . . I have, with the assistance of God through your prayers, made up a life for them. And I believe no deception is involved, for they were chaste and almsgiving preachers and procurers of men's souls for God. And if any among you should wonder how I was able to create the likeness I have drawn, you should know that a picture taught me.[16]

Such a writer was not unaware of the difference between truth and falsehood, as he makes clear when he defends himself against the charge of "deception." But to him the Truth was not the same as the truth, if the latter is used to mean historical accuracy, or correspondence to the observed facts of reality—a meaning that did not fully disentangle itself until the later fourteenth century from the older meaning of truth as that which is personally guaranteed by word or oath or ordeal and that is ultimately underwritten by God.[17] In the interests of this kind of Truth, fiction and invention are not falsehood. As Reginald of Canterbury explains in the Preface to his Latin verse *Life of St. Malchus* (c.1100):

> Malchus, whom it is sinful to believe was not just, holy, and beloved of the Lord, was filled with the spirit of all the just, so that however many miracles we may ascribe to Malchus personally, we will not have deviated from the truth. In addition, we do not deny that we have invented many things, as is the custom of versifiers. But those who wish that we credit their fictions will give credit to ours, and God will credit both ours and theirs.[18]

Such statements had the backing of Augustine, who recognized that a legend or fiction referring to a true meaning was not a lie but a way of presenting the truth.[19]

The invention of stories to fill spaces where they are needed is an important activity, and not confined to the Middle Ages, though there are changes in the kinds of need that are supplied. I suppose we are pleased nowadays that doctors are not inventing too many stories of the Galenic kind to fill in the spaces in their knowledge of the working of the human body, though maybe they invent some. The great makers-up of stories to fill spaces in our age are of course the astronomers, whose fantasies of big bangs, exploding universes and black holes fill spaces literally and have somewhat the same ontological status as Agnellus of Ravenna's saints. These are the stories that we need, where they needed those.

One last example: Geoffrey of Monmouth's *Historia regum Britanniae* (1135) is one of the most important books ever written, the origin of most of the Arthurian story. It is an almost complete fabrication: in modern terms, forgery on a grand scale. It supplies the lack of a foundation history for the British nation by tracing its origin to the Brutus who left Troy, founded Britain and gave it his name. The *Historia* supplies a long lineage of British kings to succeed Brutus, culminating in Arthur, the once and future king who never was. It was a story that was needed by the emergent Anglo-Norman aristocracy in England. Geoffrey had before him the model of monastic invention—documents drawn up long after the date to which they refer and relating to estates which the monastery had held undisputed for generations but which were now being eyed enviously by secular lords. Geoffrey alleges that he derived the new parts of his work, the stories so far untold, from "quendam Britannici sermonis librum vetustissimum," owned by his friend Walter, archdeacon of Oxford, and originating in Brittany (which would conveniently explain why no one in England had come across it before).[20] The book had unfortunately disappeared since he had used it.

The "very ancient book in the British language" most probably never existed, but it is unlikely that Geoffrey's purpose was to practice upon the gullibility of his audience and patrons, or to share a joke with them about the gullibility of others, or to induce a whimsical and amused complicity such as later authors might indulge when they constructed elaborate framing narratives of pseudo-authentication, like Umberto Eco in *The Name of the Rose*. What Geoffrey was chiefly doing was to secure authority and credit for his version of the history that needed to be written by claiming for it a lost and venerable antiquity. He was supplying the written record of the British history that had been lost.

His claims are similar to and may indeed owe something to those made by the two early Latin prose writers through whom the story of Troy came down to the Middle Ages.[21] The first (writing in the fourth century A.D.) claimed in the *Ephemeridos belli Troiani* to be translating into Latin the diaries and journals kept by one Dictys Cretensis. Dictys was a Cretan who bore arms on the Greek side at the siege of Troy and, like a good soldier, kept a journal, in Phoenician characters. The journal was buried with him in a tin trunk and lay there until exposed by an earthquake in the thirteenth year of the Emperor Nero. The manuscript was carried to Rome and translated on the orders of Nero as the *Ephemeridos*. Since Rome claimed descent from the Trojans (as, later on, did most of the peoples of Western Europe), Dictys labored under some disadvantage in being a Greek. Fortunately, inside the walls of the beleaguered city was Dares Phrygius, who gave a day-to-day account of the war from the Trojan point of view which was translated as the *De excidio Troiae historia* and attributed by its sixth-century translator to Cornelius Nepos (d. 24 BC). Dares was naturally much more to be relied upon, and his version of events was generally preferred to that of his predecessor.

Both of these works are commonly called 'forgeries,' but again the word is not appropriate. The writers are not practicing a deception the uncovering of which would undo them, for there are no facts to set against their stories. They work with the material they have, which may have been not insubstantial, and in a plain and circumstantial style simply fill out the narrative with the details of the battles fought, soldiers killed and truces signed that have unfortunately been lost in the passage of time. Like Geoffrey, they supply the gaps in the historical record and, in the absence of information, provide it.

Geoffrey may have derived some of his material from written sources now lost or from oral sources, and Archdeacon Walter may have played a part in providing him with materials. But it is difficult to take any longer a very keen interest in the question of Geoffrey's veracity as a historian. Some of what he said may be true; some is not true; some could conceivably be true. He did not expect that everything he said should be believed as literally true, nor did he expect that everything he said should be dismissed as false. It is a not unsophisticated understanding of the reality of the past that acknowledges its unknowability except in the terms that are provided by the writer of history. There is another way of looking at the matter, too. The most objective form of historical enquiry we have for the more distant past is that of the archaeologist: From that form of enquiry we shall accumulate large numbers of incontrovertibly true facts concerning the contents of the stomachs of people who lived thousands of years ago. From Geoffrey of Monmouth, on the other hand—a wealth of fine fabling and an inspiration for generations of storytellers.

It is disappointing, therefore, to find a cultural historian as good as A. B. Ferguson, in his recent book *Utter Antiquity*, reading the Middle Ages and Renaissance against an old-fashioned evolutionary paradigm of fact/truth triumphing over fiction/falsehood.[22] He gives an account of changes in sixteenth and seventeenth-century views of classical and British history as writers who were no longer content with the fabled past shuttled between belief and skepticism. For him the story is of how the Renaissance gradually freed itself from the ambivalence with which it viewed the traditional stories of the past even when a new critical spirit of historical analysis was emerging. "Renaissance minds," he says, "were notoriously capable of thinking on apparently divergent lines with no sense of incongruity." Ferguson is mildly surprised by such shilly-shallying ("To modern eyes, the distinction between fact and fiction appears obvious"), and he speaks of the Renaissance as an age "plagued by ambivalence," when even "select minds" like Bacon's could fall into the belief that there was wisdom in the ancient fables. Ferguson sees Renaissance scholars growing fitfully to the understanding of a "primitive mentality" among early people, evidenced in their contemporary experience in the record and observation of the American Indians, but he himself clearly sees those scholars as part of the same progressivist narrative of evolution, part of the later childhood of the race. Their ambivalence, their confusion between belief and half-belief, is compared to that of a child, their "threshold of credulity" so low as to make the "American aborigines seem, by contrast, only a bit eccentric."[23]

It might be that we could do without "the Renaissance mind" as well as "the medieval mind," especially as singular categories in a narrative of progressive cultural evolution. The term "ambivalence" is certainly due for a rest, suggesting as it does a suspension between two definable forms of "valence" to which the will might attach itself. What we need is something like "recognition of the impossibility of deciding," or "non-recognition of any need to decide," perhaps construed not as an intellectual defeat but as an achievement, the capacity to hold on to one's lack of certainty. Some of the ambivalences that the "modern mind" finds so frustrating can be explained perfectly simply. Spenser, we are told, failed to reconcile "poetic history and history proper," but almost immediately it is added, "He treated the same material very differently, according to whether his own purpose was primarily poetical or historical."[24] Isn't this what any sensible person, unaware of his part in the unfolding drama of intellectual progress, would do?

Triumphalist accounts of history, and of the emergence of a new Baconian spirit of critical and historical understanding which freed people from the traditional stories of the past and enabled them to see clearly the difference between fact and fiction, are themselves uncritical. The belief-systems of the past do not crack up and collapse because they have been subjected to the searching scrutiny of superior minds: They go away because they no longer serve their original purpose. The idea of forgery is a serious need in a belief-system predicated upon a clear-cut distinction between what is factually true and what is not; in the Middle Ages it was not so important.

Notes

1. See *Oxford English Dictionary*, s.v. imposture, sb.; fake, v.; forge, v. (the earliest date recorded for 'forgery' is 1574).

2. These examples are from the *Middle English Dictionary*, ed. Hans Kurath and Sherman M. Kuhn (Ann Arbor: University of Michigan Press, 1952–), s.v. forgen, v. The first example is from one of the London Letter Books (annual summaries of court proceedings) and the second from records of proceedings in the Court of Chancery. The influence on society, culture, and language of the increase in writing, literacy, and written instruments during the Middle Ages is exceptionally well documented in books by M. T. Clanchy, *From Memory to Written Record, England 1066–1307* (London: Edward Arnold, 1979; 2nd edn, Oxford: Blackwell, 1993, with many important additions—this is the edition used here), and Richard Firth Green, *A Crisis of Truth: Literature and Law in Ricardian England* (Philadelphia: University of Pennsylvania Press, 1999).

3. See T. F. Tout, 'Mediaeval Forgers and Forgeries,' *Bulletin of the John Rylands Library* (Manchester), 5 (1918–20), 208–34 (p. 212).

4. See Green, *A Crisis of Truth*, p. 37; Clanchy, *From Memory to Written Record* (2nd edn), pp. 148–9, 318–27. Clanchy's general argument is that stricter definitions of forgery and stricter distinctions between 'genuine' and 'forged' documents became necessary as written records replaced oral testimony more and more.

5. Giles Constable, 'Forgery and Plagiarism in the Middle Ages,' *Archiv für Diplomatik*, 29 (1983), 1–41 (p. 26). See also Christopher N. L. Brooke, 'Approaches to Medieval Forgery,' a lecture (1967) reprinted in his *Medieval Church and Society: Collected Essays* (London: Sidgwick and Jackson, 1971).

6. See G. G. Coulton, *Five Centuries of Religion*, 4 vols. (Cambridge: Cambridge University Press, 1923–50), Vol. III, pp. 310–12.

7. Clanchy, *From Memory to Written Record*, pp. 324–5.

8. H. E. Malden, 'The Possession of Cardigan Priory by Chertsey Abbey (A Study in some Mediaeval Forgeries),' *Transactions of the Royal Historical Society*, Third Series, 5 (1911), 141–56.

9. For other examples of this kind of unwitting anachronism, see Tout's account of the Crowland Chronicle of the pseudo-Ingulf, a late fourteenth-century narrative, with fictitious charters, of the foundation and history of Crowland Abbey, in 'Mediaeval Forgers and Forgeries,' pp. 224–5.

10. Clanchy, *From Memory to Written Record*, p. 322.

11. Clanchy, *From Memory to Written Record*, p. 149.

12. See G. G. Coulton, *Five Centuries of Religion*, Vol. III, p. 440.

13. Green, *A Crisis of Truth*, pp. 248–9.

14. Brian Stock, *The Implications of Literacy: Written Language and Models of Interpretation in the Eleventh and Twelfth Centuries* (Princeton: Princeton University Press, 1983), p. 60.

15. Montague Rhodes James, *A Descriptive Catalogue of the Manuscripts in the Library of Corpus Christi College, Cambridge*, 2 vols. (Cambridge: Cambridge University Press, 1912), No. 449 (Vol. II, p. 363). I owe this reference to Martha Driver.

16. Agnellus of Ravenna, *Liber pontificalis ecclesiae Ravennae*, cited and translated by Charles Jones, *Saints' Lives and Chronicles in Early England* (Ithaca, New York: Cornell University Press, 1947), p. 63.

17. The history of the developing distinction between these two kinds of truth, and the eventual triumph of 'objective truth,' is the theme of Richard Firth Green's book, *A Crisis of Truth*. See also Constable, 'Forgery and Plagiarism,' pp. 4–6, 23–6.
18. Reginald of Canterbury, *Vita S.Malchi*, cited and translated by James W. Earl, 'The Typological Structure of Andreas,' in John D. Niles (ed.), *Old English Literature in Context: Ten Essays* (Cambridge: D. S. Brewer; Totowa, New Jersey: Rowman and Littlefield, 1980), pp. 66–89 (p.70).
19. See Constable, 'Forgery and Plagiarism,' p. 4, n. 14.
20. See J. S. P. Tatlock, *The Legendary History of Britain: Geoffrey of Monmouth's Historia regum Britanniae and its Early Vernacular Versions* (Berkeley and Los Angeles: University of California Press, 1950), pp. 422–5.
21. For a brief account of the early history of the Trojan story, with further references, see C. David Benson, *The History of Troy in Middle English Literature* (Woodbridge: D. S. Brewer; Totowa, New Jersey: Rowman and Littlefield, 1980), pp. 1–12.
22. Arthur B. Ferguson, *Utter Antiquity: Perceptions of Prehistory in Renaissance England*, Duke Monographs in Medieval and Renaissance Studies 13 (Durham, North Carolina: Duke University Press, 1993).
23. References in this paragraph are, successively, to Ferguson, *Utter Antiquity*, pp. 70, 114, 136, 140, 66, 78–9, 2, 6.
24. Ferguson, *Utter Antiquity*, p. 124.

CHAPTER 2

Forging a Past

The Sibylline Books and the Making of Rome*

SAROLTA A. TAKÁCS

The tapestry of Rome's foundation is intricately woven: There is a consciously produced coherence so that one pattern glides smoothly into the next and forced seams are visible only on close examination. There is the mythological Romulean foundation of 753 BCE, the gaining of an active poetic voice as a result of two Carthaginian Wars (264–241 BCE and 218–201 BCE), and Augustus' reshaping of Rome and its empire (31 BCE–14 CE). The senator Quintus Fabius Pictor, who participated in the Second Punic War, was the first Roman to record the history of Rome from the Trojan Aeneas' coming to Italy until the time of Rome's wars with Carthage. Pictor wrote in Greek.[1] The connection with Troy gave Rome a claim to a heroic foundation based within a Greek cultural context. Besides Trojan ancestry that generations later resulted in the birth of Romulus and Remus, Rome's foundation stories also include prophecies.

Since the time of the dictator Sulla (88–79 BCE), the Sibylline Books consisted of Greek sayings and were understood in the context of Rome's Greek cultural heritage. However, there was also an Etruscan component that disappeared from the historical record. These Books of mixed heritage played an important part in the making of Rome, in particular, its religious

*My sincere thanks go to the two conference organizers and editors of this volume, Judith Ryan and Alfred Thomas. I am also grateful to Maureen McGeary for her editorial suggestions.

formation. The first part of this paper will deal with the Greek aspect. The second part will focus on literary sources that, in my opinion, reveal some of the obscured Etruscan heritage.

Although the history of the Sibylline Books is obscure and the Books themselves were hardly authentic, they played a crucial role in the legitimation of religious innovations and the formation of Roman religion. The Roman Senate ordered the consultation of these books during political crises in order to find alleviation for predicaments that its society confronted. In general, a political crisis was linked to a religious failing that warranted remedy so that Rome could continue to prosper. In Roman thinking, politics and religion were intertwined. Even the most skeptical Roman knew and acted within the understanding that religious *disciplina* (discipline) was crucial for the *salus publica* (well-being of the state) and that *religio* (religious practice) could provide it. The underlying mythological, albeit actual, belief was that Rome was founded by *auspicio augurioque* (by auspices and augury), which generated a contract between Rome and the gods, above all Jupiter, and that binary reciprocal mechanisms were at work. Thus, the relationship between the divine and the human sphere (the Roman senate and the Roman people [*senatus populusque Romanus*]) was defined. Society, the web of human interactions and interrelations, is a nonmaterial component of culture. "Religion legitimates social institutions by bestowing upon them ultimately valid ontological status, that is, by locating them within a sacred and cosmic frame of reference."[2] Religious rituals remind society of its ontological definition and legitimation. They also link the changing present with a constant, that is, the timeless sacred and cosmic frame of reference.

Rome's historical tradition has been termed a "confused mass of truth and fiction, of legend and patriotic invention."[3] Literary sources, above all the works of Livy (59 BCE—17 CE) and Dionysius of Halicarnassus (in Rome 30—8 BCE), provide us with the most detailed information of Rome's early history. Both authors relied on earlier authors whose writings are more or less lost to us. Archaeological discoveries, especially since the 1960s, have shed light on the development of small village communities in Latium from the neolithic to the archaic period. These villages had "a subsistence economy based on the cultivation of primitive cereals and legumes, supplemented by stock-raising."[4] However, the settlements' character changed in the mid-seventh century BCE. Monumental chamber tombs, public market places (*fora*) and stone houses with tiled roofs were built. Aristocrats began to display their wealth and prestige by building permanent structures. Rome, an aggregate of small hilltop villages, became urbanized.

The city-state began to exercise political control over Latium and eventually, by the first part of the third century BCE, over the whole Italian peninsula. Rome's expansion beyond Latium brought it ultimately in contact with Greek colonies in the south (*Magna Graecia*). Greek historians, consequently, began to investigate the origins of this new power. Hellanicus of Lesbos and Damastes of Sigeum, at the end of the fifth century BCE, were the first of these historians to refer to Aeneas as the founder of Rome. Their focus was on the Homeric hero and not on the city. By the fourth century BCE, that focus had changed. It was the city now that commanded interest. Timaeus of Tauromenium and Hieronymus of Cardia were the first Greek writers to stress the importance of Rome and describe the origins of the city to their audience. The first Roman historians, in turn, would use these writers as their sources. Consequently, Rome's foundation legend was one of indigenous and Greek layering. The Trojan Aeneas became the ancestor of Romulus and Remus. Even before the Trojans' arrival, Heracles and the Arcadian Evander made their way to the region which would become Rome. By the time of Augustus, the traditional narrative that explained the city's foundation had been fashioned into a chronologically coherent account. What is more, the premier poet of the Augustan age, Vergil, would point out that Aeneas' ancestor, Dardanus, had come from Italy before settling in Troy. Hence, Aeneas and his descendants were simultaneously strangers and ancestral natives to Italy.[5]

The Sibylline Books present a duality as well. They were connected to Rome's assimilated Greek cultural past but underneath all the molding, forging, and layering hid an indigenous aspect. A college (*collegium*) of two (*duumviri*), ten (*decemviri*) and then fifteen men (*quindecimviri*) were in charge of the Sibylline Books and the ceremonies prescribed in them (*sacris faciundis*). While their title referred to religious ceremonies (*sacra*), it did not include the Sibylline Books (*libri Sibyllini*). This group consulted the books only after an official request from the Senate. Plague, famine, or prodigy was most often the impetus for a consultation. All three occasions indicated political discord, and in Roman terms, the human sphere was not in order. As a result, the reciprocal relationship between humans and gods (*pax deorum hominumque* [the peace among gods and humans]) was no longer functioning properly. Romans were a most religious people; augury and auspices founded their city, and its success depended on the proper and timely performance of religious rituals. No Roman ever dared to stop performing the state ordained rituals. He was vested in the system, which, in turn, relied on him; the dialectic was inescapable. On account of this, the remedies the Sibylline Books ordered were religious in nature.

Women who were "with gods" (*entheoi*) and spoke prophecies were called Sibyls. According to the chronological list of the first century BCE antiquarian Varro, there were ten Sibyls. The first and oldest one was the Persian; the youngest, the Tiburtine Sibyl.[6] Persia, forever the nemesis of Greco-Roman city-states, features prominently throughout ancient sources as the accepted source of millennia-old traditions linked to astrology and astronomy. The most prominent oracular shrine was that of Apollo at Delphi. Whenever a Greek city established a colony abroad, an embassy was sent to Delphi to incur the god's support. It does not come as a surprise, then, that Rome's foundation was also linked to prophetic sayings and Apollo. In Lycophron's poem *Alexandra*, Cassandra prophesies the coming of a new Troy, Rome. Cassandra, a daughter of Priam, Troy's last ruler, had refused Apollo's advances. The god's punishment for her refusal was that no one could understand the meaning of Cassandra's prophetic utterance. In the *Alexandra*, the Trojan princess recalls the "memory of ancient oracles" and proclaims that "Trojans must wander till they were forced to eat their tables" and would "found their city where they encountered a white sow with thirty piglets."[7] Dionysius of Halicarnassus has Aeneas receive this very prophecy from "a Sibylla, a local nymph, who was a prophetess dwelling in the red soil of Ida" and then once more from Zeus at Dodona, the oldest Greek oracular site.[8] Dionysius had turned Lycophron's prophesying Cassandra into a god inspired woman, a Sibyl.

Vergil separates these two prophecies in his *Aeneid*. The greatest of the furies, Celaeno, inspired by Apollo, speaks of these tables.[9] At the moment of the prophecy's fulfillment, however, Aeneas does not recall Celaeno's prophecy but his father's arcane sayings about destinies (*fatorum arcana*).[10] Helenus, one of Cassandra's brothers, relates the prophecy of the white sow and the thirty piglets to Aeneas when he and his companions land at Buthrotum in Epirus.[11] The river-god Tiber, who urges Aeneas to seek out Evander reveals also the meaning of the white sow and thirty piglets.[12] The historian Livy reports that Evander's mother, Carmenta, was considered to be divine and revered by the people as a prophetess before the actual Sibyl came to Italy.[13]

Carmenta was, like the Camenae, a water nymph. Ancient sources stressed the chthonic nature of water, and as such, it had mantic powers.[14] There was also a perceived linguistic link between the name Carmenta and *carmen*, which we translate as poem but in its primary meaning is a ritual utterance or a magic spell. Livy had to convey a chronological coherence in his historical narrative. History develops in linear fashion; there is progression. In Rome's case, there was a foundation, a regal period, a republic, and then a principate, all while an empire came into being. The Cumaean Sibyl, the fourth in Varro's list and the one who plays such a pivotal role in the Vergilian narrative, appeared during the regal period. This period was not much more tangible than the time of pre-foundation. However, by the third century BCE and then once more in the Augustan period (the principate), the narrative traditions had solidified to such a degree that they functioned as accepted explanations of a chronological coherent past. Ancient writers relate explanations that perpetuate a consistent chronology of events. The Augustan elegaic poet Tibullus has a Sibyl, either the Marpessian (Hellespontine) or the Cumaean, describe Aeneas' coming to Italy and the foundation of the *imperium Romanum*.[15] The Sibyl had been connected to Rome's regal period (the time of the Etruscan Tarquin). Campania (Cumae) as well as the Hellespontine region (Troy and Asia Minor) were for generations Roman-controlled territories. Tibullus moved the foundation prophecy from a classical Greek literary to a Roman context.

Varro, our earliest source regarding the introduction of Sibylline Books to Rome, relates the story of an old woman trying to sell King Tarquin nine books filled with Sibylline oracles. In his version, this old woman was the Cumaean Sibyl. In all the other sources though, this woman remains nameless. Tarquin rebuked the woman twice. Each time, she burned three of the nine books. In the end, augurs convinced the king to purchase the remaining three books. He did and had to pay the initial nine-book price for them; no bargain here. Asked to take great care of them, Tarquin chose two men of distinction (*duumviri*)[16] and two public slaves to guard his acquisition. The books were deposited in the temple of Iuppiter Optimus Maximus (Jupiter the Best and Greatest), Rome's premier god.[17] A Marcus Acilius (or Atilius) is the only *duumvir* (one of the two men in charge of the Sibylline Books) recorded for the regal period. He secretly copied some of the text and received the death penalty. Acilius (Atilius) was sewn up in a sack and thrown into the sea; the same punishment for parricide required by the ancient law code. Since the Acilii and Atilii were plebeian families, they could not have held office during the regal period.[18] Whoever these original guardians of the Books might have been eludes us and it can only be said that they like the *duumviri* (two men), *decemviri* (ten men), and *quindecimviri sacris faciundis* (fifteen men in charge of the Sibylline Books and the ceremonies prescribed in them)[19] of later times must have been members of leading Roman families. The *oracula Sibyllina* (Sibylline sayings in Greek), arranged in acrostic hexameter texts, and their interpretation were to be kept secret as Acilius' story taught.[20]

The reported Sibylline instructions could be horrific (bury a Greek and a Gaul alive in order to avert a foreign invasion) but most often they prompted the introduction of a foreign god and the building of a temple. The introduction of new cults, those performed according to Greek rite (*Graeco ritu*),[21] depended on the college's interpretation of the Sibylline Books. The most dramatic introduction of a cult at the behest of the Sibylline Books was the introduction of the Great Mother from Ida (*Mater Magna Idaea*) in the Troad, Aeneas' home region, at the end of the Second Punic War. The Romans were urged to fetch this goddess, for her presence in Rome would bring an end to the struggle with Carthage. The Romans did as instructed, but they also double-checked with the oracle in Delphi. Rome's victory over Carthage occurred in 201 BCE, one year after the goddess' arrival in Rome.[22] As a consequence of this victory, Rome's hegemonial supremacy over the Mediterranean world was firmly established. Although the war had turned in Rome's favor already in the late 210s BCE, historical tradition linked the final triumph to the coming of the Great Mother. The Sibylline Books had given instructions, the Roman people carried them out, and victory was assured.

The Roman elite was responsible for the consultation of the Sibylline Books, the visitation to the oracle at Delphi, and the transfer of the goddess to Rome. The early war period had been disastrous for the Romans, whom Hannibal had outmaneuvered. The balance between leaders and led within Roman society became strained. Because any prophecy questioning the status quo would have been perceived as playing into the hands of the enemy, the Senate ordered an investigation into prophetic books. This inquiry took place in 213 BCE. The Senate was specifically interested in examining freely circulating and prohibited versions that could potentially undermine the strained status quo. In 212 BCE, a two-volume set of prophecies authored by a Marcius had been handed over to them. Using Homeric metaphors, Marcius prophesied the battle of Cannae in 216 BCE, a catastrophic moment for the Romans. He predicted Roman success, if an annual game in honor of Apollo was held and a sacrifice was given. When the Senate asked the men in charge of the Sibylline Books to consult the collection regarding this prediction, the Books ordered the same.[23] The unauthorized version had anticipated the disaster; thus, Marcius' collection was judged genuine and incorporated into the existing set of sayings. This is an illustration of how the commission in charge of the Sibylline Books could add newly found sayings to the existing corpus if they were judged to be authentic; that is, if they proved to be true in their prediction.

Ancient sources report that when Sulla marched on Rome (83 BCE), the temple of Iuppiter Optimus Maximus burned down and with it, the *original* Sibylline books. A senatorial commission was instructed in 76 BCE, after Sulla's dictatorship, to put together a new collection of Sibylline sayings. A committee was sent to the Greek East and not to Cumae in Campania. The best collection of utterances (consisting of 1000 lines) was found on Samos.[24] None of the surviving sources speaks of a deception. The college in charge of the Sibylline Books judged the sayings from Samos to be authentic.[25] The search for this new set of prophetic utterances had been a legitimate and authorized task. As in earlier times this new collection prophesied most accurately. In 18 BCE, when Augustus wanted to move the Sibylline Books into the newest temple of Apollo, which was opportunely situated next to his home on the Palatine, the Books were deemed "damaged by age."[26] Augustus ordered the college to make new copies. While doing so, a passage was found that prescribed the *ludi saeculares*, games that celebrated the empire and Augustus' achievements. There is no indication in the sources that claim this particular passage might have been a contemporary interpolation, a blatant manipulation of the sources, to support the emperor's decision. But, even as early as 18 BCE, when Augustus' position was not as secure as it would eventually become, no one dared to challenge Augustus on a religious point.

As Caesar's heir, Augustus was accumulating all powers in and around himself, even symbolically appropriating it. His private house on the Palatine nicely demonstrates this. Next to his house complex, which included the villa of his wife Livia, was the temple of Victoria. This edifice housed the Great Mother from the Troad (a sacred stone) until her temple was built and dedicated in 191 BCE. Below the western corner of the Palatine was the Lupercal with the Ficus Ruminalis, the sacred fig tree, where the she-wolf suckled Rome's twin founders, Romulus and Remus. Augustus had surrounded himself with the symbols of Trojan ancestry, Roman foundation, and the victory over the new Isis, Cleopatra VII, and her Dionysian lover, Mark Antony, at Actium in 31 BCE. The victor Augustus, who had embraced cerebral Apollo, in contrast to Mark Antony's emotional Dionysius, made the Palatine the center of the world. By a senatorial decree, an altar and a statue of Vesta were placed at the end of Augustus' house, opposite to the new temple of Apollo. They were dedicated on April 28, the festival day of Vesta, in 12 BCE, after Augustus became the high priest of Roman religion (*pontifex maximus*). The goddess, whose fire was never allowed to go out (*ignis inextinctus*), symbolized the state.

During the reign of Augustus' successor, Tiberius, a *quindecimvir* tried to revitalize the practice of consultation after the Tiber had flooded:[27] but to no avail. During the republican period, the Books were consulted over fifty times.[28] However, during imperial times, the Books were hardly consulted. Besides the fact that the Senate had faded into rubber-stamping oblivion, Roman religion was established and Rome had put internal strife to rest under Augustus' leadership. A secure Rome ruled the world. The Sibylline Books were rarely consulted. Famine, plague, and prodigies—all indicators of political strain—simply no longer presented themselves as they did during the republican period. When Rome experienced a crisis in 19 CE, chiefly brought about by Germanicus, a burning of unauthorized books was ordered.[29] Like wandering astrologers, prophets, and dream interpreters, prophecies could upset the established order and societal stability. In order to prevent such perturbation, unauthorized books were burned, prophesying persons were killed, exiled, or placed under the direct control of the sole ruler, who alone needed to know what the future held in store.

Nero had the Sibylline Books consulted in 64 CE, after a devastating fire that had destroyed Rome.[30] The destruction gave him a chance to build his dream palace, which also fueled the belief that he had the fire set. After Nero, the sources are silent until the short reign of Julian the Apostate (361–363 CE). He put it to the college to find out whether the auspices were in favor of a campaign against Persia. The answer was negative but Julian was already on his way. While Julian invaded Persia in the Spring of 363 and was killed, the temple of Apollo on the Palatine burned down. The Sibylline Books were saved only to be destroyed a generation later by Stilicho, the Christian general in charge of the West. The omen of 363 CE had come to pass, and even Julian's attempted pagan reforms could not prevent Christianity's triumph. Prudentius, known as the Christian Vergil, noted that the Sibylline Books would no longer prophesy.[31] The pagan Sibyl fell silent as the Judeo-Christian began to speak. Like her pagan sister, she spoke Greek.

Greek culture, however, cannot completely veil an original Etruscan aspect. Scholars of Roman religion such as Georg Wissowa discussed the *Etrusca disciplina* (inspection of livers, interpretation of lighting and unnatural phenomena) in connection with the Sibylline sayings. If they were thought not altogether different,[32] the conclusion was that the *disciplina* sought to explain the phenomena while the Books suggested expiation.[33] Indeed this is true. Ancient sources make it clear that the Sibylline Books were a collection of nothing else but Greek oracular sayings. Since the discovery on Samos of the 1000 lines immediately after Sulla's dictatorship, this certainly has validity. Nevertheless, one can argue that they were grafted onto an Etruscan pedicel that Greek layering had obscured until it eventually disappeared. In contrast to the Greco-Roman religious system of rituals and cultic actions, Etruscan religion was one of books.[34] The surviving sources speak of three types, the *libri haruspicini* (books of divination), *libri fulgurales* (books of lightning), and the *libri rituales* (books of rituals). The second century CE grammarian Festus noted (358, 21L):

> *Rituales* are called the books of the Etruscans, in which is described, by which rite cities are founded, altars, shrines are sanctified, by which religious sanction walls, by which legal sanction gates (are sanctified), in what way tribes, curiae,[35] centuriae[36] are divided, armies are set up, arranged, and other things of this kind pertinent to war and peace.

There were also subcategories to the *libri rituales* like the *ostentaria* (explanations of prodigies) and the *libri fatales* (books of things destined by fate).[37]

Throughout his history, Livy uses the term *libri fatales* and *libri Sibyllini* interchangeably. The most telling episode can be found in Book Five, which deals with the siege of Veii, an Etruscan city, and ends with the destruction of Rome by the Gauls in 390 BCE. Livy ends his fifth book with a speech by Camillus, the Roman general who had brought Veii to its knees in 396 BCE. The historian notes that Camillus particularly moved his audience when he touched upon issues of religion.[38] Rome's strength was its religion and its beneficial reciprocal relationship with the gods. In the summer, three years before Veii's destruction, a grave pestilence was afflicting all living creatures. The senate voted that the Sibylline Books (*libri Sibyllini*) ought to be consulted. The *duumviri* decreed a *lectisternium*,[39] the first ever held in Rome.[40] This was primarily a cultic action with expiation as a subsequence. A couple of chapters later, Livy speaks once more of the pestilence of 399 BCE, but this time he uses the term *libri fatales*.[41] Ogilvie, in his commentary, writes as an explanation for the latter: "The term is wider than and inclusive of the Sibylline books. It would also include the books of Etruscan discipline."[42] For Ogilvie, the term *libri fatales* is a neutral, overarching category.

Livy's account, however, continues. More portents were reported. The Romans were at war with the Etruscans, which deprived them of any access to Etruscan *haruspices* (interpreters/diviners of internal organs, lightning, and prodigies). The Delphic oracle, however, was open for business. Roman envoys were sent there. But then, an old man from Veii, an *interpres fatis* (interpreter of fates), a *haruspex*, presented himself. He declared that "it was written in the books of fate (*libris fatalibus*), thus handed down by the Etruscan discipline (*disciplina Etrusca*), that when the Alban water should overflow, a Roman should draw it with all due formalities, then victory over the Veientes was to be given. Until that should come about, the gods would not abandon the walls of the Veientes."[43] Although the *haruspex* explained the method of drainage, the senators did not follow his advice. Eventually, the Roman envoys returned from Delphi, and the oracle's response corresponded with that of the Etruscan "priest." Delphi, however, was not a cheap oracle. "When you have ended the war of conquest, as victor bring an ample gift to my temple, repeat as well as bring about in customary way the ancestral rites you have neglected."[44] Two points come to the forefront here. One, the Etruscan *haruspex* did not just explain a phenomenon. He referred to a recorded prophecy and then went about expounding it. Second, the Romans consulted the Delphic oracle, which reminded them of their ancestry, and not the Sibylline Books, which were supposedly in their possession at that time. In this story, the Etruscan *libri fatales* functioned and were used very much like the *libri Sibyllini*.

Livy has an annalistic note in Book Ten, which he leaves unexplained. Even in its condensed form, it holds pertinent information. "A happy year

(295 BCE) on account of war was disturbed by a grave pestilence and prodigies; it was reported that it rained earth in many places and in the army of Appius Claudius many were struck by lightning, on account of these things the books (*libri*) were consulted."[45] The books were not, as translators have it, the Sibylline Books but the Etruscan *libri fulgurales* and *rituales* (subcategory *ostentaria*). Unless, of course, the *libri Sibyllini* included these Etruscan books, which would make them the all-encompassing collection; in a sense, the opposite of Ogilvie's suggestion.

Another episode from Livy points in the same direction. Quintus Fabius Maximus, Rome's dictator in 217 BCE, convinced the senate that the Sibylline Books should be consulted on account of Hannibal's success that was somehow linked to the gods' displeasure with the Romans. This was an extraordinary request, since no dreadful prodigies had been reported. The ten-man commission was ordered to consult the Sibylline Books (*decemviri libros Sibyllinos adire iuberentur*). After they had inspected the books of fate (*inspectis fatalibus libris*), they reported to the fathers that the vow, which was made to Mars regarding this war, had not been properly performed. It needed to be performed again but on a larger scale.[46] The *libri rituales* dealt with religious rites and performance and so Livy's choice of words is not exact, but it is close enough. Again, the commission in charge of the Sibylline Books seems to have checked material very akin to the content of the Etruscan books.[47]

Maybe, to make a bold suggestion, even the nameless old woman in the acquisition story points to an Etruscan root. Women played an important role in Etruscan society.[48] Without the powerful Tanaquil, who was skilled in reading omens, Lucius Tarquin (the Elder) would not have left Tarquinia to find his fortune in Rome, where he became king. Roman historians and antiquarians place the purchase of the Sibylline Books in the time of the Etruscan kings (Tarquins), fusing, in effect, an Etruscan element (king) with a Greek one (Sibyl). For all his details, Livy does not relate the acquisition story at all, although, as we have seen, he speaks about the consultation of Sibylline Books quite often. Why does he keep this story from his readers, when he recounts the one of Numa's sacred books?

The king's sacred books were written in Greek, despite the fact that Numa was a Sabine. In this there is a parallel to the Sibylline Books. Tradition, strongly influenced by Greek sources, had made Numa a learned, Pythagorean, nymph-inspired[49] wise man. The *libri Sibyllini* offer a glimpse at Rome's cultural assimilation, the buried Etruscan, and the actively embraced Greek layers. They also unveil how the past was created and how it then, in turn, helped shape Augustan Rome.

The Books, edited and copied, were consulted for a millennium, from the time of pagan Rome's foundation until one god controlled all aspects of life and death. Fire destroyed them once, but a new set of sayings, perhaps even with a different content, did not make them less authentic. It was never a matter of original but of accepted authority. The college of the fifteen men guaranteed this authority by its continuity as well as its never-changing method of inquiry. While we might ponder the problem of authenticity, material and historical truth concerning the Sybilline books, we should not forget that even we are surrounded and culturally marked by the genuine faux that fashion our history.

Notes

1. Cato the Elder was the first to use Latin to record the city's past and make it an acceptable prose language.
2. P. L. Berger, *The Sacred Canopy: Elements of a Sociological Theory of Religion* (New York, Garden City: Doubleday, 1969), p. 33.
3. F. Heichelheim and C. Yeo, *A History of the Roman People* (Englewood Cliffs, N.J.: Prentice-Hall, 1962) p. 47. This is a general (and maybe the best English) introductory book to Roman history.
4. Tim Cornell, *The Beginnings of Rome: Italy and Rome from the Bronze Age to the Punic Wars, c. 1000–264 BC* (London: Routledge, 1995), p. 54.
5. M. DiLucia *The Sabine Versions* (diss.: Harvard), p. 7.
6. The second one was the Libyan (Euripides), the third the Delphian (Chrysippus), the fourth the Cimmerian (Naevius and Piso), the fifth the Erythraean (Apollodorus of Erythrae), the sixth the Samian (Eratosthenes), the seventh the Cumaean (Varro), the eighth the Hellespontine (Heraclides), the ninth the Phrygian. See H. W. Parke, *Sibyls and Sibylline Prophecy in Classical Antiquity*, ed. B. C. McGing (London and New York: Routledge, 1988) for details and discussion.
7. Lycophron *Alexandra*, 1250–1262. On the poem as a whole and Vergil's adaptation see West 1983. These tables turn out to be flat bread on which food was placed. The story of the sow follows Hellenic patterns of city foundations. The city was founded on the spot where a guiding animal found a resting place. The thirty piglets (!) suggest incredible fecundity and may even be interpreted as the future *curiae* (division of Roman people) of the same number.
8. 1.55.4. In Dionysius' story, the sow about to be sacrificed runs off and leads Aeneas and his men to the future site of Lanuvium.
9. *Aeneid*, 3.230.
10. *Aeneid*, 7.123, also West, "Notes on the Text of Lycophron," *Classical Quarterly*, n.s. 33, 1 (1983): 114–135.
11. *Aeneid*, 3.359.
12. *Aeneid*, 9. 42–85.
13. AUC 1.6. *Ab Urbe Condita: From the Founding of the City*, trans. B. O. Foster (Cambridge, MA: Harvard University Press, 1960-); abbreviated as AUC throughout this paper.
14. M. Ninck, *Die Bedeutung des Wassers in Kult und Leben der Alten: Eine symbolgeschichtliche Untersuchung* (Darmstadt: Wissenschaftliche Buchgesellschaft, 2nd ed. 1960).
15. 2.5.19–64; B. Cardauns, "Zu den Sibyllen bei Tibull 2.5," *Hermes* 89 (1961), 357–366, and F. Cairns, *Tibullus: A Hellenistic Poet at Rome* (Cambridge and New York: Cambridge University Press, 1970), pp. 73–78.
16. In 348 BCE the number was raised to ten (*decemviri*) and in the late 80s BCE to fifteen (*quindecimviri*).
17. The temple was located on the Capitoline Hill. It was dedicated to the Capitoline triad: Jupiter, Juno, and Minerva. Tarquin the Elder (Tarquinius Priscus) vowed the temple during his war with the Sabines, Tarquin the Proud (Tarquinius Superbus), however, is thought to have brought the building project to completion. Tarquin the Elder was Rome's fourth king, Tarquin the Proud was Rome's seventh and last king. Both were Etruscans. See L. Richardson,

A New Topographical Dictionary of Ancient Rome (Baltimore and London: Johns Hopkins University Press, 1992), pp. 221–224 for more details.

18. F. Münzer, *Roman Aristocratic Parties and Families*, ed. T. Ridley (Baltimore and London: Johns Hopkins University Press, 1999), Atilius 57–59 and Acilius 87–88. An interesting fact is that the Atilii were a very prominent plebeian family from Campania, the region in which Cumae is located. The first Atilius was consul in 335 BCE, another in 294 BCE. Other Atilii became prominent during the First Punic War and the clan was instrumental in keeping Campania loyal to Rome when Hannibal had the upper hand in Italy.

19. The *collegium* (college) started to have ten members (five patricians and five plebeians) in 367 BCE. Sulla (dictator, 83–79 BCE) increased the number to fifteen, Caesar to sixteen. The name of the priestly college remained the same, even though its membership was over twenty during the principate. The college in charge of the Sibylline Books was one of the four most important priestly colleges (*quattuor amplissima collegia*) in Rome.

20. The traditional dates of Rome's foundation (753 BCE) and the beginning of the republic (509 BCE) reverberate Greek/Athenian dates: the first Olympic Games in 776 BCE and the murder of the Athenian tyrants, Peisistratos' sons, in 514 BCE. Since early Roman history is very much a literary invention, these close chronological parallels come as no surprise. The Peisistratides (the sons of Peisistratos) deposited an oracular collection on the Akropolis. The Akropolis was like the Capitoline Hill, the location of the temple of the city's guardian deity. Peisistratos' son employed a diviner (*chresmologos*) and an editor (*diathetes*) of oracles. The editor, Onomacritus, was to work on sayings from earlier times. These sayings were attributed to Musaeus. Onomacritus, however, was caught improving the oracles; that is, interpolating, and was fired from his job. The Peisistratides wanted a coherently arranged set. Unlike the Homeric poems, which received their first standardization during this period, interpolations could not enter the oracular corpus.

21. This in contrast to Etruscan rite (*Etrusco ritu*). The cults Romans introduced were, according to the literary sources, Greek (*Graeco ritu*). It is not surprising that new cults were incorporated with their original cultic action. As the empire encompassed more than the Greek East, new cults kept being performed *Graeco ritu*.

22. On the introduction of the cult, see S. A. Takács, "Magna Deum Mater Idaea, Cybele, and Catullus' *Attis*," in *Cybele, Attis and Related Cults: Studies in the Memory of M. J. Vermaseren*, ed. E. Lane. *Religions in the Ancient World* 133 (Leiden and New York: E. J. Brill, 1996), pp. 367–386.

23. AUC 23.12.

24. Samos, like Ephesos, did have a Sibyl but not a cult of Apollo. An interesting fact insofar as prophesying women (be they the Delphic Pythia or a Sibyl) is concerned, was that they were thought to be the mouthpieces of Apollo. The myth has Apollo slay the dragon Python, a monstrous son of Ge (Earth) and guardian of her oracle at Delphi. From that moment on, Apollo controlled the oracle.

25. K. Latte, *Römische Religionsgeschichte* (Munich: Beck, 1960), 160–161 and Parke, *Sybils*, pp. 136–7. The dissemination of Sibylline prophecies from different places is conjecturally assigned to the Mithridatic period (80s BCE).

26. Vergil, *Aeneid*, 6.69ff., Dio Cassius *Roman History*, 53.1.3, Suetonius *Augustus*, 31.

27. Tacitus, *Annales*, 1.76.

28. Parke, *Sibyls*, 212 n. 5.

29. Dio Cassius *Roman History*, 57.18.4 discussed in Newbold, "Social Tension at Rome in the Early Years of Tiberius' Reign," *Athenaeum* 52 (1974), 110–143.

30. Tacitus *Annales*, 15.44; Dio Cassius *Roman History*, 52.18.4

31. *Apotheosis*, 4.39.

32. Latte, *Römische Religionsgeschichte*, pp. 160–161.

33. G. Wissowa, *Religion und Kultus der Römer* (Munich: C. H. Beck, 1902), pp. 461–475, esp. 470 n. 2. The first study of Roman religion in English, M. Beard, J. North, and S. Price, *The Religions of Rome*, vol. 1: *A History* (Cambridge and New York: Cambridge University Press, 1998) does not, unfortunately, provide any new insights on the Sibylline Books.

34. G. Capdeville, "Les Livres sacrés des Etrusques," in *Oracles et prophéties dans l'antiquité*, ed. J. G. Heintz (Paris: De Boccard, 1997), pp. 465–66: "Car justement, parmi les traits qui distinguent la religion étrusque—que les Romains appelaient l'*Etrusca disciplina*—, notamment par opposition aux religions romaine et grecque, il y a les deux caractéristiques

suivantes: c'est une religion du livre, ou plutôt des livres, ceux-ci étant constamment mentionnés par nos sources dès qu'il est question d'un acte relevant de cette *Etrusca disciplina*; c'est une religion révélée, comme le rappelle avec emphase Cicéron lui-mème (*Har. resp.* 20) . . ."

35. A *curia* was a division of the Roman people. There were thirty such groupings. The assembly of the thirty *curiae* voted on issues related to religion.

36. A *centuria* was a military unit (nominally 100 soldiers) but also a unit into which the Roman people were divided for voting purposes. The issues voted in the centuriate assembly had military overtones.

37. Detailed discussion of ancient sources in Capdeville, "Les livres sacrés."

38. AUC 5.55.1.

39. A supplication festival. Images of the gods were placed on couches so that they could be part of the banquet in their honor.

40. AUC 5.12.4–8.

41. AUC 5.14.4.

42. Ogilvie, 1965, p. 658.

43. AUC 5.15.11.

44. AUC 5.16.8–11. The last time a Roman had consulted the Delphic oracle in Livy's account was the Etruscan Tarquin the Proud, Rome's last king, shortly before he was overthrown. The prodigies were such that the most famous oracular site in the world needed to be consulted (AUC 1.56.5–6).

45. AUC 10.31.8.

46. AUC 22.9.7–11.

47. We know that by the first century BCE Etruscan was no longer spoken. Etruscan material, however, had been translated into Latin. For the emperor Claudius (41–54 CE) *Etrusca disciplina* was *vetustissima Italiae disciplina* (the most ancient discipline of Italy; Tacitus *Annales* 11.15.1–3). A good example of cultural (including religious) transference is the myth of Tages (best discussion on this, Wood, "The Myth of Tages," *Latomus* 39 [1980]: 325–344, but also Briquel, "Le cas étrusque: le prophétisme rejeté aux origines," in *Oracles et Prophéties*, 439–455). A being born from cultivated earth, who goes through the stages of life in a day, gives the farmer Tarchon religious instructions. The myth is recorded on an Etruscan mirror engraving (3rd century BCE), in Cicero, Ovid (Latin sources), and Lydus (Byzantine source). The most intriguing fact for our discussion here is that Tarchon is represented on the mirror as a *flamen* (a priest appointed to carry out rituals) and not a *haruspex* (diviner). The conclusion is that "all representations of *flamines* and *pontifices* [*pontifex* = priest belonging to a college] found in Etruria depict *haruspices* (Wood, p. 330)." One of the four most important priestly colleges is the one in charge of the Sibylline Books. One could conclude that aspects of Etruscan *haruspicium* actually fell into the sphere of the flaminate as well as the office of the *pontifices*, hence the position of the commission among the four most important religious colleges. In addition, Tarquinius is the Latin transliteration of the Etruscan Tarchon. The Romans had two kings of that name. J. R. Wood ("The Myth of Tages," *Latomos* 39, p. 344) concludes his article: "Truth to tell, perhaps, the Etruscan engraving would teach us more: that, rather than a mere continuity of *tradition*, there was a continuity of *culture* between Etruria and Rome. Tarchon and Tages in the regalia of *flamines*, the most Roman of priests! When, one must ask, was there more than the Tiber between Roman and Etruscan culture? . . ."

48. A short and insightful discussion in L. Bonfante, "Etruscan Women," in *Women in the Classical World: Image and Text*, ed. E. Fantham et al. (New York and Oxford: Oxford University Press, 1994), pp. 243–259.

49. A water nymph called Egeria (Dionysius of Halicarnassus 2.60, Ovid, *Metamorphoses* 3.273ff. and 15.487ff., Plutarch, *Numa* 4.13).

CHAPTER 3

Forging Czechs

The Reinvention of National Identity
in the Bohemian Lands

ALFRED THOMAS

What is a nation? According to Ernest Gellner and Eric Hobsbawm, nationalism is an "invented tradition" that has little relation to the premodern past.[1] Other historians such as Adrian Hastings maintain that nationalism is not a purely modern phenomenon at all but has deep and ancient roots in the medieval nation-state.[2] Hastings focuses on the example of England as an early unified kingdom; but France could serve as an equally good example of what he has in mind, since, in spite of its political transformation from feudalism to republicanism in the late eighteenth century, it has remained a united nation with a strong sense of its own unique identity rooted in a separate language and distinct customs.[3]

The case of the ancient kingdom of Bohemia, however, does not fit readily into either of these modern or premodern paradigms. Although it has been a geo-political entity since the early medieval period, this east-central European state has rarely been politically stable or independent for any length of time, a process of discontinuity that has led to divergent and ever changing notions of "national" identity.[4] How, then, can the complex case of Bohemia, for so long possessing a national consciousness without a national status, be classified in terms of current historiographical debates about the nation?

Turning his attention to the question of Bohemia, R. J. W. Evans argues that the year 1848 witnessed the clash between two senses of the term "nation," one pre-modern, the other modern:

> We can identify two basic senses of the term, one older in origin, on the whole, the other younger. On the one hand, a nation is a community bound together by residence in a given territory. On the other, it is a community bound together by ties of language, tradition, religion, or culture in general. The first kind of nation defines itself through citizenship, the second through ethnicity. In 1848, these two principles first confronted each other directly. Patriotism, allegiance to one's country, found itself outflanked by nationalism, allegiance to one's ethnic kin. From that time on, nationalism progressively became the dominant motive force, threatening the break-up of existing states, forcing strategists of the prevailing political order to take on board its own weapons.[5]

This transition from Bohemian citizenship (encompassing both Czech and German speakers) to an ethnic sense of Czechness, as exemplified by František Palacký's *Dějiny národu českého* (The History of the Czech Nation, 1848), has recently been documented by the American historian Hugh Lecaine Agnew in his book *The Origins of the Czech National Renascence* (1993).[6] In this essay, I would like to broaden the parameters of the discussion about the construction of national identity in the Bohemian Lands to encompass the period before and after the National Revival. Focusing mainly, but not exclusively, on the years which define this movement (1774 to 1848), I shall argue that the shift in 1848 from national identity understood as *Landesgemeinschaft* to national identity based on a specific language and ethnicity partakes of a larger and continuous process of "reinvention" that began in the Middle Ages and postdates the consolidation of the National Revival. This model of "reinvention" mediates between Hobsbawm's construct of "invented tradition" and Hastings' pre-modern model of national identity as an historical given. The term "reinvented tradition" thus has the advantage of overcoming what Benedict Anderson has perceived to be the constructionist fallacy in Hobsbawm and Gellner's theory of national identity:

> The drawback to this formulation, however, is that Gellner is so anxious to show that nationalism masquerades under false pretences that he assimilates "invention" to "fabrication" and "falsity," rather than to "imagining" and "creation." In this way he implies that "true" communities exist which can be advantageously juxtaposed to nations. In fact, all communities larger than primordial villages with face-to-face contact (and perhaps even these) are imagined.[7]

Anderson's analysis deftly reveals the essentialist underpinnings of Gellner's model of "invention" in necessarily implying the existence of its immutable and fixed opposite: the true community. The virtue of Anderson's "imagined community" is that it collapses the constructionist-essentialist opposition inherent in Gellner and Hobsbawm's model by suggesting that nationalism, like any other form of collective identity, is neither "true" nor "false," neither "authentic" nor "forged," but somewhere in between these polarities. This syncretic response to reality involves the simultaneous discovery and fabrication of real facts, the partial reclaiming of history from oblivion and its partial erasure in the interests of ideological self-fashioning. I shall argue that the construction of national identity in the Bohemian Lands has always been shaped by this collusion of forgetting and memory, fiction and history, a paradoxical continuum of discontinuity that I shall attempt to highlight with reference to several key texts from the twelfth-century *Chronica Boëmorum* of Cosmas to the neo-revival movement of the 1880s.

The Middle Ages

In the medieval period a collective identity based on the Czech language, as distinct from the neighboring languages of German and Hungarian, was constructed by the Bohemian nobility to reflect their role as the most powerful element in the state.[8] But in distinction to the modern period when national identity came to be understood in the immutable and fixed terms of ethnicity, medieval writers conceived of identity in the fluid terms of language and community; hence, the Old Czech word *jazyk* meant both "language" and "people."

The earliest articulated definition of national identity in the Bohemian Lands was provided by the Latin writer Cosmas in his twelfth-century *Chronica Boëmorum*, the first history of the region in any language. As a high-ranking cleric and a loyal adherent of the Přemyslid dynasty of dukes, Cosmas (1045–1110) represented Bohemian history in terms of the ruling ducal house and the church. We see a visual expression of this close alignment of dynastic and ecclesiastical interests in the wall-paintings from the Romanesque rotunda of St. Catherine at Znojmo in southern Moravia. Painted about 1134, several years after the completion of the chronicle and patently influenced by it, these images of worldly rulers and saints are intended to reflect the perfect congruence of the earthly and heavenly realms. The central scene on the upper level depicts how the nobles of Princess Libuše, the mythic foundress of Prague, invited Přemysl the Plowman, the alleged founder of the dynasty that ruled Bohemia until its extinction in 1306, to become her husband and the ruler of the land. Visual and literary treatments of this foundation myth continued right into the modern period.

Writing on behalf of the nobility and clearly antagonistic to the pro-German policies and cultural leanings of the rulers of Bohemia (by now styled kings rather than dukes), the anonymous author of the first Czech-language chronicle, known since the early modern period as the *Dalimil Chronicle*, is at pains to distance himself from the pro-ducal ideology of Cosmas. In his prologue, the former disparages and disavows the influence of his Latin predecessor (whose text he refers to obliquely as the "Prague Chronicle"), even though his subsequent treatment of events reveals his extensive dependence on the latter's account of Bohemian history. In order to camouflage his true source, the later writer claims that his principal inspiration was provided by an old priest near Boleslav, a detail that has led historians in recent years to rechristen the text *The Boleslav Chronicle*. But this renaming of the *Dalimil Chronicle* (an appellation itself based on a spurious author named "Dalimil" to whom the chronicle was first attributed in the sixteenth century) risks taking the author at his word. Given his obvious dependence on Cosmas and his tendency to invent things as he goes along, it is possible that the later author made up the detail about the old priest near Boleslav, a fabrication not uncommon in an age when reliable sources were deemed indispensable to any story worth its salt.

This is not to say, of course, that the medieval chronicler fabricated his account of Bohemian history entirely, but rather that he combined fact and fiction, history and myth, by drawing upon literary sources, oral-derived tales, and even invented material of his own to create the impression of a seamless flow of historical events. Intrinsic to this impression of actual events speaking on their own behalf is the eradication of Cosmas's distinction between myth and history proper. This impression of continuity allows the author to reinforce his claim that Bohemian history has been a purely linear process originating in the founding of the Tower of Babel (with its confusion of tongues) and culminating in the author's own time with the triumph of the Czech language as the unifying and univocal principle of Bohemian history.

A good example of this crucial departure from Cosmas is the episode of the War of the Bohemian Maidens, an account of a female rebellion against male rulers.[9] This account may or may not have been invented by Cosmas; at any event, he treats it in the ludic spirit of myth and concludes it with the assertion that the failure of the rebellion marked the transition not only from myth to history, but from a matriarchal to a patriarchal society. The later Czech chronicler expands the episode into eight chapters, and invents some elements such as the episode of the entrapment of the knight Ctirad by the cunning maiden Šárka, in order to give the impression of a real flow of historical events; and in so doing he suggests that the female rebellion was an aberration from a patriarchal norm rather than an organic and sequential process, a view he drives home by ordaining a grisly fate of mutilation and immolation for the hapless female rebels. This subordination of random events to a uniformly patriarchal ideology is consistent with the author's insistence that the Czech language (as opposed to Latin and German) and the Czech-speaking nobility provide the sole key to the meaning of Bohemian history, a belief that he asserts in the prologue where he contrasts his own intention of providing a "complete meaning" to events with the "empty speeches" of his Latin precursor.

That the later author does not ignore Cosmas's brief fable of the Bohemian Maidens altogether, however, reinforces both his dependence on his Latin source and his basic acceptance of Cosmas's point that the rebellion marked the beginning of the absolute rule of Přemysl the Plowman. The common link between Cosmas and the later author is that patriarchy—whether understood in terms of the rule of kings or magnates—is normative. Thus our Czech writer did not simply "invent" a new model of Bohemian identity but refashioned a pre-existing one to fit his ideological purpose as the representative of the Czech-speaking gentry. This process is literally exemplified by a manuscript of Cosmas's *Chronicle* from the late twelfth and early thirteenth centuries in which a later illumination of the mythic patriarchal figures Čech and Krok has been superimposed on the upper half of the narrative.

Following the tradition established by the author of the *Dalimil Chronicle*, Bohemian identity in the later fourteenth and early fifteenth centuries became deeply associated with the Czech-language preachers of the pre-Hussite and Hussite reform movement. Influenced by the writing of the Oxford theologian John Wyclif, Jan Hus advocated the reform of abuses in the Church at the Bethlehem Chapel in Prague, a site specifically intended for the preaching of God's word in the Czech language. Being a good Bohemian now meant being a faithful adherent of the reformed religion without regard to a specific class, which marked an important departure from the model of identity constructed by the author of the *Dalimil Chronicle*. But at the same time Hus's attempt to purge the Czech language of many of its Germanisms and his insistence on the use of native Slavic words clearly looked back to the earlier author's assertion in his prologue that Czechs should not marry German women and that Bohemia was "for the Czechs."[10]

The Early Modern Period

Following the signing of the Compacts of Basel (1436), which brought an uneasy compromise between the warring factions of the Catholic Church and the moderate wing of the reformers, the Czech language re-emerged as a vibrant medium of religious identity in the writings of the Bohemian Brethren, a Protestant group whose ideas were based on the radical teachings of Petr Chelčický. Their sponsorship of a vernacular translation of the

Bible from the original Greek and Hebrew tongues—the *Kralice Bible*—reinforced their identification with religious non-conformism in the heart of Europe. This momentous cultural and religious event was the continuation, rather than the beginning, of a long tradition of biblical translations into Czech, which date back to the early fourteenth century. Even some medieval versions of the Vulgate bear the trace of their Bohemian identity, such as the *Velislav Bible* with its ink drawings of the life and martyrdom of the national patron St. Wenceslas and other members of the Přemyslid dynasty. As Hastings has pointed out, a strong vernacular, and especially the translation of the Vulgate into the native language of an ethnic group, is a major factor in the eventual construction of its national identity, since people tend to identify with a particular language and the ideological values expressed and encoded in the literary form of that language.[11] One reason why the Hussites had such a strong sense of political and national identity was that they were able to read the Bible in their own language.

Following the defeat of the Protestant cause at the Battle of the White Mountain in 1620, the majority of the Bohemian nobility, patriciate and clergy lost their positions as the most powerful players in the state. Their legacy of religious non-conformism was erased from official memory: The twenty-seven leaders of the rebellion were hanged, drawn and quartered on the Prague Old Town Square, as illustrated in contemporary prints which represent the grisly scene with all choreographed precision of public theater. Other adherents of the Protestant cause, including the great Moravian pedagogue Comenius (later to be offered the first mastership of the fledgling Harvard College), were driven into exile, and many more were forcibly reconverted to Catholicism. The physical evidence of Bohemian non-conformism was effectively obliterated for centuries to come: Churches were razed to the ground and replaced by triumphalist monuments to the Counter-Reformation. The Cathedral of St. Nicholas in Prague is a good example of this act of political forgetting since it was built on the site of a demolished Hussite church, a fact vividly demonstrated in the interior statue of the eponymous St. Nicholas crushing the heretical foe underfoot with his bishop's crozier. Protestant books and Bibles were confiscated and burned, to be replaced by their Catholic counterparts.

But although political and cultural control now passed into the hands of the Habsburg rulers and their religious ally, the Roman Church, Bohemian history (in spite of its reputation for heresy) continued to serve the ideological interests of the new establishment. The Jesuits, who were in the vanguard of the Counter-Reformation push to reconvert the Bohemian Lands to the old faith, looked back to the "glorious" past and its culture as a means of legitimizing—and sometimes criticizing—the present. Notable in this respect were the Latin writings of the Catholic antiquarian and Jesuit priest Bohuslav Balbín (1621–88), who glorified the nation's history in his *Epitome rerum Bohemicarum* (Epitome of the Bohemian Kingdom) and *Miscellanea historica regni Bohemiae* (Miscellanea from the History of the Kingdom of Bohemia). In these works Balbín invokes the classical topos of the *laudatio temporis acti* to comment on the present political situation, in particular, the appropriation of landed estates by foreign aristocrats and the excessive centralizing power of imperial counsellors in Vienna. In this sense, his strategy of invoking the mythic past to explain the present not only recalls the author of the *Dalimil Chronicle* but also anticipates the idealization of the medieval period by the myth-makers of the National Revival in the nineteenth century.[12] A further indication of this process of reinvention is the deployment of the figure of St. Wenceslas as symbol of Bohemian nationhood in seventeenth- and eighteenth-century art and literature.[13]

If being a good Bohemian now meant being a faithful Catholic and an obedient subject of the Habsburg emperor, it did not always mean articulating that new identity in Latin. The mystic and devotional writings of the Jesuits Bedřich Bridel (1619–80) and Adam Michna z Otradovic (c. 1600–76), among others, aspired to provide an impression of cultural and religious continuity by writing in the affective and courtly manner of medieval Czech literature. Michna's hymns in his first collection *Česká mariánská muzyka* (Czech Marian Music, 1647) are directed at a humble audience of Czech-speaking burghers and peasants, which perhaps explains the partial oral and folkloric features of his compositional style and lexicon. The famous Christmas carol "Vánoční noc" (Christmas Night) from the same collection successfully fuses the oral form of the lullaby (with its popular lexicon) and the high courtly style of the medieval past to create the impression of cultural continuity.[14] The fourteenth-century Czech *Life of St. Catherine*, which exemplifies many of the high-style elements adopted by Michna, had been intended for an exclusively courtly audience, which no longer existed in the seventeenth century. Thus the Jesuit poets of the Counter-Reformation were in effect *reinventing* a medieval courtly tradition for a humbler public of merchants, artisans and peasants, precisely those social classes which did not emigrate and which had either remained Catholic or were forcibly reconverted to the old faith after the Battle of the White Mountain.

The National Revival

Toward the close of the eighteenth century, a new economic situation led to the increased prosperity of the bourgeoisie of the Bohemian lands. Allied with an increased exposure to the secular and rational ideals of the Enlightenment emanating from the West, this class conceived of literature first and foremost as a medium for the expression of political ideals and scientific knowledge. Although Catholic, they turned away from the purely religious values of the past and began to embrace new secular values. But, unlike in France, the expression of these new values in the Habsburg Lands was devoid of any revolutionary attitude toward the existing social order. As in Catholic Germany and Austria, a compromise was established between the new Enlightenment ideals and Catholic orthodoxy. The form this took in Bohemia was nostalgia for the "glorious" medieval past, when the nation had been a powerful kingdom in the heart of Europe. Ironically (since the bourgeoisie was mainly Catholic), it was the Hussite reform movement that was identified with the greatness of the nation's past. Thus the martyr Hus and the Hussite military leader Žižka were appropriated by the writers of the Revival as heroes in preference to the Counter-Reformation icon St. John of Nepomuk. At the same time, the bourgeoisie of the Bohemian Lands was undergoing a rapid Germanization. This process led to an increased awareness on the part of many members of the literate bourgeoisie that Bohemian identity (distinct from that of the Habsburg Empire) should be identified with the former glories of its history.

The reinterpretation of medieval Bohemian history played a pivotal role in this newly conceived national identity. As Hobsbawm has pointed out, the study of invented traditions cannot be separated from the wider study of the history of society. Hobsbawm goes on to argue that invented traditions use history "as a legitimator of action and cement of group cohesion."[15] Even revolutionary movements justified their innovations by reference to a "people's past" (for example, Saxons versus Normans in England). For the revivalists, Bohemian history, especially the religious turmoil of the fifteenth century, provided a fictional pedigree for their own decidedly secular investment in the ideals of the Enlightenment. A good example of this secularization of Bohemian history is the figure of Jan Hus himself, whose life was not interpreted in the specific context of a religious crisis in the late medieval Church but as a modern struggle between the forces of absolutism and democracy. Hence nineteenth-century accounts of Hus's life tend to emphasize his trial at the Council of Constance in 1415 rather than his subsequent martyrdom at the stake. Typical of this reinvention of the past in the ideological interest of the present is Josef Kajetán Tyl's patriotic drama *Jan Hus* (1848), which casts the religious reformer as a spokesman of democracy and human rights, and Václav Brožík's neo-revivalist painting of an heroic Hus at his trial.[16] As Hobsbawm states, such representations of the past depend for their claim to truth not on what is preserved in popular memory but on "what has been selected, written, pictured, popularized and institutionalized by those whose function it is to do so."[17]

If this impression of continuity was a product of fiction, it was also contingent on the historical reaction against German dominance in the region. Just as the medieval writers were frequently antagonistic to the Germans in their midst, so were the revivalists reacting to the nascent German nationalism in their quest for their own Slavic culture and identity. The construction of a new Slavic identity was thus itself contingent upon a pre-existing German nationalism whose influence on the Slavs had to be camouflaged or even erased completely. Ironically, the impetus for Slavic nationalism was provided by two foreign (and Western) influences: the principles of liberty enshrined in the French Revolution and the German idealism of Johann-Gottfried Herder. Under the Enlightenment influence and Herder's Romanticism, the first phase of the Revival (1774–1810) saw the scholarly reconstruction and codification of the Czech literary language by means of German-language grammars and dictionaries, followed by modest attempts at the construction of a national literature, based mainly on German sources, after decades of decay and decline. This was a period of scholars, journalists, and imitative poets. Amongst the principal scholarly figures were Gelasius Dobner (1719–90), the father of Czech historiography, Mikuláš Adaukt Voigt (1733–87), a numismatist who wrote encyclopedic works on Czech and Moravian scholarship and Czech literature, František Martin Pelcl (1734–1801), the first professor of Czech Language and Literature at Charles University, Václav Fortunát Durych (1735–1802), a Hebrew scholar and writer on early Slavonic literature, Karel Raphael Ungar (1743–1807), and František Faustín Procházka (1749–1809), who wrote a history of Czech literature and published popular editions of Old Czech texts.

The most important Czech scholar of this generation was undoubtedly Josef Dobrovský (1753–1829), who began his scholarly life as a biblical scholar and then turned to historical studies of Czech literature. He then turned to Czech prosody and grammar, and here he really came into his own. In his *Böhmische Prosodie* Dobrovský advocated a natural accentual metre based on the trochaic rhythm of Old Czech poetry and rejected *časomíra*, verse based on the quantity of syllables rather than stress. His most important work, however, was his *Ausführliches Lehrgebäude der böhmischen Sprache* (1809, revised second edition, 1819), the first systematic grammar of the Czech language. It achieved a great deal toward the normalization of written Czech in the literature of the Revival. With his works on Czech and other Slavic languages, Dobrovský became the founder of comparative Slavic philology. He was also the author of *Geschichte der böhmischen Sprache und Literatur* (1792). At the beginning of his studies, he considered Czech to be a dead language, but toward the end of his life he became something of a patriot and Slavophile.

According to the Harvard Slavist Edward Keenan, Dobrovský may have had a hand in forging *The Tale of Igor's Campaign*, a medieval Russian poem (allegedly composed some time before 1187) and extant in a single manuscript which is thought to have perished in the Moscow fire of 1812, but not before it had been copied for Catherine the Great's private library in 1795–96 and published in 1800. Keenan has established that the style and lexicon of the text betrays the influence of works written subsequently to it, such as the Old Czech *Alexandreida* (c. 1290) and even the Czech Forged Manuscripts of the early nineteenth century. If Keenan is correct in his hypothesis, Dobrovský's highly skillful act of forgery has to be seen in the ideological context of the National Revival as a Slavic counterpart to the *Nibelungenlied*, a medieval German poem that was itself being "reinvented" in response to nineteenth-century German nationalism, and the legends of King Arthur which were being adapted to accommodate the interest of incipient British imperialism.[18]

The second phase of the National Revival consisted of minor poets who attempted to create a national literature proper. Foremost among these was the Thám School or *thámovci*, who contributed to Václav Thám's (1765–1816) two-part anthology or "almanac," *Básně v řeči vázané* (Poems in Verse, 1785). Most of the poems in this almanac were written or adapted by Thám himself. But he also includes poems by older poets to prove that Czech poetry had not died out in the period immediately preceding the battle of the White Mountain and the Counter-Reformation. One of the older poems he adapts in this way is "Zdoroslavíček" ("The Defiant Nightingale," 1665) by the Baroque Jesuit Felix Kadlinský, itself a paraphrase of the German "Trutznachtigall" (published 1649) by Friedrich von Spee (1591–1635) with its dualist love of Christ and love of nature.[19] In the poem "Láska" (Love) Thám obviates the religious aspect of the Baroque model while amplifying the pastoral-nature theme.[20] For example he substitutes the devotional voice of the female-connoted soul addressing Christ with that of a young shepherdess who burns with desire for her beloved, changing the divine "Ježíše" (Jesus) into the anacreontic lover "Meliše" and thus transforming a Baroque mystical poem into a Rococo lyric. In claiming to preserve the older tradition of Czech poetry, Thám reinvents the poem to make it reflect the secular values of the Enlightenment age in which he was writing. In spite of Thám's secular values, he was unable to shed completely the previous model of religious thought. In his ode "Na zpěvořečnost" (To Poetry),[21] he feels compelled to praise the Creator for making art "divine" and in his pastoral lyric "Máj" (May),[22] he ends with a paean to God as the benevolent creator of nature, although in both these cases the emphasis is typically rational and deistic rather than intuitive and Catholic.

In addition to his services to Czech poetry, Thám was also active on the newly reinvented Czech stage. Although a thriving tradition of vernacular drama had existed since the Middle Ages, it had suffered frequent interruptions, firstly by the Hussite prohibition of theatrical performances in the fifteenth century and, secondly, by the decline of the Czech literary language in the eighteenth century. But religious plays such as *Komedie o svaté panně Dorotě* (The Play of the Holy Virgin Dorothy) as well as secular subject matter such as *Hra o turecké vojně* (The Play of the Turkish War) and *Salička* (a domestic drama) continued to be performed between the Counter-Reformation and the eighteenth century. By the end of the eighteenth century, however, the theaters of Prague performed plays primarily in German and operas in Italian, for example, Mozart's *Don Giovanni* received its premiere at the Count Nostitz Theater (1781–1797) in 1787. Although Czech translations by Thám, Jakub Thändler, and Prokop Šedivý (among others) of German-language plays were performed on Sundays and holidays to enthusiastic audiences, it was not until several years after the Nostitz Theater was founded in 1781 that this became a common practice. The first Czech-language performance at the Nostitz Theater was a translation of a German piece titled *Der Deserteur aus Kindesliebe* and the first play originally written in Czech was Thám's historical drama *Břetislav a Jitka* (Břetislav and Judith), performed on January 10, 1786.

The second group of poets were the Puchmajer school (*puchmajerovci*) who wrote much more varied and even talented verse. A great deal of it was published in five almanacs edited by Antonin Jaroslav Puchmajer (1769–1820), which appeared between 1795 and 1814. One of Puchmajer's aims was to fill in perceived gaps in Czech literature. Therefore most of his verse consists of imaginative adaptations of other works by classical German, French, and Polish poets. In some cases this involved more or less translating poems like Friedrich Schiller's famous "An die Freude" with its celebration of the Enlightenment belief in the brotherhood of mankind and the principle of freedom. Puchmajer derived other poems from mainly German models but camouflaged them by giving them Czech names and settings from Bohemian history, for example, he based the ballad "Král Jiří a Vaněk Všeboj" (King George and Vaněk the Fight-All) on "Der Kaiser und Der Abt" by Gottfried August Bürger (1747–94) and set it during the reign of the Hussite King George of Poděbrady.[23] In addition to providing a Bohemian historical setting for the ballad, Puchmajer endowed his version with local color by introducing lively Czech folk idioms and expressions.

The most talented member of this group was Šebastián Hněvkovský (1770–1847), whose greatest work was the long mock-heroic poem, *Děvín* (1805).[24] The poem relates the legendary War of the Bohemian Maidens first recorded in Cosmas of Prague's twelfth-century *Chronica Boëmorum* and expanded in the *Dalimil Chronicle*. Hněvkovský reinvents the legend of the Bohemian Maidens to make it conform to his Enlightenment ideals. The problem he faced was that if he made the Maidens into fighters for democracy and freedom, he ran the risk of incurring German derision at the implication that the only true Czech heroes of the past were women. If, on the other hand, he presented the Maidens in purely negative terms, he would end up glorifying their male opponent, the weak and petulant Přemysl the Plowman, traditionally associated with monarchical tyranny and now equated with Austrian absolutism. Hněvkovský circumvents this problem by writing his poem in the mock-heroic vein and treating the rebellious maidens in a tongue-in-cheek fashion. Thus his harmonious denouement in which the men and the Maidens establish a truce marks a significant ideological departure from the violent ending of *The Dalimil Chronicle* in which the female rebellion is bloodily crushed, their bodies hacked to pieces, and their dismembered remains thrown from the ramparts of their castle at Děvín.

Thus Hněvkovský's *Děvín* "reinvents" the medieval legend of the Bohemian Maidens as an Enlightenment fantasy of brotherhood and freedom realized in the final rapprochement between the sexes. In general, the early revivalists saw the medieval legend of the Maidens as clear evidence of a Bohemian tradition of the love of freedom from tyranny as personified by the Maidens' leader Vlasta and the cunning seductress Šárka. Thám's play *Šárka aneb děvčí boj u Prahy* (Šárka or The Maidens' Battle near Prague) had already been performed at the Prague Bouda (Hut) Theater (1786–1789), founded by a group of actors formerly employed at the Nostitz Theater for the regular performance of works in the Czech language; and as early as 1792, Prokop Šedivý's chivalric romance *České Amazonky aneb Děvčí boj v Čechách pod správou řekyně Vlasty* (The Czech Amazons or the Maidens' War under the Rule of the Heroine Vlasta) had appeared in Prague to enthusiastic acclaim. Later in the century this same legend would be reinvented yet again by Symbolist writers like Jaroslav Vrchlický and Julius Zeyer and set to music by the young Leoš Janáček. Whereas for the early revivalists the legend connoted the Enlightenment principles of liberty, equality and fraternity, for the neo-revivalists—as we shall see later—it served to reinforce the tragic perception of Czech history.[25]

The third phase of the National Revival (1810–48) comprises the beginning of Czech Romanticism with its attachment to an emotional nationalism which contrasted with the reason and restraint of the former "classical" generation represented by Dobrovský, Pelcl, Dobner, and other exponents of the Enlightenment. The fund of themes used by Romantic writers can be divided into four areas: the sphere of folk art; the history of the nation (especially the influence of Sir Walter Scott's historical novels); nature, near and remote; and man in his relation to his fellow men and eternity. From these four thematic groups, the early Czech Romantics were attracted mainly by the first two. They paid little attention to the third group and ignored the fourth altogether. Czech literature would have to wait until the advent of Karel Hynek Mácha (1810–36) to witness the integration of these elements into a unified whole. The most significant figures of the third phase of the National Revival were Josef Jungmann (1773–1847), Václav Hanka (1791–1861), Jan Kollár (1793–1852), and František Ladislav Čelakovský (1799–1852).

The period was dominated by the lexicographer and literary theoretician Josef Jungmann, who was an elegant, if uninspired poet. But his work as a translator and lexicographer was highly influential. His most important translations were those of Chateaubriand's *Atala* (1805) and especially Milton's *Paradise Lost* (1811). With these masterly translations, which makes use of Russian and Polish lexicon, Jungmann helped to shape modern literary Czech. Yet as well as creating Slavic neologisms to purify the language of its Baroque dependency on German lexicon, Jungmann was deeply indebted to the medieval and early modern forms of the Czech language and drew upon works like the *Alexandreida* and the *Dalimil Chronicle* to restore the language to its erstwhile vigor and flexibility. Also influential was Jungmann's textbook of Czech literature, *Slovesnost* (Literature 1820; second edition, 1845), which included a theoretical introduction on generic categories and an anthology of what he considered best in Czech literature. In 1825, he published his *Historie literatury české* (History of Czech Literature). But his greatest work of scholarship was his five-volume explicatory Czech-German dictionary (1835–39), which has never been superseded. Jungmann's restoration of the Czech language to its former glory may be said to have partaken of the overall reinvention of tradition delineated in this chapter: Just as the revivalist poetry mediated between tradition and invention, history and fabrication, so did Jungmann's dictionary bring together neologisms—whether calques derived from German, neologisms based on native Slavic roots or loan words imported directly from other Slavic languages—and older diction culled from the medieval and Baroque periods of Czech literature.

Apart from Jungmann, the so-called Zelená Hora and Dvůr Králové Manuscripts, allegedly "discovered" in 1817, provided the greatest impact on the second phase of the National Revival. The Forged Manuscripts, as they have come to be known, were once thought to have been fabricated by Václav Hanka (who claimed to have discovered them) and Josef Linda (1789–1834). They purportedly dated from the ninth-tenth and thirteenth centuries, respectively. Whoever the forgers were, they believed that Slavic folk songs were the equal of the German *Nibelungenlied* and the Greek *Odyssey* but, seeing no epic tradition in their own culture, they felt the need to create one by drawing upon Hájek's sixteenth-century chronicle as well as Russian and Serbian heroic folk songs, certain authentic works of Old Czech literature, Homer, Tasso, Milton, Ossian, Chateaubriand, and Jungmann. A team of empiricist scholars exposed these works as forgeries, but this happened quite belatedly, in 1886.

It is typical that the Czech forgers did not simply invent their texts but drew upon foreign models to assert their own literary pedigree. In this respect, they were following the Romantic example of the Scottish "translator" of Ossian, James Macpherson, who drew upon Irish Gaelic poetry as the raw material for his fabrications. And like Macpherson, the forgers used this foreign, older material to assert the alleged superiority and greater antiquity of Slavic culture over its foreign—especially German—rivals, just as the Hussites had advocated that Czech was superior to German.

If ethnicity played a role in this process of reinvention, so did class. The Romantics wished to give the impression that the medieval past reflected their bourgeois values of liberty rather than those of an aristocratic and religious culture; hence the need to forge a body of medieval texts that never really existed. Their act of forgery, however, has to be seen in its overall historical context, since they were simply taking to the extreme a process of reinvention which, as we have seen, had its origins in the Middle Ages and which was continued by the baroque poets of the seventeenth century and the revivalists of the modern period. Synchronically speaking, the forgers were also following a pan-European trend by emulating the successful example of the Scottish writer Macpherson, whose partially fabricated Gaelic poems attributed to the mythic Ossian had come to assume a central and prestigious place in the canon of European Romanticism.[26]

As we have seen, a central feature of this new Slavic nationalism conceived along ethnic lines was the denigration of all things German, a trend exemplified by the Slovak Jan Kollár, who wrote his verse in Czech, some of his prose in German, and some of it in Slovak. Kollár studied theology at Jena from 1817 to 1819, where he came into contact with German nationalism. Influenced by the German Herder's theories of national essence as embodied above all in folk songs, Kollár expounded the idea of Panslav fellowship and "Slavic reciprocity" (*Slovanská vzájemnost*), along cultural rather than political lines, in *Über die Wechselkeit zwischen den verschiedenen Stämmen und Mundarten der slawischen Nationen* (1837).[27] His first volume of verse, *Básně* (Poems, 1821), contains 86 sonnets which form the germ of his cycle of lyrical and narrative sonnets, *Slávy dcera* (The Daughter of Sláva), which, by its fourth edition (1854), consisted of an introductory elegy in *časomíra* and 645 sonnets.

An important personal influence on the composition of this highly idiosyncratic poem was the daughter of a German Protestant pastor, Wilhelmina Schmidt (nicknamed Mina), whom Kollár met while studying at the University of Jena but who refused to marry him until 1835. In the poem, the real Mina is transformed into the allegorical daughter of Sláva (Glory), the goddess of the Slavs. In the work the author wanders from one Slav, or formerly Slav, land to another, bewails the present lot of the Slavs and glorifies their past. At the same time, he sings the praises of his German parson's daughter whom he equates with the beautiful spirit of Slavdom. This female ideal is in fact a hybrid of a Teutonic cult of pagan goddess worship and the Czech legend of Libuše, just as the poem itself is a formal and generic blend of heroic epic and love lyric. Thus Kollárian Panslavism emerges as a reinvented tradition without authentic origins, an artificial amalgam of Herderian Romanticism and Czech foundational myths.

In a series of books and sermons, Kollár elaborated his notion of cultural Panslavism. As a Slovak, a group with no independent literary culture at that time, he saw salvation in a unified Slav nationalism to match German nationalism. He invariably presents the Slavs as peace-loving and passive in contrast to the sadistic Germans and Hungarians. This distinction between the peaceful Slavs and their virile neighbors is typified by the sonnet "Ku Barbarům" (To Barbarians)[28] in which the gentle Slavs, enamored of music and song, are contrasted with their belligerent Avar captors. This fusion of the personal and the political corresponds to the fact that this epic confrontation between nations is narrated in the lyric form of a sonnet:[29]

> To savage Avars in the days of old
> Came journeying three messengers, in their hands
> Slavonic harps with trembling strings they hold.
> Upon his throne the haughty Khan demands:
>
> "What men are you? From what land of you ride?
> "We are the Slavs, O Lord," the bards replied,
> "Our homelands verge upon the Baltic sea,
>
> We know no wars—no arms to us belong
> We cannot swell your regiments, O lord
> Our people's fancy is for play and song."
>
> They played for him. They played so tenderly
> The tyrant bade his slaves, as their reward,
> "Lead off these men to close captivity."[30]

Although the poem would appear to be purely fanciful in its opposition between peace-loving Slavs and belligerent Avars, it is typical of the Revival as a whole in harnessing the scientific fruits of up-to-date scholarship to reinforce its Romantic ideology. The reference to the Slavic homeland verging on the Baltic, for example, subscribes to the contemporary archeological and philological belief that the *Urheimat* of the Slavic peoples was much further north than is considered to be the case today. In this way, Kollár weaves together fiction and fact, poetry and science, to forge his Panslavic vision. This collusion between Romantic literature and the empirical sciences is equally characteristic of the so-called Forged Manuscripts, which also deploy the conclusions of empirical science (in this case historical philology) to promote their authenticity. In steering a middle course between literature and science, these poems cannot be termed forgeries in the strict sense of the word since they incorporate discourses that were respected as truthful and historically authentic at the time they were written. If the Forged Manuscripts deploy poetry in the service of history, *The Daughter of Sláva* may be said to deploy history in the interests of poetic fiction. The Romantic *modus operandi* was in a sense analogous to the way medieval poets went about reinventing the past. For example, the author of the *Dalimil Chronicle* does not simply reproduce verbatim what his "truthful" sources attest; he also amplifies and modifies those sources in the interest of his own ideology.

Kollár became more and more of a fanatic as he grew older. In his travel diaries (1841–63), his autobiography (1862) and *Staroitalia slavjanská* (Ancient Slav Italy, 1853), he found Slav roots wherever he went, and where he did not find them, people had an unpleasant appearance and even the weather was bad. Kollár's Panslavic ideas were very influential and later found a renewed expression in the work of the neo-revivalist Svatopluk Čech (1846–1908). In his poem *Slávie* (1884), Čech presents Slavic unity as a solution to the decrepit state of European civilization.

The fourth and last phase of the National Revival (1848–58) began with the revolutionary year 1848 and ended with the founding of the *May Almanac* in 1858. By this time, the linguistic and literary ambitions of the revivalists had been more or less fulfilled. But political aspirations were not in synchrony with cultural achievements. The failure of the Czechs' attempt to take part in the revolution of 1848, which was spreading all over Europe, dashed the political hopes of the Czech liberal intelligentsia and ushered in a decade of Austrian reaction known as the Bach Repression, named after Baron Alexander von Bach (1813–93) who in his years as head of government (1852–59) tried to subject the Habsburg lands to a strong centralized bureaucracy.

This repressive period witnessed a powerful literature of political resistance in the journalistic prose and poetry of Karel Havlíček-Borovský (1821–56), most notably his brilliant epigrams and his satires on absolutism, *Křest svatého Vladimíra* (The Baptism of St. Vladimír, published posthumously in 1876), *Tyrolské elegie* (Tyrolean Elegies, 1861) and *Král Lávra* (King Lávra, 1870).[31] Born near Německý Brod, Havlíček attended German schools and was initially an enthusiastic disciple of Kollár. He wanted to become a priest but was expelled from his seminary for propagating Panslavism. The historian Pavol Jozef Šafařík (1795–1861) was instrumental in having Havlíček appointed as a private tutor in a noble household in Russia. Here his enthusiasm for the Panslavic ideal rapidly evaporated in the face of the sordid reality of Russian life. Instead of brotherly love, Havlíček encountered a brutal feudal system in which serfs were regularly beaten by their masters; in fact, he was eventually dismissed from his teaching position when he tried to prevent his pupil from beating a serf. On his return journey from Russia, Havlíček witnessed even more evidence of the falsity of Panslavism in the Russian oppression of the Poles.

In 1845 Havlíček published his *Obrazy z Rus* (Pictures from Russia), the first truly realistic work in Czech literature.[32] He now began to publish literary criticism in the newspaper *Česká včela* (The Czech Bee). Notable among his literary criticism was his negative review of K. J. Tyl's novel *Poslední Čech* (The Last Czech), which he dismissed as sentimental and false. In 1846 the owner of the only existing Czech newspaper, *Pražské noviny*, asked František Palacký to recommend an editor-in-chief; and the name of Havlíček was proposed. He now began a brilliant journalistic career by defining his attitude to the Panslav ideal in his influential article "Slovan a Čech" (The Slav and the Czech, 1848) in which he dismisses Panslavism as outdated.[33] Havlíček relates how in his student days it was fashionable to recite passages from Kollár's *The Daughter of Sláva*, but that the time has come to dismiss the idealistic notion of the Slavs as one nation and to see them in a more realistic light as distinct cultural groups (Czechs, Slovaks, Poles, Silesians, and so on.) This reassessment implied a constructed rather than a purely essentialist understanding of Slavdom. Havlíček insists that what constitutes identity is not merely language and ethnicity but also laws, customs, and government: For the first time Czech nationalism went beyond the cultural sphere and entered mainstream politics.

But Havlíček's constructionist view of Czech identity was still reliant to some extent on the Panslavic essentialist model of identity that he criticizes in Kollár. For example, when he turns his attention to the Slovaks, an ethnic group also moving toward a cultural sense of differentiation from other Slavs, Havlíček criticizes the Slovak leaders Ludovit' Štúr and V. K. Hurban for threatening to tear the Slovaks from their historical association with the Czechs in the name of Panslavdom.[34] Here Havlíček invokes the very essentialist argument he objects to in Panslavism when he states that the Czechs and the Slovaks are tied together by a common language and literature, thereby contradicting his insight expressed earlier that identity is constituted by cultural factors like government, laws and customs—all of which differentiated the Hungarian-dominated Slovaks from their Austrian-dominated Czech cousins. Thus Havlíček is in effect reinventing Kollár's Panslavic model of identity in the interest of his own position rather than rejecting it outright.

Crucial to Havlíček's political realism was an awareness that the political plight of the Czechs as a small nation dominated by a great power was analogous to the situation of other marginalized ethnic groups. Hence his support for Irish resistance to British rule. In distinction to Kollár and his Panslavist idea, what constituted "Czechness" for him was not a subcategory of Slavic identity; in fact, it was not uniquely different from what constituted being, say, Irish, or a member of any other politically oppressed ethnic group. Havlíček exemplified his view of Czech identity as the struggle of a small nation against the great European powers by juxtaposing it with the Panslavic myth of Mother Russia in his satirical poem *The Baptism of St. Vladimir.* The saintly Vladimir of Panslavic myth is more akin to the autocratic tsar of nineteenth-century Russia than the medieval Grand Duke (c. 955–1015) who (according to Russian national legend) converted Rus to Christianity. When at the beginning of the poem, Vladimir orders the Slavic pagan god Perun to produce thunder bolts on his name day, his command is motivated by personal vainglory. The Slavic God Perun becomes a crude Russian peasant mercilessly persecuted for refusing to carry out the tsar's command. Havlíček presents his eventual execution as the founding act of violence that leads the way to the christianization of Russia.

In addition to contrasting Panslavic myth with the reality of the contemporary political situation, Havlicek creatively compares the political system of Austria and Russia by mingling Russianisms and Germanisms to great satirical effect. For example, Perun's servant is described as a Russian peasant girl, while the tsar's messenger becomes a low-level village policeman from Austria:[35]

> The village policeman came-a-calling,
> Knocked on Perun's dome;
> Asked the girl straight out:
> "Is Grandpa at home?"

The description of Perun evokes the world of Russian literature, in particular the one-eyed tailor in Gogol's story "Shinel'" (The Overcoat), which Havlíček translated into Czech:[36]

> "He's at home, he's at home,
> Sir, in that wooden shed,
> Sewing up his breeches
> On his nice warm bed."

At the same time, Perun speaks like an uncouth Czech peasant, and his speech is larded with Czech folk idioms that displace the medieval Russian legend from its mythic origins onto the reality of contemporary life:[37]

> "Little pay and heavy service,
> slogging all day long;
> and in addition I'm supposed
> to sing a grateful song?"

And the message Perun sends back to the Tsar via the shocked messenger is unequivocally coarse with Czech oaths:[38]

> "Be he tsar or peasant,
> I do not care a bit.
> I will not, will not thunder
> And couldn't give a shit."
>
> The village policeman stood transfixed
> As though kicked by a mule:
> "Grandpa, remember who you are,
> And don't talk like a fool."[39]

By contrasting the Christian story of St. Vladimír with contemporary political reality in which the Russians were more than willing to oppress their fellow Slavs when it suited their interests, Havlíček skillfully exposes Panslavism as itself a forgery. What distinguishes Czech identity is not their ethnic kinship with the Russians but their subordinate role as a small nation dominated by great European powers like Austria and Russia. The conclusion to be drawn from the satire is that the answer to the Czech question is not to relinquish one form of tyranny for another by turning from Austria to Russia for political salvation, but to seek political reform within the context of the Habsburg Empire. Just as Havlíček's views on the Czech question involved the repudiation of an essentialist Panslavic ideal in favor of a constructionist model of nationhood based on realistic political principles, so does the satirical effectiveness of *The Baptism of Saint Vladimír* consist in the way it highlights the glaring discrepancy between idealistic and realistic models of national identity.

Havlíček's demystification of Panslavic idealism reflected his realistic political insight that the Czechs were as vulnerable to the tyranny of their fellow Slavs as they were to Austrian absolutism. Ironically, however, Havlíček does not repudiate Panslavism altogether: His proposition that the Austro-Slavs (the Czechs, Slovaks, and Yugoslavs) should support each other and cooperate for their mutual interest harnessed the Kollárian ideal of the Slavs as a collective unit in the interests of political realism. Thus Havlíček's political realism did not fully supersede Panslavism but reinvented it to serve his own political ends.

I would like to end this essay by discussing a later treatment of the Legend of the Bohemian Maidens by the Symbolist writer Julius Zeyer (1841–1901) who, along with Jaroslav Vrchlický (1853–1912), was extremely interested in the medieval legends of the past. In spite of his debt to modernity and cosmopolitanism, much of Zeyer's works betray a fascination with Czech nationalism, perhaps in part because he was himself of German-Jewish origin and wished to identify more closely with the language in which he wrote. Foremost among these is his novel *Jan Maria Plojhar*, whose cosmopolitan hero, the tubercular and passive Jan Maria, becomes the symbol of the martyred Czech nation. A more explicit example of Zeyer's nationalist fervor is his long narrative poem *Vyšehrad*, the fourth part of which ("Ctirad") was adapted as a libretto at the request of Antonín Dvořák (1879) who wished to turn it into an opera.[40] But Dvořák never set the libretto to music, perhaps because its representation of Šárka as a *femme fatale* was too provocative and modern for the composer's nationalist temperament. It was later used by the young Leoš Janáček as the basis of his first opera *Šárka* (1887, revised 1888). The third tone poem of Smetana's *Má vlast* (My Fatherland) is also titled "Šárka" (1880) as is Fibich's best-known opera (1897).

"Ctirad" relates how the eponymous hero comes to Přemysl the Plowman's castle to guard the tomb of Libuše against the attacks of the rebellious Maidens. Here he finds the invincible hammer (a Slavic equivalent to King Arthur's Excalibur) which formerly belonged to the warrior Trut, a companion of his father, and which has now been bequeathed to him. Armed with Trut's phallic hammer, Ctirad is able to foil Šárka's attempt to steal Libuše's magical crown for the female leader Vlasta. This provides the motivation for Šárka's revenge against Ctirad: She orders the Maidens to tie her to an oak tree and, while the Maidens prepare an ambush in the forest, calls out for help. Discovering the girl tied to the tree, Ctirad releases Šárka, who explains that she is the victim of Vlasta's envy. Once untied, Šárka summons the waiting Maidens who surround Ctirad. Unable to recover his former strength, which has been sapped away by the serpent-like embrace of the *femme fatale* Šárka, Ctirad is helpless before the Maidens and is subsequently murdered by them.

In order to negate the disturbingly sadomasochistic implications of his retelling of the legend, Zeyer makes Šárka fall in love with the heroic Ctirad so that her triumph ceases to be a victory of *femme fatale* guile and becomes a reaffirmation of Czech national goodness. As he dies, Šárka assures Ctirad that she truly loves him in spite of her betrayal, a confession that allows the fallen hero a joyful death and permits his female captor to be morally exonerated. Significantly, Zeyer refuses to depict Ctirad's physical torment in a graphic fashion and he dies without any real causal explanation. Although the Bohemian Maidens are no longer fighters for freedom in the revivalist mold but satanically dangerous and sexually provocative in the Symbolist tradition, their entrapment of Ctirad by magical means lends a passive determinism to the entire poem so that Ctirad's tragic fate becomes a foregone conclusion, an affirmation of Czech goodness with undeniably sadomasochistic overtones.

In spite of the obvious differences between Hněvkovský's revivalist poem and Zeyer's Symbolist poem, both can be seen to neutralize the potential threat of female sexuality to male well-being, although this effect is achieved in different ways: In the former closure is brought about by uniting the sexes in life, whereas in the latter it is achieved by reconciling them in death. Such closure enables both writers to narrow the gap between their subjective male fantasies and their nationalist agendas. If Ctirad and Šárka are reconciled in life (by Hněvkovský) and in death (by Zeyer), this allows nationalist collectivism (transcending gender difference) to emerge as the undoubted hero of both versions. Thus in spite of its Symbolist décor, Zeyer's poem serves the larger agenda of Czech neo-revivalism and in so doing effectively reinvents an ancient legend in the interests of contemporary national politics.

Conclusion

In favoring the term "reinvention" over the Hobsbawmian notion of "invention," I have implied that national identity in the Bohemian Lands mediates between an historical and fictional interpretation of the past. This "forging" of Bohemia was neither an act of pure invention nor an absolute historical given but a curious combination of both. The root cause of this dialectical tension is the constant interplay between the invented and the real, the subjective and social, in Czech writing itself. The origins of Czech writing in the Middle Ages have to be seen against the political and cultural primacy of Latin as the official discourse of the Church and government, and German as the preferred cultural medium of the kings. In reacting against this Latin-German hegemony, medieval Czech writers felt the need to assert the primacy of their language over those of their rivals, even if this meant inventing some facts and ignoring others. If propagating the Czech language often called for the denigration of Latin as well as German, the price to be paid for this claim to ultimate primacy and authenticity was an inferiority complex that reached its most extreme and compensatory manifestation during the National Revival. But if this national habit of reinventing tradition attained its most fraudulent climax with the case of the Forged Manuscripts in the nineteenth century, the periods preceding and succeeding the National Revival—as I hope to have demonstrated—have had their own considerable part to play in this ongoing process of "forging Czechs."

Notes

1. *The Invention of Tradition*, edited by Eric Hobsbawm and Terence Ranger (Cambridge: Cambridge UP, 1983); Ernest Gellner, *Nations and Nationalism* (Ithaca and London: Cornell UP, 1983).

2. Adrian Hastings, *The Construction of Nationhood: Ethnicity, Religion and Nationalism* (Cambridge: Cambridge UP, 1997).

3. For national consciousness in pre-modern France, see Colette Beaune, *The Birth of an Ideology. Myths and Symbols of Nation in Late-Medieval France,* translated by Susan Ross Huston and edited by Fredric L. Cheyette (Berkeley, Los Angeles, and Oxford: Univ. of California Press, 1991).

4. For the changing definition of Czech identity throughout the Middle Ages, see František Šmahel, "The Medieval 'Rebirth' of the Czech Nation," *Acta Universitatis Carolinae - Philosophica et Historica 3 Studia Historica XLIV* (1996), pp. 33–39.

5. R. J. W. Evans, "The Magic of Bohemia," in *The New York Review of Books,* Vol. XLVI, No. 16 (October 21, 1999), pp. 61–63 (p. 61).

6. See Hugh Lecaine Agnew, *The Origins of the Czech National Renascence* (Pittsburgh: Univ. of Pittsburgh Press, 1993).

7. Benedict Anderson, *Imagined Communities: Reflections on the Origin and Spread of Nationalism,* second edition (London: Verso, 1991), p. 15.

8. See Alfred Thomas, *Anne's Bohemia. Czech Literature and Society, 1310–1420* (Minneapolis and London: Univ. of Minnesota Press, 1998), pp. 54–55.

9. For the origin of the myth of the Bohemian Maidens and its treatment in Czech chronicles, see Pavel Spunar, "Dívčí válka v českých středověkých kronikách," *Tvar* 6/19 (1995), 161–17.

10. See *Výbor z česke literatury doby husitské,* vol. 1, edited by Bohuslav Havránek, et al. (Prague Nakl. Československé akademie věd, 1963), p. 147. See also: Vladimír Karbusicky, *Anfänge der historischen Überlieferung in Böhmen: Ein Beitrag zum vergleichenden Studium der mittelalterlichen Sängerepen* (Cologne and Vienna: Böhlau, 1980).

11. Hastings, pp. 15–18.

12. For the construction of the myth of the Battle of the White Mountain, see Josef Petráň and Lydia Petráňová, "*The White Mountain as a symbol in modern Czech history,*" in *Bohemia in History,* edited by Mikuláš Teich (Cambridge: Cambridge UP, 1998), pp. 143–63 (p. 148).

13. Ibid., p. 150. See also Jan Royt, *Svatý Václav v umění 17. a 18. století* (Prague: Národní galerie v Praze, 1994).

14. For the text in question, see *České Baroko,* edited by Zdeněk Kalista (Prague: Evropský literární klub, 1941), p. 53.

15. Hobsbawm, *The Invention of Tradition,* p. 12.

16. See *Dějiny v obrazech. Historické náměty v umění 19. století v Čechách,* edited by Naděžda Blažíčková-Horová (Prague: Národní galerie, 1996), p. 98 (illustration reproduced on p. 96).

17. Hobsbawm, *The Invention of Tradition,* p. 13. See also Vladimír Macura, "Problems and Paradoxes of the National Revival," in *Bohemia in History,* pp. 182–197.

18. See Maike Oergel, *The Return of King Arthur and the Nibelungen. National Myth in Nineteenth-Century English and German Literature,* European Cultures, Studies in Literature and the Arts, vol. 10 (Berlin, New York: Walter de Garytes, 1998).

19. For the Baroque poem adapted by Thám, see *České Baroko,* p. 77.

20. See *Počátky novočeského básnictví*, edited by Karel Polák (Prague: Československý spisovatel, 1950) pp. 9–11.
21. Ibid., p. 15.
22. Ibid., p. 12.
23. Ibid., pp. 33–40. For Bürger's ballad, see Gottfried August Bürger, *Gedichte*, edited by Günther E. Grimm (Stuttgart: P. Reclam, 1997), pp. 101–8.
24. Šebastián Hněvkovský, *Děvín* (Prague, 1805).
25. Jitka Malečková, "Nationalizing Women and Engendering the Nation: the Czech National Movement," in *Gendered Nations: Nationalism and Gender Order in the Long Nineteenth Century*, ed. Ida Blum, Karen Hageman and Catherine Hall (Oxford, New York: Berg, 2000), pp. 293–310. For the Libuše myth in the National Revival, see also Vladimír Macura, *Český sen* (Prague: Nakl. Lidové noviny, 1998).
26. See Hugh Trevor-Roper, "The Invention of Tradition: The Highland Tradition of Scotland," in *The Invention of Tradition*, pp. 15–41 (pp. 17–18).
27. For Kollár and Šafařík's myth of Slavness, see Robert B. Pynsent, *Questions of Identity. Czech and Slovak Ideas of Nationality and Personality* (Budapest, London and New York: Central European UP, 1994), chapter four.
28. Jan Kollár, *Básně* (Prague: Československý spisovatel, 1981).
29. Ibid., p. 80.
30. Translated by John Bowring. See *Czech Prose* ed. William E. Harkins *An Anthology*, (Ann Arbor: Slavica, 1983), p. 175. I have changed Bowring's "minstrels" (line two) to "messengers" in the interests of accuracy.
31. For Karel Havlíček-Borovský's satires, see Marie Řepková, *Satira Karla Havlíčka* (Prague Academia, 1971).
32. Karel Havlíček-Borovský, *Obrazy z Rus* in *Dilo* I (Prague: Československý spisovatel, 1986), pp. 13–116. For an English-language study of this work, see Michael Henry Heim, *The Russian Journey of Karel Havlíček-Borovský*, Slavistische Beiträge, 128 (Munich: O. Sagner, 1979).
33. Karel Havlíček-Borovský, "Slovan a Čech," in *Dilo* II (Prague: Československý spisovatel, 1986), pp. 57–81.
34. Ibid., p. 59.
35. Havlíček-Borovský, *Dilo I*, p. 455.
36. Ibid., p. 455.
37. Ibid., p. 456.
38. Ibid., p. 457.
39. The English translation of the poem is my own.
40. Julius Zeyer, *Vyšehrad* (Prague: Militký a Novák, 1885). For the libretto of "Šárka," see Zeyer, *Spisy*, vol. 25 (Prague, 1918), pp. 177–97. For a study of Zeyer, see Robert B. Pynsent, *Julius Zeyer. The Path to Decadence* (The Hague and Paris: Mouton, 1973).

CHAPTER 4

Eclectic Fabrication

St. Petersburg and the Problem of Imperial Architectural Style

JULIE A. BUCKLER

Since the time of St. Petersburg's founding in 1703, the Russian imperial capital has been much reviled. Nineteenth-century writers such as Nikolai Gogol and Fedor Dostoevsky characterized Petersburg as a citadel of hollow rhetoric—utopian in conception, yet inhumanly indifferent to its humbler citizens. The humanist literary tradition that regards Petersburg as a phantasm has, moreover, a counterpart in strictly aesthetic judgments of the city as counterfeit. This aesthetic critique of Petersburg addresses the presumptuous Russian project of creating a Western-style capital in an alien cultural and topographical setting, since Peter the Great's showpiece city seemed at odds with its surroundings, the famously chilly and damp expanses of the low-lying Neva delta. While eighteenth- and nineteenth-century visitors marveled at the resources expended to produce Petersburg's effects, they often dismissed the result as a shoddy imitation of other capital cities, and thus an inauthentic copy of foreign cultural achievements.

It is true that St. Petersburg took shape through reference to its predecessor cities, buildings, and monuments. As the capital of a vast empire, "Petropolis" employed a plan of rayed, straight avenues reminiscent of Rome and Versailles. The city claimed the Byzantine legacy from Constantinople, but also called itself a "New Jerusalem." Petersburg adopted the name of its patron, Saint Peter, according to the Dutch form Sankt-Piter-Burkh, and modeled itself as a great port city after Venice and Amsterdam, but also imitated the carefully planned gardens and elaborate fountains of French royalty. Like Alexandria, Petersburg commemorated its creator-conqueror, celebrating Peter the Great's victory over the "barbarian" Swedes, but Petersburg also identified itself as a city of culture akin to Athens, Paris, and London. Often referred to as "the Northern Palmyra," Petersburg administered a visual shock to early visitors with its unexpected classical façades and pillars rising from the northern swamplands, analogous to the sight of similar structures gracing an oasis in the Syrian desert.[1]

Perhaps St. Petersburg represents a pastiche of styles according to Gerard Genette's definition of this relatively "pure" and "neutral" hypertextual practice: "a texture of *imitations.*"[2] Although the spirit of pastiche is often playful, there is nothing to prevent a pastiche from being received in a serious spirit as an original work. Pastiche may thus offer sincere homage to its multiple inspirations, as Petersburg does to the European and ancient capitals. A *forgery*, on the other hand, is analogous to an apocryphal text, "whose challenge would be to pass for an authentic text in the eyes of a reader of absolute and infallible competence."[3] To meet its own goals, declares Genette, a forgery must avoid anachronisms as well as literal borrowings. Since the Russian capital was found guilty of both, directly appropriating a diverse array of seemingly incompatible urban referents, observers declared the city inauthentic. For foreign visitors, Petersburg was an imposter because it displayed a lack of finesse in copying the West.

Nineteenth-century Russian fictional texts that comprise the so-called "literary mythology of St. Petersburg" reject the eighteenth-century neoclassical ideal in favor of an increasingly critical, realist literary aesthetics.[4] Another branch of nineteenth-century critique—one that extends to the present day—denounces St. Petersburg for *departing* from the classical eighteenth-century vision and regrets the inappropriately varied architectural effects that cluttered the cityscape as the nineteenth century progressed. A third tradition of Petersburg-bashing condemns the city as inauthentic at its very heart, thereby denying the existence of any true, originary vision of St. Petersburg. Still, none of these critical views fully represents the artful fake that is St. Petersburg. There exists another possible characterization of St. Petersburg, neither dismissive nor reactionary, which finds an intentional quality in the city's juxtaposition of diverse urban models and traditions. A revisionist description of the Petersburg cityscape in terms of *eclecticism* casts the city in terms of nineteenth-century Russian cultural poetics, according to which a loose, encyclopedic literacy is the only recourse in the absence of a single, dominant aesthetic.

As the familiar story goes, St. Petersburg represents the material embodiment of the definitive shift made by Peter the Great—from Russia's tradition-bound and culturally isolationist past, as exemplified by its former capital city Moscow, toward the European-oriented future he envisioned for his country. Peter imported Western technologies and architects to create his city, whose initially Baroque, then rococo and neoclassical features were elaborated during the reigns of Elizabeth (1741–61), Catherine the Great (1762–96), and Alexander I (1801–1825). Architectural histories of St. Petersburg comprise a litany of foreign architects, such as Dominico Trezzini, Bartolomeo Francesco Rastrelli, Giacomo Quarenghi, and Carlo Rossi, who executed extraordinary feats of design and engineering. Cultural histories characterize St. Petersburg at the end of the eighteenth century as a chronicle of artistic masterworks—the Cathedral of SS. Peter and Paul, the Alexander Nevsky Monastery, the Kunstkammer, the Twelve Administrative Colleges, the Smolnyi Cathedral and Convent, the Winter Palace, the Academy of Fine Arts, the Tauride Palace, the neoclassical Bronze Horseman monument to Peter the Great, and the sumptuous palace-parks at Peterhof and Tsarskoe Selo, to name only a few. These buildings were executed in Western architectural styles, with suggestive old-Russian features in the case of Smolnyi. The architectural narrative of St. Petersburg extends into the nineteenth century through the reign of Alexander I, with grand projects such as the General Staff Headquarters, the Stock Exchange, the redone Admiralty, the Kazan Cathedral, and finally, the massive St. Isaac's Cathedral. The story of the city after Alexander's death in 1825 grows more confused, however, in both aesthetic and cultural terms. The coherent architectural ensembles of Alexandrine classicism became part of Petersburg's living past. Around them sprung up the architectural structures of mid- to late-nineteenth-century St. Petersburg, whose profusion of ornamentation proclaimed their full or mixed allegiances to neo-Grecian, neo-Byzantine, neo-gothic, neo-renaissance, and neo-baroque aesthetic revivals. Architectural eclecticism, the much-disparaged product of these changes, refers to those in-between, non-monumental spaces of the Petersburg cityscape that represented an increasingly dominant aspect of the imperial capital during the nineteenth century.

"Eclecticism" is a blanket designation for the architectural tendency that falls between Neoclassicism and the evolution of the Art Nouveau style (known in Russia as *moderne*). "Eclecticism" in Russian architecture also corresponds to the period in literary history between romanticism and modernism, a span of years usually associated with realism (1830s–1890s), the great flowering of Russian prose. Unlike literary realism, however, architectural eclecticism is rarely treated as a style in its own right, and considered merely a "transitional" poetics between two distinct period and style designations.

History credits the repressive Tsar Nicholas I (1825–55) with initiating the breakdown of a unified aesthetic vision for St. Petersburg when he gave his blessing to the hurried construction of many utilitarian structures for the growing government bureaucracy, realized in a style known as barracks-like (*kazarmennyi*), bureaucratic (*kazënnyi*), or conventional classicism.[5] In doing so, Nicholas inadvertently opened the door to architectural eclecticism. The ensuing "crisis of classicism" in architecture reflected the shift in national consciousness, from celebrating the victories of the Napoleonic wars to grieving over the crushed hopes of the Decembrist uprising. City-dwellers grew weary of relentlessly classical façades that no longer seemed to proclaim eternal civic precepts or to embody Johann Joachim Winckelmann's neoclassical ideal of "noble simplicity and calm grandeur." Furthermore, the dull sameness of these buildings made it impossible to determine whether a given structure was public, private, cultural, commercial, military, or industrial. The "crisis of classicism" came as the need for varied architectural forms responding to urban modernization and industrialization began to make itself felt.

The decline of classicism in Russian architecture, as the story goes, corresponds to the passing of imperial Russia's "Golden Age," a conceit that evokes the elite Pushkinian literary and social culture as well as the consolidation of Russia's status as an imperial power during the period 1762–1855.[6] Eclecticism arose in response to the diffusion of cultural currency toward the end of this period, and with it came a powerful, if sloppy nostalgia for the seeming certainties of the past. It is possible, however, that the flexible and inclusive notion of eclecticism might be partly a foil, useful for shoring up the potent mythology of Alexandrine architectural coherence. After all, the "Empire" style of Alexander's time combined elements from Roman and Greek architecture with those appropriated from diverse foreign cultures in a decorative expression of Napoleonic imperialism.[7] Furthermore, Alexandrine Petersburg has by no means been universally celebrated for its gloriously harmonious wholeness. O. A. Przhetslavskii's memoirs of the 1820s, for example, refer to the "unfinished" look of the capital, complaining of the "monotonous" streets and squares with uniform pale-yellow façades.[8] Perhaps the story of Petersburg architecture has grown no less rote than the tired classicism of Nicholas's reign, and perhaps the evolution of architectural "eclecticism" is due for re-examination.

Was nineteenth-century eclecticism motivated and coherent as an architectural style, or is "eclecticism" a term simply used to convey the absence of a dominant, identifiable architectural style—a catch-all for an awkward period that predates the emergence of "modern" architectural shapes? The questions that eclecticism raises about aesthetics and value have proved challenging for anyone attempting a synthetic overview of the nineteenth-century cityscape. Soviet-era architectural histories characterize the second half of the nineteenth century in St. Petersburg as the "capitalist epoch," due to the boom in private entrepreneurial construction, apartment housing in particular, rather than building projects funded by the imperial family and the state.[9] Architectural eclecticism is thus negatively linked in Petersburg cultural history with the decline of cohesive city planning and the rise of a prominent new class of professional moneymakers.

Did eclecticism simply seek to distract the viewer's eye with excessive ornamentation, to hide the cheap construction of apartment buildings and commercial facilities? At its worst, architectural eclecticism stands accused of "indifferentism" and "uncommitted romanticism" in its haphazard mixing of stylistic elements from different cultures and historical periods.[10] But rather than unthinking recourse to tired architectural conventions, can "eclecticism" be considered an explosion of the imagination, resulting in a fragmentation of the available architectural vocabulary into the space of the possible? Perhaps eclecticism is related to *both* cultural and territorial imperialism and social-climbing desperation, in that eclecticism literally tries to have it all. This suggested link is supported by the fact that, beginning with the first part of the eighteenth century, there have *always* been those who considered Petersburg architecture to be eclectic.

Eclectic Rhetoric: Critical Responses to St. Petersburg

Many foreign visitors and Russian cultural critics have gone on record denouncing Petersburg's architectural eclecticism. In attributing a mongrel quality to Petersburg's borrowings from the West, such statements sometimes significantly predate the second half of the nineteenth century, when the notion of eclecticism arose. One of the first such characterizations came from Count Francesco Algarotti, who visited Russia during the first half of the eighteenth century, a decade and a half after Peter the Great's death, describing Petersburg as "this new city . . . this great window lately opened in the north, through which Russia looks into Europe."[11] Algarotti describes his first sighting of the imperial city, which at first glance struck him as sumptuous and brilliant. Upon disembarking from his ship, however, Algarotti found the city less impressive: "There reigns in this capital a kind of bastard architecture, which partakes of the Italian, the French, and the Dutch." The palaces of the courtiers, notes Algarotti, were already in disrepair: "Their walls are all cracked, quite out of perpendicular, and ready to fall. It has been wittily enough said, that ruins make themselves in other places, but that they were built at Petersburg." According to Algarotti, Petersburg architecture exhibits a derivative, hybrid tastelessness whose effect is heightened by the inadvertent illusion of age.

Algarotti conceded, "the situation of a city built upon the borders of a great river, and formed of different islands, which give room for a variety of points of view and effects of optic, cannot but be fine." Still, he insistently enumerated the city's shortcomings: "the ground upon which it is founded is low and marshy, the immense forest, in the middle of which it stands, is frightful, the materials of which it is built are not worth much, and the plans of the buildings are not those of an Inigo Jones or a Palladio." Petersburg does not manifest the vision of an artistic genius boldly integrating elements from the past, but is inferior even in its basic conception.

Algarotti's famous metaphor of the great window (*finestrone*) "through which Russia looks into Europe" suggests that Petersburg is doomed to remain an outsider, its nose pressed up against the glass, no matter how assiduously it imitates the West. Perhaps, however, Algarotti's "window" metaphor—adapted and immortalized by Pushkin in the Prologue to "The Bronze Horseman"—has overshadowed his equally compelling characterization of Petersburg's "bastard architecture." Algarotti's assessment suggests that Petersburg was eclectic even as an eighteenth-century project.[12]

In 1839, a century after Algarotti, the Marquis de Custine declared, "[T]he streets of Petersburg present a strange appearance to the eyes of a Frenchman."[13] He stated flatly, "A taste for edifices without taste has presided over the building of St. Petersburg." For Custine, the incongruous effect of St. Petersburg architecture reflected the incompatibility between European architecture and the Russian natural landscape. Antique statues, ornamental columns, and temple-like façades all seemed to him "captive heroes in a hostile land." Situated near swamps and unprepossessing woods, the beauty of classical architecture resembles "mere heaps of plaster and mortar" and classical art seems no more than "an indescribably burlesque style of modern decoration." Like Algarotti, Custine refers to Petersburg's eclecticism without naming it as such, in advance of the later periodized phenomenon, blaming the hodgepodge effect on the ill-advised transplantation of European architectural conventions. Custine was in part mollified by "the form and multitude of turrets and metallic spires which rise in every direction," about which he pronounced with evident satisfaction, "This at least is national architecture." He declares that Russia's cultural debt to Greece and Byzantium permits the country "to seek for models at Constantinople, but not at Athens."[14] In this, Custine anticipates Emmanuel Viollet-le-Duc's 1877 treatise, *L'Art Russe*, which urged Russia to recover its own native genius in architecture by forswearing sterile imitations of Italy, France, and Germany and turning anew to Eastern influences.[15] He dismisses Petersburg with the sweeping claim that "Partially to imitate that which is perfect is to spoil it. We should either strictly copy the model, or invent altogether."

The lost, once powerful unity of neoclassicism in St. Petersburg—the "stern harmonious aspect" invoked by Pushkin in "The Bronze Horseman"—might well be an aspect of Russian cultural mythology that reflects a fond notion held only by Russians about their city.[16] For foreign visitors, the architectural history of St. Petersburg has been characterized in terms of "faux classical" and "hopelessly eclectic," two period designations that convey an equal sense of the city's aesthetic illegitimacy. Where did Russian views fit in?

Peter Chaadaev's views on Russian cultural eclecticism began as a Custine-like condemnation of indiscriminate copying, but developed into an appreciation of eclecticism as the proper aesthetic for his country at its particular moment of historical evolution. The first of Chaadaev's *Philosophical Letters* (1829) refers to the Russian people as "illegitimate children," members of a culture "based wholly on borrowing and imitation" who accept only "ready-made ideas." Chaadaev claims that Russians have not contributed a single great idea to the progress of humanity, and have adopted "from the inventions of others . . . only the deceptive appearances and the useless luxuries."[17] In his 1837 "Apology of a Madman," however, Chaadaev declared that Peter the Great "opened our minds to all the great and beautiful ideas which are prevalent among men; he handed us the whole Occident, such as the centuries have fashioned it, and gave us all its history for our history, and all its future for our future." Chaadaev came to view Russia's importing of new ideas as simply "a truth" that "has to be accepted."[18]

Fedor Dostoevsky, in contrast, accomplished the reverse trajectory, evolving from celebratory to disparaging assessments of eclecticism. Early in his career, Dostoevsky looked upon Petersburg's eclecticism positively, seeing in the city's architectural diversity a truly contemporary, national quality. Polemicizing with Custine, Dostoevsky wrote in his 1847 feuilleton series "Petersburg Chronicle" (*Peterburgskaia letopis'*):

> All this diversity testifies to a unity of thought and a unity of movement. This row of buildings of Dutch architecture recalls the time of Peter the Great. This building in the style of Rastrelli recalls the century of Catherine; this one, in the Greek and Roman style, the latest time; but all together recall the history of the European life of Petersburg and all Russia. Even up to the present, Petersburg is in dust and rubble; it is still being created, still becoming.[19]

For Dostoevsky, spatial diversity becomes temporal continuity, as Petersburg's cityscape speaks the history of the world and "the European life of Petersburg and all Russia" simultaneously. The "dust and rubble" of St. Petersburg undergoes a comparable transformation, becoming a sign of creation rather than destruction. But Dostoevsky changed his tune in his 1873 "Little Pictures" (*Malen'kie kartiny*) from *Diary of a Writer*, in an extended nationalistic polemic against the eclectic architecture of St. Petersburg, which, he declared, perfectly reflected the city's characterless, faceless quality:

... there is no other city like it; in the architectural sense, it is a reflection of all architectures in the world, all styles and fashions; everything has been gradually borrowed and everything in its own way disfigured. In these buildings, as in a book, you can read all of the influxes of big and small ideas, which flew ... to us from Europe ... But now, ... one doesn't even know how to define our current architecture. It is a kind of disorder of the present moment.[20]

Once again, Dostoevsky renders St. Petersburg legible, but this time negatively so. Now St. Petersburg tells the story of Russia's wide-eyed worship of the West and the disfigurement of European tradition. Instead of writing history, the St. Petersburg cityscape *erases* history by redoing its façades "for chic." Instead of creating order and narrative, the St. Petersburg cityscape expresses chaos, and is original only in its absolute lack of character. At times, architectural eclecticism tells the story of the world, but elsewhere, it embodies an anti-narrative and thus anti-historical principle in architecture. Accounts of eclecticism almost never find a middle ground that would allow for *selection*, a principle mediating between the two extremes.

Dostoevsky rants against Petersburg's juxtaposition of diverse styles, and its phony invocations of imperial traditions from Egypt, Rome, and modern France. He paints a vivid picture of rotting wooden houses interspersed between marble palaces, and a jumbling together of Roman-style imitations, public hospitals, and institutes evoking the epoch of Napoleon III, Italian palazzos, and pre-revolutionary aristocratic French chateaux. Huge hotels with their "American" air of business, and new industrial structures complete the picture. Dostoevsky's critique in "Little Pictures" establishes the connection between eclecticism and the market that reflected so negatively upon the qualities of the former in Soviet architectural histories. He expresses ironic concern that the newly-built Venetian-style mansions—designed to suggest their arriviste occupants' ancient lineage—might soon bear signboards advertising themselves as pleasure gardens or French hotels for foreign visitors.

In an 1882–1883 four-part survey of the arts during the reign of Alexander II, the critic Vladimir Stasov similarly employed the language of trade and commerce in characterizing eclecticism as a shopper's greed that attempted to establish a history overnight. According to Stasov, architecture was a Janus-like art with two faces, one of which looked backward and represented:

... architecture copied from old models, from books and albums, from photographs and drawings, the architecture of clever people who get smart in class and then with great indifference turn out goods by the yard and by the pound. They only have to stretch out an arm and retrieve what is needed from the shelf. If it suits you, here are five yards of Greek "classicism"; if not, here are three and a quarter of Italian "Renaissance." Don't like that? Well then, here, if you please, is a little piece of the highest sort of "Rococo Louis XV," and if that's not it, here is a nice bit of "Romanesque," six ounces of "Gothic," or a whole gross of "Russian."[21]

In Stasov's characterization, culture and education are reduced to architectural commodities, and the precious legacy of the past becomes useful only insofar as it can be assigned a price.

Stasov's protests emphasize the relationship between eclecticism in Russian architecture and the nineteenth-century search for a national identity. That is, eclecticism overtly performed the operation toward which so much of post-Petrine Russian culture directed itself: to subsume and appropriate the legacy of world culture, especially of Western Europe, for itself. Russian Slavophiles and nationalists also made use of eclecticism, but to forge a modern Russian identity from Eastern cultural referents—Byzantium and old Russia. The second face of architecture, in Stasov's view, was thus the new "Russian" style, of which he heartily approved.

Those who advocated a return to a more authentic past could thus conceive this past in terms of medieval Byzantine as well as classical aesthetics. In the case of the latter, the passing of time dignified the Western-style architecture that Algarotti and Custine had dismissed as mongrel, and eclecticism became a useful whipping boy, accused of degrading an imaginary classical unity. In the nationalists' view, however, eclecticism constituted the logical outgrowth of a Western-style classicism that already excluded Russia's own cultural legacy, if a slight improvement in aesthetic terms.

In this way, even a critic such as Stasov who so favored the pseudo-Russian style could favor architectural eclecticism with a kind word. Stasov granted that the new private homes with their Italian and French excesses were an improvement over "those barracks, gloomy, unadorned, and dull to the point of nausea," from the time of Tsar Nicholas. Recalling this "barracks" classicism drew a lyrical outburst of spleen from Stasov, who invoked "pediments everywhere, endless columns like rows of classical corpses, occasional garlands, wreaths, vases . . . dark and awkward staircases . . . a lifeless correctness everywhere, tastelessness, misery, cold, wide dark corners, walls like those in a political prison, something shed-like and soulless."[22] In comparison, he conceded, the colorful, graceful, and even capricious forms of the Renaissance and Rococo were very welcome.

Although Stasov saw the national trend in architecture as a solution to the excesses of eclecticism, many critics considered the pseudo-Russian style to be part of the problem. In a series of essays that appeared in the journal *World of Art*, preservationist Alexander Benois revived the old notion of classical Petersburg, casting himself as the city's defender. In the 1902 "Painterly Petersburg" (*Zhivopisnyi Peterburg*), the most notable of these essays, Benois declared:

It seems that there is no city on earth that has been less liked than Petersburg. Which epithets has it *not* earned: "putrefying swamp," "absurd invention," "without individuality," "bureaucratic department," "regimental office." I have never been able to agree with all of this, and must, in contrast, confess that I love Petersburg, and even, to the contrary, find a mass of charms that are absolutely distinctive, and characteristic of it alone.[23]

Benois considered Petersburg admirable "as a whole," or at least, "in large pieces, big ensembles, and wide panoramic views." He urged readers to rehabilitate what he saw as Petersburg's colossal, pitiless, and stony Roman beauty, whose larger lines had remained in place despite the ravages of eclecticism, and regretted the developments of the later nineteenth century, which obscured St. Petersburg's essential nature with frivolous, eclectic flourishes.[24] Benois attempted to rally the Russian public, protesting the destruction of perfectly proportioned old mansions to make room for the new architectural "buffoons, loaded with an enormous quantity of cheap and vulgar plaster ornamentation."[25] He deplored the nationalists' misguided attempts to make Petersburg seem more Russian by scattering bogus stylized onion domes and multicolored tile decorations amid the Empire-style structures.

Benois sought to restore the authentic Petersburg masterpiece that has been painted over by unsure amateur hands. To this end, he called for artists to take Petersburg as a subject, to defend the city's classical consistency against the onslaught of "barbarian mutilation."[26] This artistic call to arms points to Benois's creative project of reconceiving Petersburg in aesthetic terms, positing a pure and unitary style for an architectural "classicism" of the Golden Age that had always constituted a mix of styles and elements. Ironically, if there were an architectural style in Petersburg's past that might be immune to accusations of impurity, it would be the reactionary classicism instituted by Nicholas!

Benois's claims about Petersburg nevertheless grow more grandiose as his essay unfolds. He denies the commonplace that Petersburg developed by imitating the West, stating instead that Petersburg "grew and developed in a surprisingly original fashion."[27] While Benois concedes that basic constitutive classical motifs were borrowed from Europe, he declares them to have been recombined into an unprecedented and magnificent new form that is neither European nor Russian. Petersburg's empty spaces and lack of history inspired foreign architects to create on a grander and more original scale than had been possible in their native countries, claims Benois. In this sense, Benois saw Petersburg as more truly representative of eighteenth- and nineteenth-century architecture than its predecessor cities, since only Petersburg offered a "pure" manifestation of period spirit. Benois does not even employ a term to dignify the eclectic phenomenon from the 1830s onward that he refers to as "dilettantish imitation" and "a vinaigrette of *all* styles."[28]

Eclecticism has long suffered a poor reputation as a result of the perplexity it has generated in critics and scholars, and this situation has yet to be fully remedied. A recent popular history in Russian by Natalia Glinka subtitled "The Golden Age of St. Petersburg Architecture" stops pointedly with the last of Carl Rossi's "ensemble" projects, the construction of the Alexandrinskii Theater complex in the early 1830s.[29] This contemporary historical survey follows the early-twentieth-century example set by preservationist Igor Grabar, whose history of Petersburg architecture purports to cover the eighteenth and nineteenth centuries, but goes no further than "Nikolaian Classicism," providing a traditional categorization by architect and individual monumental structure.[30] Architects who were active during the eclectic period may grace the Petersburg architectural pantheon only if their early work was thoroughly grounded in the neoclassical style, or if they were responsible for any of Petersburg's most celebrated buildings. Such was August Montferrand (1786–1858), who designed and built the lavishly eclectic St. Isaac's Cathedral, but receives much less qualified approval for his Alexander Column on Palace Square. Similarly, Alexander Briullov (1798–1877) created interiors in Gothic, Renaissance, and Moorish styles for the Winter Palace after the 1837 fire, but is perhaps best known for his work on the General Staff Headquarters.[31] Grabar's contemporary Vladimir Kurbatov reserved particular contempt for the contributions of Andrei Stakenschneider (1802–1865), who built the Mariinsky palace and the Beloselsky-Belozersky palace, both completed in the 1840s, and Constantine Thon (1794–1881), architect of the 1830s St. Catherine church, which combined an essentially neoclassical structure with early Russian and Byzantine motifs.[32]

Russian historians may have neglected eclecticism, but many writers have gone so far as to obliterate it, instead canonizing the ideal classical Petersburg they wish to remember. In this spirit, Alexander Solzhenitsyn's 1960s prose poem titled "The City on the Neva" celebrates Petersburg's "perfect, everlasting beauty."[33] "It is alien to us," he declares, "yet it is our greatest glory." Solzhenitsyn expresses his gratitude that Petersburg will remain its classical self, immune to the innovations of modern times: "What a blessing that no new building is allowed here. No wedding-cake skyscraper can elbow its way on to the Nevsky Prospekt, no five-storey shoebox can ruin the Griboyedov canal. There is no architect living, no matter how servile and incompetent, who can use his influence to build on any site nearer than the Black River or the Okhta . . . What a pleasure it is today to stroll down those avenues." Like Benois, Solzhenitsyn turns back the clock to an imaginary era and reconceives Petersburg according to the city's insistent mythology—without the architectural eclecticism that was a major part of its history.

Petersburg's most sophisticated contemporary cultural theorists and elegists also purvey the prevailing view on architectural eclecticism. In his 1979 essay "A Guide to a Renamed City," Joseph Brodsky characterizes the gradual decline of Petersburg architecture from the perfect abstraction of classicism to the unlovely shapes of capitalism: "This was dictated as much by the swing toward functionalism (which is but a noble name for profit-making) as by general aesthetic degradation."[34] Brodsky, like so many others, evokes the "barrack-like style of the Nicholas I epoch," and the "cumbersome apartment buildings squeezed between the classical ensembles." "Then came the Victorian wedding cakes and hearses," notes Brodsky, referring to eclecticism's heyday with the same phrase Solzhenitsyn had used to characterize a thankfully *absent* feature of the cityscape. "And, by the last quarter of the century, this city that started as a leap from history into the future began to look in some parts like a regular Northern European bourgeois." Brodsky attributes the diseased spread of eclecticism to the pernicious influence of late-nineteenth-century capitalist Europe, and not to Petersburg's own unique copycat style. Still, the aesthetic effect remains the same.

And yet, Brodsky invokes the imperial capital's architecture before Nicholas I as a phenomenon no less haphazard, and thus implies continuity between "classical" and "eclectic" Petersburg. When the infamous "window on Europe"—or in Brodsky's words, the "sluices"—were opened, he declares, European architectural motifs "gushed into and inundated" St. Petersburg, in a variation on the ubiquitous Petersburg flooding motif. Petersburg represents European aesthetic surplus; the city has been overwhelmed by Western architectural motifs, just as the Russian language was flooded by a thoroughly unregulated influx of foreign words during the eighteenth century. Because the vastness of the surrounding space demanded a proportionate deployment of European architectural styles, however, Russia resembled a "blown-up projection" of European civilization "through a *lanterna magica* onto an enormous screen of space and waters."[35] This overdone quality attributed to Petersburg—in marked contrast to restrained and tasteful classical proportions—extends to the scale of the buildings themselves, characterized by Brodsky as an enlarged projection and an ephemeral image, rather than a verifiable reality. Brodsky's vision of Petersburg conflates two aspects of the city's persistent failure to be authentic: the aesthetic and the ontological. Regarding the European tradition, Petersburg remains a fake: "whatever the architects took for the standard in their work—Versailles, Fontainebleau, and so on—the outcome was always unmistakably Russian."

Despite his description of the city's eclectic history, however, Brodsky ultimately insists that classical form has remained a Petersburg precept. Brodsky rejoices that Lenin's fateful arrival at Finland Station "froze" St. Petersburg, since the Bolsheviks soon transferred the seat of their government to Moscow and paid little attention to the former capital, which escaped major intrusions of monumental Stalinist architecture. In fact, the motif of freezing speaks to Brodsky's own desire to protect an imaginary authentic Petersburg, not from the ravages of the twentieth century, but from the truths of nineteenth-century architectural history. Even Brodsky, who acknowledges Petersburg's eclecticism more fully than any other modern cultural critic, seems vulnerable to the potent mythology of the city's aesthetic authenticity. Although Petersburg has so often been termed *inorganic,* lacking the subtle temporal and stylistic layering of cities that have gradually evolved, Russian writers such as Brodsky and Solzhenitsyn themselves wishfully hold this process of organic evolution at bay by freezing time.

Interestingly, however, Brodsky gives eclecticism its due in another essay: "I must say that from these façades and porticoes—classical, modern, eclectic, with their columns, pilasters, and plastered heads of mythic animals or people—from their ornaments and caryatids holding up the balconies, from the torsos in the niches of their entrances, I have learned more about the history of our world than I subsequently have from any book. Greece, Rome, Egypt—all of them were there."[36] The great poet and essayist briefly renders Petersburg's eclecticism entirely legitimate as a source of cultural literacy and an essential part of his own artistic evolution. Of course, Brodsky is speaking of the Soviet period, when citizens were not free to travel abroad and Petersburg architecture was the closest they could get to the "real" thing.

Perhaps it is more accurate to distinguish between those such as Brodsky and Benois, who acknowledge Petersburg's eclecticism, even if most do so regretfully, and those such as Solzhenitsyn who ignore it entirely. Twentieth-century deifiers of the mythical "Pushkin's Petersburg" fall into this latter category, among them the cultural semiotician Yurii Lotman, whose essay "The Symbolism of Petersburg and Semiotic Problematics of the City" was written five years after Brodsky's essay and belongs to the same tradition of Petersburg critique.[37] Reprising the early Dostoevsky, Lotman asserts that in its intense contrasts and metaphysical paradoxes, Petersburg represents a "unique phenomenon in world civilization." Sounding like Benois, Lotman cites "[T]he architecture of the city, unique in the consistency of the huge ensembles which cannot be divided up into buildings of different periods, as is the case in cities with long histories."[38] According to Lotman, Petersburg is thus distinguished precisely by the *absence* of diversely blended styles in random juxtaposition, as is usual in most cities.

What has become of Petersburg's infamous eclecticism? To be fair, Lotman's Petersburg is a historicized one, pertaining to the early decades of the nineteenth century—a particular and much-beloved moment in the city's cultural history. But the architecture of Lotman's imperial capital seems frozen much in the way of Brodsky's Soviet-era Petersburg.

Lotman describes the first half of the nineteenth century as a time of "cultural and semiotic contrasts which served as the soil for an exceptionally intense intellectual life" in St. Petersburg, characterized by a struggle between "Petersburg the literary text" and "Petersburg the [normative] metalanguage."[39] He evokes the constant collisions between the heterogeneous texts and codes that collide within the "cauldron" of the city environment. Lotman neglects to treat architectural eclecticism on its own terms, however, as part and parcel of the heterogeneous mix. Instead, Lotman implicitly assigns Petersburg architecture to the monolithic "metalanguage," which literature sought to subvert. He celebrates the city's literary, social, and cultural eclecticism, but only against the background of a Petersburg that he renders architecturally much more coherent than it truly was.

Only recently have twentieth-century Russian sources started to treat eclecticism's low status in explicit terms as part of Russian cultural history. The 1988 exhibition catalogue *Lost Architectural Monuments of Petersburg-Leningrad*, for example, provides an unusually subtle perspective on the relative distribution of cultural value, noting that the term "monument" (*pamiatnik*) became a distinct historical-artistic category for the city only at the beginning of the twentieth century: "For Petersburg, this included the surviving constructions of the entire eighteenth century and the first third of the nineteenth century, that is, of baroque and classicism. Eclecticism on the whole was despised, *moderne* was selectively respected, but not counted in terms of 'monuments' because of its recent appearance."[40] A few Russian architectural historians have concentrated their efforts on the problematic second half of the nineteenth century in an affirmatively revisionist spirit, among them Andrei Punin, who pointedly titled one of his monographs *Architectural Monuments of Petersburg: The Second Half of the Nineteenth Century*.[41]

The architectural historian Evgenia Kirichenko was one of the first to take eclecticism on its own terms, rather than assessing eclecticism negatively against the conventions of classicism. She thus advocated a serious effort at "deciphering" the architectural language of later nineteenth-century Russian buildings.[42] In Kirichenko's view, the democratic diffusion of cultural influences is a deliberately manifested philosophical feature of eclecticism, the operative values of eclecticism being distribution (*ravnomernost'*) and equivalence (*ravnoznachnost'*). In short, eclecticism constitutes "a multiplicity of forms and a single device," resulting in a profusion and democratization of expressive means.[43]

Recent trends thus link eclecticism positively with Petersburg's essential qualities and with its status as a "meta-city" that reproduces and creatively combines images from other world capitals and, in fact, the spirit of the times seems almost to dictate seeing Petersburg in this way. N. B. Ivanova considers Petersburg a "style-engendering" city, in "adapting, transforming, assimilating, and processing diverse urban styles."[44] I. V. Sakharov links Petersburg architecture with its inhabitants, who comprised a "Pan-European world," a synthetic "sign of European unity," even a "Europe in miniature," that surpassed Western Europe itself.[45] Sakharov attributes this phenomenon to the fact that Petersburg residents, even those who were Russian, were all immigrants in some sense. There existed no "indigenous ethnocultural nucleus" in Petersburg to exert a dominant influence on new arrivals from different parts of the Empire—Finland, Poland, the Baltics, and Armenia, to give a few examples—and these residents were thus compelled to reinvent themselves as "Petersburgers." At the same time, Europeans of all kinds—Germans, Dutch, French, and Swedes—also made their way to Petersburg and became permanent members of the community. Sakharov suggests a link between the inhabitants and the cityscape, whereby the Petersburg human cultural synthesis manifested itself visually in architecture.

The historian K. G. Isupov similarly argues for considering eclecticism as Petersburg's "stylistic dominant," invoking the city's "stylistic polyglossia" in an "aesthetic-historical" sense, and not according to eclecticism's more narrow discipline-specific connotations in architecture and art criticism.[46] For Isupov, eclecticism constitutes a stylistic rather than period designation, and forms the basis for Petersburg's essential character of "city-compilation," "city-collection," and "city-museum."[47] In his view, St. Petersburg presents an ideal object of study in its "hypersemiotic" aspect and in the city's consciousness of itself as an aesthetic artifact. Of course, Isupov's affirmation of Petersburg's composite qualities is not a new characterization of the city, but an old characterization given a new, positive spin. Given the central role that eclecticism has historically played in the persistent view of St. Petersburg as an inauthentic capital, however, it is ironic that eclecticism offers the solution to Petersburg's current identity crisis.

Nineteenth-century eclecticism is not simply another name for the culminating confusion of the "crisis in classicism," but rather a poetics that represents a natural and logical outgrowth of the time.[48] Eclecticism represents a deliberately horizontal and relational, and not a vertical or hegemonic expressive strategy, and in this, eclecticism corresponds to the literary realism of the time and its exploratory movements across the city surface. What is more, Petersburg did not merely pass through an eclectic period during the latter part of the nineteenth century, in a highly regrettable departure from its authentic neoclassical self. St. Petersburg has always been eclectic.

Eclecticism: The Unprincipled Principle

Criticism of eclecticism as sloppy and indiscriminate ignores the principle at the word's very root, however, as well as eclecticism's history as a philosophical movement. The term comes from the Greek *eklektikos* (selective) and *eklegein* (to select), meaning to choose out of a selection, or to distinguish. Etymologically, at least, eclecticism is not perverse or random, but rather intentional. Eclecticism's primary meaning, moreover, implies an evaluative basis for selection—choosing what appears to be *best* from diverse sources, systems, or styles. Eclecticism is democratic in its array of choices, but privileges the freedom of the creator, and in this, prefigures modernist art techniques such as pastiche and bricolage.

Eclecticism as a philosophy arose in Greece in the second century B.C., as a fusion of three major schools of thought—Academic, Peripatetic, and Stoic—that sought to combine doctrines about nature, life, and the divine from different schools of thought. Eclecticism was, moreover, implicated in the relationship between Greece and Rome, once Greece had become part of the Roman Empire. The Romans were prone to eclectic borrowing, since they had not developed their own independent philosophical systems, and in this, they are paralleled by the nineteenth-century Russian Empire's aesthetic predicament.

The generic mixing and matching specific to nineteenth-century aesthetic eclecticism was a cultural phenomenon inspired by the teachings of Victor Cousin, whose 1818 course at the Sorbonne, *Du Vrai, du Beau et du Bien* referred to his system of philosophy as "éclecticism." Cousin attempted to combine and distill the teachings of diverse English, Scottish, French, and German philosophers, creating a synthetic approach to the discipline that combined elements of spiritualism and scientism.[49] Cousin's work provided the basis for French academic philosophy, which was taught throughout the French lycée system and at universities from a common syllabus known as the *programme*. In its nineteenth-century incarnations pertaining to philosophy and then architecture, eclecticism retains a strong pedagogical component, stressing the need for a discriminating receptivity to diverse traditions. In this, true eclecticism represents an antidote to unreflective "revivalism," not an example of it.

Nineteenth-century "eclecticism" applies as a period and style designation to European architecture beginning with neo-Gothic experiments, and with what Claude Mignot calls "a more liberal use of the whole vocabulary of the Graeco-Roman tradition," which had been too narrowly interpreted during the "crisis of classicism."[50] Mignot distinguishes "typological eclecticism," according to which an architect adapts a model from the past to meet contemporary requirements, from "synthetic eclecticism," which allows an architect to combine elements of different periods. Typological eclecticism in the nineteenth century selected classical architecture for public buildings, and medieval architecture—generally Byzantine, Gothic, or Romanesque—for religious structures. But architectural treatises such as Thomas Hope's *Historical Essay on Architecture* (1835) also called for a new composite style that borrowed individual features selectively from the past as appropriate for a particular nation's climate, topography, and cultural environment. Eclecticism in architecture is often linked to the work of Charles Garnier, builder of the ornamental neo-baroque Grand Opera building in Paris (1861–1874), perhaps the most famous building of the nineteenth century and an exemplar of the so-called "Second Empire" or "Napoleon III" style.

Eclecticism represented an all-encompassing language of culture. In this sense, eclecticism was more worldly than classicism, since eclecticism did not confine itself to Greek, Roman, and Renaissance influences, but reveled in Eastern motifs, and in architectural styles such as Baroque, Gothic, and medieval Russian, whose aesthetic reputations had declined by the latter part of the eighteenth century.

An 1837 periodical article attributed to the Russian writer Nestor Kukol'nik evaluated the new aesthetic standard for architecture in connection with the author's visit to Peter the Great's summer palace, Peterhof, whose surroundings were undergoing rapid expansion and development. With cautious enthusiasm, Kukol'nik noted the coexistence of small summer dachas, sumptuous private residences in diverse architectural styles, and the new neoclassical Peterhof theater:

> Our age is an eclectic one, in everything its characteristic feature is intelligent choice (*umnyi vybor*) . . . variety is superb, enchanting, but only if it is exquisite. The Parthenon and other remnants of Greek architecture; the Moorish Alhambra; Gothic cathedrals of the old and new styles; the Italian architecture of Palladio . . . and so on. Ancient Venice . . . Indian architecture with its Byzantine development, in a word, all kinds of architecture can be exquisite, and all of them reciprocally employ their means, intermingle and produce new kinds. But these kinds are only exquisite and original when they preserve the harmony of their parts and their majesty . . . as a whole.[51]

Kukol'nik supported the creation of "new kinds" combining diverse influences, but called upon the principles of taste, proportion, and harmony to guide these choices.[52] Eclecticism as originally conceived manifested precisely this balance between free choice and traditional values.

Kukol'nik's remarks are part of an ongoing polemic about artistic form and function in Russia during the 1830s–40s that was often directed against classicism. As Kukol'nik's declaration illustrates, one of the signs of architectural eclecticism in its early days, related to Romantic views of art, was a broader access to all past civilizations, not only to the most familiar aspects of Western classical antiquity. Initially, the eclectic impulse was connected with a general trend toward "historicism," as expressed in a well-known statement by the critic Vissarion Belinsky:

> Our age is primarily a historical one. Historical contemplation powerfully and irresistibly penetrated all spheres of contemporary consciousness. History became the general basis for and only condition of any living knowledge: without it, the apprehension of art and philosophy would be impossible. Moreover, art itself has now become primarily historical in character.[53]

Belinsky here invokes the heightened interest in the history, architecture, and culture of different epochs that became one of the defining features of nineteenth-century thought during the 1830s–40s, an orientation that continued through the 1890s.[54] Growing out of the philosophies of history proposed by Herder and Hegel, historicism countered Enlightenment philosophy of the preceding century, and maintained that historiographical thinking alone, and not universal principles, could account for human culture. In this, historicism provided a marked contrast to classicism's reliance on the "timeless" and "abstract" forms of antiquity. Historicism was eclecticism's better-behaved older sibling, who dignified its less pedantic relative by association.[55]

During the 1830s and even 1840s, eclecticism seemed a positive development—as in Kukol'nik's declaration—heralding a new freedom in the use of architectural features. Only during the second half of the nineteenth century did eclecticism acquire its negative connotations of sloppiness, ahistoricity, and tastelessness. But were these criticisms of eclecticism justified? In his Encyclopedia entry on "eclecticism," Diderot takes pains to distinguish eclecticism from "syncretism," which he terms a less principled approach to combining heterogeneous sources. "Imagine a poor insolent fellow," writes Diderot of a hypothetical syncretic, "ill content with the rags that cover him, who throws himself upon the best-dressed passers-by, tears from one a blouse, from another an overcoat, and makes from his plunder a bizarre outfit of every possible color and part."[56] Syncretism, as Renate Lachmann defines it, is "antistylistic," anarchic, transgressive, dehierarchicizing, detotalizing, and semiotically promiscuous.[57] Eclecticism, in contrast, takes a more benign, non-judgmental view of its diverse inspirations. Like syncretism, eclecticism juxtaposes diverse historical and cultural referents.[58] But syncretism is defiant and doctrinaire, whereas eclecticism is admiring of its sources, even as it culls from them selectively. If eclecticism is sometimes confused with the later phenomenon of syncretism, it is also reviled in the same terms as the earlier eighteenth-century style of rococo, which rejoiced in anachronistic combinations of ornamentation and its concomitant rejection of both organic Nature and culturally-imposed symmetry.[59]

As mentioned in connection with Cousin, however, eclecticism also possesses a scholarly component: its citations of diverse architectural detail are meant to be historically accurate, if not pedantically or fanatically so. Juxtaposing elements from diverse periods and places offered a new artistic "language" for representing culture, since the choice of motifs was meant to be both artistically *and* functionally motivated, in order to signal a building's identity to viewers. A revisionist view of eclecticism might thus assert that eclecticism strove to re-forge the connection between form and function that had been lost during the long period of undifferentiated classicism. Eclectic buildings signaled their identities through associative visual strategies, making clear eclecticism's preoccupation with cultural literacy. Detractors have argued, however, that eclecticism's recourse to the architectural past extended only to the surface structures of buildings, not to their larger forms and underlying design. Evgenia Borisova counters these objections with the assertion that eclecticism was related to the general influence of literature on art during this period, since eclectic buildings required their audience to process the complex, allegorical associations conveyed by details of structure and ornamentation.[60]

It can also be argued that eclecticism is worldlier and more open-minded than neoclassicism. Eclecticism does not confine itself to influences from Greek, Roman, and Renaissance culture, but revels in Eastern motifs and lines, and in architectural styles like Baroque, Gothic, and medieval Russian, whose aesthetic reputations had declined by the latter part of the eighteenth century. A new reality could be constructed from pieces of the past, since invoking this past in fragmented form pays tribute to history, while denying history's power to determine the future.

At its best, eclecticism represents a meditation on tradition, on multiple conceptual unities, alike in their diversity. Eclecticism is inherently democratic and non-hierarchical, since no single style or historical period is privileged over all others. Petersburg's architectural eclecticism points backwards in time to the imaginary neoclassical union of all artistic forms and genres, but transforms that hierarchical, vertical structure of cultural meaning into a horizontal network of semiotic connections. Petersburg's eclecticism may well be related to what Philippe Hamon has more generally identified as a nineteenth-century poetics of "expositions," whose aspects include "a delight in the encyclopedia of novelties and in the universal exposition of knowledge and products," and the creation of "a site for eclecticism."[61]

Although aesthetic denunciations of the Petersburg cityscape are numerous, support for architectural eclecticism turns up in unexpected quarters, as in Nikolai Gogol's essay "On the Architecture of the Present Day" (1831), which preaches expansion in the use of architectural forms and ornaments. While Gogol (who hated living in St. Petersburg) argues against eclecticism operating within single architectural structures, he celebrates eclecticism as a feature of the cityscape as a whole:

> A city should consist of varied masses, if you will, so that it provides pleasure to the gaze. . . . On a single street, let there rise the gloomy Gothic, the Eastern laden with luxurious ornamentation, the monumental Egyptian, and the Greek, infused with harmonious proportions. Let there be visible the lightly-protruding milky dome, the infinite religious spire, the Eastern mitre, the flat Italian roof and the high, figured Flemish roof, the four-sided pyramid, the rounded column, and the angular obelisk. Let the buildings not merge into a single, even, undifferentiated wall, but rather incline variously up and down.[62]

Gogol thus ultimately asserts the eclectic principle in urban aesthetics overall, although he ostensibly rejects eclecticism for individual structures in favor of single, coherent forms. In Gogol's view, every part of a city should be a "vivid landscape." "Architecture," declares Gogol grandly, toward the conclusion of his essay, ". . . is a chronicle of the world: It speaks when songs and legends are silent, when no one speaks any longer about a vanished people."[63] He goes so far as to propose in a footnote that cities might designate a single street that constitutes an architectural chronicle, proceeding through the architectural styles of different ages and narrating a history of "the development of taste." Citizens too lazy to read through heavy volumes could simply walk the length of this street "in order to know everything." Gogol's proposal allows eclecticism to achieve the ultimate coherence of textual history, serving its pedagogical function, as Victor Cousin advocated, and conveying the diachronic study of history by means of a synchronic, all-encompassing cityscape.[64] If applied to Petersburg, Gogol's recommendations correspond to the now-canonical view of the Russian imperial capital as a "city of cities," a second-degree aesthetic phenomenon like literature itself.

Although Petersburg has been termed inorganic in its lack of the temporal and stylistic architectural layering typical of gradually evolving cities, Russian cultural critics have themselves held this very process at bay with their rhetoric of canonizing the classical. In fact, appropriately, Petersburg's first century, the eighteenth, was the very period during which questions of influence and originality in art began to receive full, theoretical articulation. Renate Lachmann claims that it is "the classical part of literature that provides the place where memory is shaped within a given culture."[65] The "classical" is that cultural locus from which emerge mechanisms for selecting, preserving, and transmitting cultural values through normative concepts such as genre, style, and tradition. The classical principle, in Lachmann's view, polices the cultural terrain, ever on the watch for invasive threats to canonical structures. But paradoxically, revision is a natural aspect of a canon's ongoing life within a culture. Or, as Lachmann puts it: "In order to be what it truly is, the classical has to initiate an act of destruction."[66] In this sense, the eighteenth-century classicism of Petersburg architecture, even as an ideal, already contained the seeds of its eclectic offshoots.

If St. Petersburg contains all cities and cultures within itself, moreover, then it must be more and not less than its predecessors, at once an aesthetic critique and a validation of the urban project. As Lachmann declares, "In Russian literature, Petersburg is the supreme memory place: the 'tattooed' city bearing the incisions and the inscriptions of history and of stories . . . imagined as a world, as a universe in which all cultures, all contrary and heterogeneous mythological elements are contained."[67] St. Petersburg has always been authentically eclectic—only the negative characterizations of eclecticism have cast the city as fake. In short, the aesthetics of derivation is St. Petersburg's greatest art.

Notes

1. If St. Petersburg seemed cobbled together from bits of pre-existing realia, visual representations of the city did not help matters by making patently false claims. During the first part of the eighteenth century, it was common practice to depict as complete buildings that were not yet constructed. Such drawings and lithographs also populated the bridges, streets, and squares of the under-inhabited city with a bustling crowd of imaginary citizens. See Aleksei Zubov's 1727 engraving of Saint Petersburg for an example of this phenomenon. For a comparison of this engraving with a contemporary representation of Amsterdam, see Grigory Kaganov, *Images of Space: St. Petersburg in the Visual and Verbal Arts*, trans. Sidney Monas (Stanford: Stanford University Press, 1997).

2. Gérard Genette, *Palimpsests: Literature in the Second Degree*, trans. Channa Newman and Claude Doubinsky (Lincoln: University of Nebraska Press, 1997), p. 80.

3. Ibid., p. 87.

4. The basic corpus of this "literary mythology" includes such fictional works from the 1830s as Alexander Pushkin's "The Bronze Horseman" and "The Queen of Spades," as well as Nikolai Gogol's "Nevsky Prospect," "The Nose," "The Portrait," "Diary of a Madman," and "The Overcoat." The tradition continues with Fedor Dostoevsky's "Poor Folk," "The Double," "White Nights," "Notes from the Underground," and *Crime and Punishment*, and in the twentieth century, with Andrei Belyi's *Petersburg*. This list does not even begin to exhaust the full corpus of "Petersburg" literature, but these works represent the core texts that all Russian readers know.

5. As the Marquis de Custine exclaimed, "Singular taste! Temples erected to clerks!" See Marquis de Custine, *Empire of the Czar: A Journey Through Eternal Russia* (New York: Doubleday, 1989), p. 152.

6. See the introduction to Monika Greenleaf and Stephen Moeller-Sally, eds., *Russian Subjects: Empire, Nation, and the Culture of the Golden Age* (Evanston: Northwestern University Press, 1998). For a discussion of the harmonious principles governing literature, music, and architecture of this period, see T. F. Savarenskaia, "Evritmiia v arkhitekture Peterburga pushkinskoi pory." *Arkhitektura v istorii russkoi kul'tury*, I. A. Bondarenko, ed. (Moscow: RAN, 1996).

7. Moisei Kagan declares the Empire style to be a synthesis of geometrical classicism and plastic, dynamic, and highly ornamental Baroque. See his *Grad Petrov v istorii russkoi kul'tury* (SPb: Slaviia, 1996), p. 272.

8. "Vospominaniia O. A. Przhetslavskogo." *Russkaia starina*, no. 11, 1874, p. 465.

9. *Ocherki istorii Leningrada*, t. 2 (Period kapitalizma—vtoraia polovina XIX veka) (Moscow: AN SSSR, 1957), pp. 793–809 ("Arkhitektura Peterburga").

10. Peter Collins, *Changing Ideals in Modern Architecture 1750–1950* (London: Faber and Faber), p. 117.

11. Francesco Algarotti, "Letters from Count Algarotti to Lord Hervey and the Marquis Scipio Maffei," Letter IV, June 30, 1739. (London: Johnson and Payne, 1769; Reprint in Goldsmiths'-Kress Library of Economic Literature, no. 10500). For more information about Algarotti's "Russian Journeys" and commentary on his letters, see M. G. Talalaia, "Franchesko Al'garotti: Russkie puteshestviia. Perevod s ital'ianskogo, predislovie i primechaniia" in *Nevskii arkhiv* III (SPb: Atheneum Feniks, 1997). See also M. S. Nekliudova and A. L. Ospovat, "Okno v Evropu: Istochnikovedcheskii etiud k 'Mednomu Vsadniku,'" *Lotmanovskii sbornik* 2 (Moscow: RGGU, 1997).

12. W. Bruce Lincoln also suggests something of this sort when he describes Peter the Great's 1697 Grand Embassy of the Russians to the West: "Everything Peter saw during his first trip to the West helped him create an eclectic image of what Russia might become." See his *Sunlight at Midnight: St. Petersburg and the Rise of Modern Russia* (New York: Basic Books, 2000), p. 22.

13. Custine, pp. 87–89.

14. Custine, p. 88.

15. E. Viollet-le-Duc, *L'Art Russe* (Paris, 1877), pp. 184–5.

16. The same might be true of the image of Petersburg as a "city of stone." During a 1908 visit to St. Petersburg, the English travel-writer A. Maccullum Scott strolled along Nevsky Prospect, which he identified to his readers as "the pride and boast of St. Petersburg." Scott noted the "uninspired copying of classical and Renaissance forms" and observed, "Stucco and plaster are universal, not boldly avowing itself as such, but ruled and squared into a miserable counterfeit of dressed stone." See A. Maccullum Scott, *Through Finland to St. Petersburg* (London: Grant Richards, 1909), pp. 227–8. Note that this use of plaster and stucco was also widespread in the eighteenth century, used on wooden building facades to create the effect of stonemasonry.

17. Petr Chaadaev, "First Letter," *Russian Philosophy*, vol. 1, James M. Edie, James P. Scanlan, and Mary-Barbara Zeldin, eds. (Knoxville: University of Tennessee Press, 1976), pp. 112, 116.

18. Petr Chaadaev, "Apology of a Madman," *Readings in Russian Civilization*, vol. II, Thomas Riha, ed. (Chicago: University of Chicago Press, 1969), pp. 311–312. Of course, the irony of this shift in viewpoint must be noted. The 1836 publication of Chaadaev's first philosophical letter resulted in the author being declared officially insane and placed under house arrest for more than a year. Thus the "madman" of the 1837 Apology's title was an independent thinker who became receptive to cultural eclecticism after being tormented by the repressive tsarist regime.

19. F. M. Dostoevsky, "Peterburgskaia letopis'," *Polnoe sobranie khudozhestvennykh sochinenii*, B. Tomashevskii and K. Khalabaev, eds., t. 8 (Moscow: Gosudarstvennoe izdatel'stvo, 1926–1930), p. 23. For more information about Dostoevsky's response to the Marquis de Custine's account, see E. I. Kiiko, "Belinskii i Dostoevskii o knige Kiustina 'Rossiia v 1839' " in *Dostoevskii: Materialy i issledovaniia*, vol. 1 (Leningrad: Nauka, 1974), pp. 196–200.

20. F. M. Dostoevskii, "Malen'kie kartiny," *Polnoe sobranie sochinenii v tridtsati tomakh* (Leningrad: Nauka, 1980), vol. 21, pp. 106–7.

21. V. V. Stasov, "Dvadtsat' piat' let russkogo iskusstva." *Izbrannye sochineniia v trekh tomakh*, vol. 2 (Moscow: Iskusstvo, 1952), p. 499. Translation to English from William Craft Brumfield, *The Origins of Modernism in Russian Architecture* (Berkeley: University of California Press, 1991), p. 6.

22. Ibid., p. 510.

23. Alexander Benois, "Zhivopisnyi Peterburg." *Mir iskusstva*, no. 1, 1902, p. 1.

24. This originary conception of St. Petersburg as a stern geometrical city exists as part of the city's mythology rather than its history. As historian Iurii Egorov points out, with the abandonment of Leblond's model plan for the city, "the growing capital had no coherent master plan and developed instead according to local planning efforts centering around the Peter and Paul Fortress and the Admiralty." Since the central part of the city was so "poorly balanced," later eighteenth-century and nineteenth-century planners tried to reintegrate the "disparate fragments" that constituted St. Petersburg at the beginning of Catherine's reign and afterward. See Iu. A. Egorov, *The Architectural Planning of St. Petersburg*, trans. Eric Dluhosch (Athens: Ohio University Press, 1969), p. 179.

25. Alexander Benois, "Krasota Peterburga." *Mir iskusstva*, no. 8, 1902, p. 141.

26. Benois's exhortation recalls Konstantin Batiushkov's characterization of St. Petersburg as an ideal subject for artists as well as an art academy in itself nearly a century earlier in his 1814 sketch "Progulka v Akademiiu khudozhestv."

27. "Zhivopisnyi Peterburg," p. 2.
28. Alexander Benois, "Materialy dlia istorii vandalizma v Rossii." *Mir iskusstva*, no. 12, 1903, p. 118.
29. N. I. Glinka, "Krasuisia, grad Petrov . . . " *Zolotoi vek arkhitektury Sankt-Peterburga* (SPb: Lenizdat, 1996).
30. I. E. Grabar', *Peterburgskaia arkhitektura v XVIII i XIX vekakh* (SPb: Lenizdat, 1994).
31. Interestingly, the nineteenth-century perspective on the Petersburg cityscape may not have been so uniformly anti-eclectic, however. Vladimir Mikhnevich's 1874 popular reference guidebook *Peterburg ves' na ladoni*, for example, includes a relatively short list of the city's "Remarkable Buildings," which lists the notably eclectic Moscow Railroad Station and the Beloselsky-Belozersky Palace alongside such Petersburg "classics" as the Peter-Paul Fortress, the Senate and Synod, Gostinnyi Dvor, the Stock Exchange, and the New Admiralty. See Vladimir Mikhnevich, *Peterburg ves' na ladoni* (SPb: Izdanie K.N. Plotnikova, 1874), pp. 240–51.
32. Kurbatov, pp. 149–50. Kurbatov's views are echoed by a contemporary cultural history of St. Petersburg. In a chapter called "The Search for a New Style," Yurii Ovsiannikov declares that Stakenschneider, like Thon, was "a typical architect from the epoch characterized by social stagnation and the lack of an authentic style. See his *Tri veka Sankt-Peterburga: Istoriia * Kul'tura * Byt* (Moscow: Galart, 1997), p. 217.
33. Alexander Solzhenitsyn, "The City on the Neva," *Stories and Prose Poems* (The Bodley Head, 1970), p. 233.
34. Joseph Brodsky, "A Guide to a Renamed City," *Less Than One: Selected Essays* (New York: Farrar Strauss Giroux, 1986), p. 81.
35. Ibid., p. 77.
36. Joseph Brodsky, "Less Than One," *Less Than One: Selected Essays*, p. 5. Petersburg abounds in statuary and thus teaches cultural literacy to those who learn this visual language and can identify Neptune on the Stock Exchange, Mercury on the Customs House, Athena at the Peter-Paul fortress gates and the Public Library, Nike over the General Staff headquarters archway, Apollo in his chariot on the Aleksandrinskii theater, and Mars on the barracks of the Horse Guards regiment. See Iurii Rakov, *Antichnye strazhi Peterburga* (St. Petersburg: Khimiia, 1996). See also P. N. Matveev, *Atlanty i kariatidy Peterburga* (SPb: Iskusstvo—SPB, 2001).
37. Yurii Lotman, "Simvolika Peterburga i problemy semiotiki goroda." *Stat'i po istorii russkoi literatury XVIII—pervoi poloviny XIX veka* (Tallinn: Aleksandra, 1992). Translated text from *Universe of the Mind: A Semiotic Theory of Culture*, trans. Ann Shukman (Bloomington: Indiana University Press, 1990), pp. 191–214.
38. Lotman., pp. 16–17.
39. Ibid., pp. 20–21.
40. V. V. Antonov and A. V. Kobak, eds., *Utrachennye pamiatniki arkhitektury Peterburga-Leningrada* (Leningrad: Khudozhnik RSFSR, 1988), p. 3.
41. A. L. Punin, *Arkhitekturnye pamiatniki Peterburga—vtoraia polovina XIX veka* (Leningrad: Lenizdat, 1981). Other important Russian work on architectural eclecticism includes E. A. Borisova, *Russkaia arkhitektura vtoroi poloviny XIX veka* (Moscow: Nauka, 1979), E. I. Kirichenko, *Russkaia arkhitektura 1830–1910-kh godov* (Moscow: Iskusstvo, 1978), and A. L. Punin, *Arkhitektura Peterburga serediny XIX veka* (Leningrad: Lenizdat, 1990). These three authors have also produced a number of articles on this topic.
42. E. I. Kirichenko, *Russkaia arkhitektura 1830–1910-kh godov*, p. 8. For a careful analysis of many different trends and pronouncements concerning architecture in Russia during the nineteenth century, see E. I. Kirichenko, *Arkhitekturnye teorii XIX veka v Rossii* (Moscow: Iskusstvo, 1986). See also E. I. Kirichenko, "Romantizm i istorizm v russkoi arkhitekture XIX veka (K voprosu o dvukh fazakh razvitiia eklektiki)," *Arkhitekturnoe nasledstvo* 36 (1988).
43. Kirichenko, *Russkaia arkhitektura 1830–1910–kh godov*, p. 36.
44. N. B. Ivanova, "Zagadka i taina v literature 'peterburgskogo stilia.' " *Fenomen Peterburga* (SPb: Blits, 2000), p. 96. Ivanova calls Petersburg "the most postmodern of the important world cities" because it combines entire epochs, and not merely different tendencies. But Ivanova goes on to characterize the "Petersburg style" in literature of this period as a poetics of "the secret," discussing the best-known Petersburg works ("The Queen of Spades," "The Bronze Horseman," "The Overcoat," *Crime and Punishment*) in terms of the fantastic, and not the eclectic.

45. I. V. Sakharov, "Stolitsa Rossiiskoi imperii kak proobraz ob"edinennoi Evropy: vzgliad etnodemografa i genealoga." *Fenomen Peterburga* (SPb: Blitz, 2000), pp. 143, 150–51.

46. K. G. Isupov, "Dialog stolits v istoricheskom dvizhenii." *Moskva-Peterburg: Pro et Contra* (SPb: Izdatel'stvo Russkogo Khristianskogo Gumanitarnogo Instituta, 2000), p. 17.

47. Ibid, pp. 18–19.

48. In fact, in his article "Architecture in Nineteenth-Century Russia: The Enduring Classic," Albert Schmidt links Russian neoclassical architecture *with* romanticism, declaring that the style he terms "romantic classicism" arose in late-eighteenth-century Russia and "claimed an authenticity based on historical and archeological research" (including the work of Johann Joachim Winkelmann and Giovanni Battista Piranesi). In Schmidt's view, the medieval revival of the 1840s thus represents a new phase of romanticism's fundamental approach to the architectural past, and not at all a break with an established tradition of classicism. See *Art and Culture in Nineteenth-Century Russia*, Theofanis George Stavrou, ed. (Bloomington: Indiana University Press, 1983), pp. 172–3.

49. For a detailed study of this phenomenon, see John I. Brooks III, *The Eclectic Legacy: Academic Philosophy and the Human Sciences in Nineteenth-Century France* (Newark: University of Delaware Press, 1998), especially pp. 13–66.

50. Claude Mignot, *Architecture of the Nineteenth Century in Europe* (New York: Rizzoli, 1984), p. 100.

51. N. V. Kukol'nik, "Novye postroiki v Petergofe." *Khudozhestvennaia gazeta*, 1837, no. 11–12, p. 176.

52. The notion of "intelligent," or motivated, aesthetic choice gradually evolved into the "rational" architectural principles of the 1850s–60s, most fully elaborated by engineer and pedagogue Apollinarii Krasovskii, who advocated a harmonious fusion of aesthetics and technology. During the first half of the nineteenth century, the relative meanings of "eclectic" and "rational" dovetailed, united against the common enemy, reactionary classicism. By the final quarter of the nineteenth century, however, "rational" architecture connoted a turn toward functionalism, in response to eclecticism's purported overemphasis on surface ornamentation. See the introduction to Krasovskii's 1851 *Grazhdanskaia arkhitektura: Chasti zdanii* (SPb, 1851).

53. V. G. Belinskii, *Izbrannye filosofskie sochineniia* (Moscow: Gosudarstvennoe izdatel'stvo politicheskoi literatury, 1941), p. 267.

54. See the exhibition catalogue *Istorizm v Rossii: Stil' i epokha v dekorativnom iskusstve 1820-e–1890-e gody* (SPb: Slaviia, 1996) for examples of various historicist fashions.

55. In a study of eclecticism in American architecture 1880–1930, Walter C. Kidney calls the movement "learnedly if selectively imitative of historic architecture in all aspects of its appearance, and using historic styles as expressions of various cultural institutions." For Kidney, the orientation to historic styles is a distinguishing feature between eclecticism and modernism, which is "tenuously unified by abstention from the historic styles." See *The Architecture of Choice: Eclecticism in America, 1880–1930* (New York: G. Braziller, 1974), p. viii.

56. D. Diderot, *Encyclopédie ou dictionnaire raisonné des sciences, des arts et des métiers* (Stuttgart-Bad Cannstatt: Frommann, 1966), p. 271.

57. Renate Lachmann, *Memory and Literature: Intertextuality in Russian Modernism*, trans. Roy Sellars and Anthony Wall (Minneapolis: University of Minnesota Press, 1997), pp. 122–123.

58. In fact, Diderot's own pronouncements in his 1755 article, "Encyclopédie," suggest that this massive project itself follows an aesthetics of eclecticism. As Diderot declares, the decision to use a purely conventional alphabetical ordering for the individual entries creates certain inadvertent "burlesque contrasts" in the juxtaposition of articles on extremely diverse topics. But Diderot compares the Encyclopedia's structure to "the foundation of a city," since all buildings should never be constructed according to a single model. "The uniformity of the buildings, bringing with it a uniformity in public passages would give to the whole city a sad and tiring appearance," he notes. See Denis Diderot, "Encyclopédie," in Denis Diderot and Jean le Rond D'Alembert, eds., *L'Encyclopédie, ou dictionnaire raisonné des sciences, des arts et des métiers* (New York, 1969), vol. 1, p. 642.

59. Hans-Günther Schwarz, "A Sense of Disorder: Rococo Ornament and its Criticism." *Transatlantic Crossings: Eighteenth-Century Explorations*, Donald W. Nichol, ed. (Newfoundland: Memorial University, 1995), p. 75.

60. E. Borisova, "Znak stilia." *Arkhitektura SSSR*, no. 1, January–February, 1984, p. 21.

61. Philippe Hamon, *Expositions: Literature and Architecture in Nineteenth-Century France,* trans. Katia Sainson-Frank and Lisa Maguire (Berkeley: University of California Press, 1992), pp. 9–10.

62. N. V. Gogol, *Sobranie sochinenii v vos'mi tomakh* (Moscow: Pravda, 1984), vol. 7, p. 80.

63. Ibid., p. 81.

64. Apparently, such a street was actually constructed for the London World's Fair.

65. Lachmann, p. 176.

66. Ibid., p. 193.

67. Ibid, p. 20.

CHAPTER 5

The Blankness of Dalí, or Forging Catalonia

BRAD EPPS

The Fame of an Artist

Thinking about forging a place for Catalonia in contemporary critical exchanges, I come quickly to Salvador Dalí, famous, among other things, for his participation in some rather fraudulent artistic enterprises.[1] Dalí has clearly managed to make a name for himself and, in the process, to make something of a name for his native Catalonia. *Something* of a name for Catalonia, because, in general, where Dalí is concerned, Spain, France, and the United States, all sovereign nation states, still tend to drown out Catalonia. Dalí's ties to all three states are undeniable, but he remains, regardless, profoundly marked by Catalonia. The *Persistence of Memory* hangs in New York City, but the landscape therein depicted, the ground and horizon against which the watches go soft, is firmly, as Dalí insisted, that of the Catalan coast.[2] Cadaqués, Port Lligat, and Figueres all figure prominently in Dalí's topography, the latter being the site of Dalí's museum, one of the most visited in Spain.[3] It apparently matters little that most of Dalí's most famous works are to be found elsewhere; Figueres receives thousands of visitors eager to see something by the self-proclaimed surrealist master in a place he called home. Dalí has, then, forged a place for himself, for Figueres, and for Catalonia in the world market, though not without a number of problems.

If Dalí has proved lucrative for Figueres, it is only because he had proved quite lucrative for himself. André Breton derisively restyled Salvador Dalí "Avida Dollars," an anagram that did not rankle Dalí nearly as much as Breton may have hoped.[4] After all, Dalí made no bones about being in the *business* of art, and wanted to have his say in, and share of, the profits. In so doing, he became more than a little embarrassing for the *grand artiste* who strove to transform the world, transcend time, capture eternity, and reveal the truth. This is not to say that Dalí did not also present himself as a *grand artiste*, but that he did not see artistic grandeur as at odds with personal profit, quite the contrary. His take on art, economics, and politics was as consistent as it was contradictory. If he flared in anger and frustration at the cultural conservatism of the Communist Party, he flared in anger and frustration at the cultural conservatism of capitalism, smashing a shop window of Bonwit Teller and raging about artistic integrity.[5] That he did much of this at a time of economic instability and war only increased his scandalous value, particularly in the United States. Unlike a number of surrealists, Dalí did not see the United States as a cesspool of exploitation, but as a land of opportunity, or at least as a cesspool from which he could opportunely extract a nugget of gold. He promoted nothing as much as his art and no one as much as himself. He seemed, and maybe even was, petty, frivolous, pompous, self-absorbed, obsessive, calculating, and adept at getting the most out of eccentricity. "Everything I touch turns to gold," he wrote in his *Private Dictionary*, under the section "Catalans and Catalonia."[6] In the same section he made a more pointed pronouncement: "Don Quixote was a mad idealist. I am a mad Catalan. That is to say, a madman with good commercial sense."[7] His madness, smart and studied, never drove him to tilt at windmills, cut off an ear, or fire a gun randomly into a crowd, but only to sign some 37,000 blank sheets of lithographic paper.

Dalí's brush with forgery involves withholding the brush. He does not paint pictures and try to pass them off as someone else's; he refrains from painting, drawing, engraving, or etching altogether and doodles instead his name across an empty surface.[8] He does this, as he would later declare, with the intention of returning to the once empty, now signed, surface and of providing it with an image—an after-image, one is tempted to say. But Dalí also signs the blank sheets knowing full well that others may, and indeed will, provide the image for him, in his stead.[9] While lithography and related forms make such fraud more feasible, it is the artist's own involvement that is noteworthy. Dalí engages in this curious activity relatively late in his career, in the early 1960s, though it is probable that he begins to flirt with fraud at least as early as 1945, if not earlier.[10] At any rate, certainly by the 1960s Dalí's name has acquired a value that allows it to underwrite something that others, but not necessarily he, would take to be auratic—or fetishistic. Whatever the case, Dalí's commodification is willful and theo-retically sophisticated, deploying virtually all the props of psychoanalysis then available. His fascination with mysteries, secrets, and enigmas—signi-fiers that inflect his writings, drawings, and paintings—places him in a Freudian circuit. His celebrated encounters with Sigmund Freud, whether textual or personal, only increase his cachet. So do his encounters with Jacques Lacan, with whom he exchanged ideas on paranoia and anamor-phosis. So, for that matter, do his *disencounters* with Karl Marx, whether textual or further mediated by people like Breton.

Mad or not, Dalí appears to understand, almost intuitively, Marx's un-derstanding of the fetishism of commodities (and the secret thereof), ac-cording to which "the specific social character of each producer's labour does not show itself except in the act of exchange."[11] And it shows itself, paradoxically, by hiding itself, by cloaking itself in mystery. "Value," Marx writes, "does not stalk about with a label describing what it is. It is value, rather, that converts every product into a social hieroglyphic" which, "later on, we try to decipher . . . [to] get behind the secret of our own social prod-ucts."[12] For Dalí, his value is all but inseparable from his "secret life," the seemingly inexhaustible and enigmatic variations on himself. Dalí trades in Dalí, on Dalí, on the persona, image, and name "Dalí." It is no accident that he frequently refers to himself in the third person, that he throws his I into something else and other. And even when he does not recast his I, even when he does not capitalize it in his writing (*jo, yo, je* in the three languages Dalí knew best), he can rest assured that he capitalizes on it. After a fashion, Dalí's value *did* stalk about with a label describing what it was, although the label described nothing so much as the impossibility of describing, of knowing. As Dalí was fond of saying, he himself did not *really* know what he or his works meant. Even if it is true that he did not possess the meaning of who he was or what he did, he nevertheless traf-ficked rather nicely in such self-declared indecipherability and anticipated, in the process, the profitability of such postmodern truisms as indetermi-nacy, ambiguity, polyvocality, performativity, and non-essentiality. Under-standing Marx's understanding of fetishism; understanding a certain not-so-secret share of capitalism; understanding himself as buckled by the unconscious and hence as beyond understanding, Dalí understands some-thing very valuable about art.

All of this proves too much for more serious folk, most notably André Breton.[13] Seeking to preserve surrealism and its revolution, Breton expels, or excommunicates, Dalí for his unabashed commercialism, his scatologi-cal depictions of Lenin, and his fascination with "Hitler's soft, round back-side always so tightly squeezed into his uniform."[14] The expulsion—or from Dalí's perspective, defection—occurs in the late 1930s and is one of the most notorious in a long string of expulsions, or defections.[15] By the early 1960s, Dalí, far too friendly for some with Franco, finds himself embroiled in the scandal of the blank sheets. Ian Gibson, in *The Shameful Life of Salvador Dalí*, assures his readers that Dalí could not have cared less about how the signed sheets might be used; it was enough, Dalí reportedly asserted, that he had exchanged his name, his signature, for amazing amounts of money paid up front.[16] The "blank sheets scandal" is only one among other "scandalous" events in Dalí's life, but it is significant because it implicates Dalí's art and artistry in particularly incisive ways. Dalí signs his name, his real name, his legal name, and sets in circulation some 37,000 "works" signed by him. *Signed by him*: nothing more, nothing less. He required help to do so, and journalistic reports indicate that in order to expedite matters, two assistants flanked Dalí, one passing him an unsigned sheet, the other pulling a signed sheet away.[17] The upshot was nothing less than an autographic assembly line that, according to Lee Catterall, allowed the artist to earn up to $72,000 an hour.[18] The scandal of an artist authorizing possibly inauthentic works bearing his own name eventually came to the attention of the legal authorities. As Gibson notes, in 1974 "French customs stopped a small lorry entering the country from Andorra and discovered that it was carrying 40,000 blank lithographic sheets signed by Salvador Dalí."[19] Dalí's lawyer argued "that no breach of law was involved in the importation of such sheets into France, and the consignment was allowed to continue to Paris."[20] The law, that is, was on Dalí's side. Color, tone, composition, subject matter, and the quality of the image, indeed its very presence or absence, are all irrelevant. Here, the signature is authentic; and here that is all that matters. Of course, it helps when the signature has attained a certain cachet, when the hand that signs the paper is famous.

Fame is one of the things that distinguishes Dalí from, say, Han van Meegeren, a Dutch painter who became *infamous* for falsifying works by Terborch, Frans Hals, Pieter de Hoogh and, most important, Johannes Vermeer. Dalí's fascination with Vermeer allows for an intriguing link to van Meegeren, for both twentieth-century artists took the seventeenth-century artist as an eminently (in)imitable master. Both Dalí and van Meegeren have been described as reactionary, bohemian, hypochondriacal, megalomaniacal, and unscrupulous, but it is their appreciation of Vermeer that constitutes the most *artistically* intriguing link.[21] For Dalí, Vermeer's painstaking attention to detail, his understanding of light, and his ability to suggest volume or its absence by means of the faintest of brushstrokes are the tokens of a greatness, a genius, that he would call his own. For van Meegeren, a Dutchman, Vermeer's greatness has national implications that are not available to the Catalan, but for both men, Vermeer's technical prowess is critical, constituting, in its duplication of reality, an artistry of the highest magnitude. And it is just Vermeer's extraordinarily refined technique that both men covet. Van Meegeren's duplications of Vermeer's duplicative style or technique lies firmly within the bounds of forgery and constitutes what Rudolph Arnheim calls a "demonstrative challenge" to a society obsessed with authenticity, truth, and the real thing.[22] Dalí poses a different, though related, challenge, one that plays with fraud and forgery without either, here too, being quite the real thing. For Dalí's forgeries are not quite forgeries; his fraud, legally speaking, not quite fraud. Not exactly authentic or inauthentic, the works derived from the signed blank sheets effect something like the forgery of forgery, the fraud of fraud.

Neither Dalí nor van Meegeren duplicates a work by Vermeer. Instead, as indicated, they strive to duplicate a style or technique associated with the seventeenth-century artist. Dalí, of course, never sought to pass off a work of his own making as a Vermeer, while van Meegeren did. At most, Dalí hoped to make a place for himself, by way of a sort of comparative imitation, among the masters of art. Vermeer's realism nourished Dalí's surrealism, giving body and concretizing, as Dalí was fond of saying, irrationality itself.[23] Dalí placed great stock in details, a pointed example of which is the needle and thread of Vermeer's *Lacemaker* (c. 1665). Barely insinuated in the painting, these objects appear in the first and last films by Luis Buñuel, *Un chien andalou*—in collaboration with Dalí—and *Cet obscur objet du désir*.[24] Dalí, even more than Buñuel, came to be obsessed with such details, not only because he claimed that they were woven into his own psychology, but also because they could be sewn, he believed, into the spectator's psychology. The detail places a demand on the spectator's attention, imposing itself almost imperiously, and yet setting the stage for what Dalí presents as interpretative freedom: a presumably delirious and interminable process of association, re-cognition, and re-figuration.[25] Dalí repeatedly criticizes the passive receptivity and lack of attention associated with automatism and advocates a return to various techniques that a certain avant-garde aesthetic discounts. In contrast to the futurist passion for speed, or the early surrealist passion for automation, or the dada negation of technical skill, Dalí's passion for Vermeer is, interestingly, a passion for patience.[26]

Dalí expresses the passion for patience, or patience as passion, in an essay titled "Sant Sebastià."[27] Along with more commonly accepted notions of patience, "there is also the patience that is a kind of passion, the humble patience in the maturing of Vermeer of Delft's paintings that is the same as the patience in the maturing of fruit trees."[28] Van Meegeren was also a patient painter, going to excruciating ends to endow his efforts with the patina of authenticity. According to Hope Werness, van Meegeren would cover the painted surface with varnish and coil it around a cylinder to imitate the cracks of age. He would then smear the works with India ink in "an attempt to replicate the centuries of fine dust that accumulates in the cracks of old canvases."[29] Such replications offend many a sensibility, whether moral, legal, or aesthetic, but they can also be quite appealing, even poignantly so. Alfred Lessing ends an illuminating article on forgery with reference to van Meegeren's most successful work, *The Disciples at Emmaus*, successful because, beautiful as it is, it could well stand on its own merits. "Even though it was painted by van Meegeren in the twentieth century," Lessing states, "it embodies and bears witness to the greatness of the seventeenth-century art of Vermeer."[30] Van Meegeren thus becomes something of an artist's artist, a man so intensely immersed in the world of art that he does not care for right and wrong, or, if he does care, it is only to prove himself right and the experts wrong.

Dalí effects his own peculiar testimony to Vermeer, though without the more unsavory trappings of deception. And yet, Dalí is certainly no stranger to deception, his experimentations with anamorphosis, *camera obscura, trompe l'oeil*, holography, and stereoscopy being indicative of his interest in the tricks of the representational trade. Dalí's commitment to mimesis, which he claims in his *Secret Life* to have theorized in a creative epiphany at the age of nine,[31] is practically inseparable from such representational tricks. To be sure, art as a whole is full of tricks, is itself in some way a trick. But the trick of signing blank sheets is of a different order. It embodies and bears witness to what might be seen as the emptiness of modern art, maybe even of art of any age that exists in the modern market, including, most definitely, that of museums. The signing of blank sheets represents, in a further turn of the screw, a degree zero of representation, a voidance of all the minute and partial objects that Dalí had so scrupulously sought to preserve for posterity. In a sense, Dalí here approximates the abstraction that he generally claimed to abhor: the geometric reduction of Mondrian, the monochromatic blueness of Yves Klein, the whiteness of Malevich.[32] As the precondition for ultimately uncontrollable reproduction, the blank sheets are perversely in line with some of the fundamental tenets of a more abstruse and abstract avant-garde.

Rosalind Krauss has argued that "if the very notion of the avant-garde can be seen as a function of the discourse of originality, the actual practice of vanguard art tends to reveal that 'originality' is a working assumption that emerges from a ground of repetition and recurrence."[33] Krauss focuses on "serious" attempts at originality through repetition, and hence on work by Léger, Schwitters, Malevich, Mondrian, and others. Seemingly self-same, non-spontaneous, and non-subjective, the grid signifies, for Krauss, "the sheer disinterestedness of the work of art, its absolute purposelessness, from which it derived the promise of its autonomy."[34] Dalí persistently scoffed at Mondrian's mystical geometry and other grid-like manifestations, not because they were not spontaneous but because they were not studied enough. What Dalí valorized was a form of studiousness verging on academicism, a mastery of masterful detail that proved the subject's individual talent as a function of tradition. Dalí's much-touted megalomania, his "extravagant narcissism,"[35] and his "thirst for fame"[36] are bound up in a respect for the achievements of others; his claims to be unique are matched by his claims to be like, or almost like, a select group of predecessors. He seemed all but in thrall to the proverbial majesty of the masters. According to Robert Radford, however, "[Dalí] was not impressed by any sense of 'aura' that might attach to the specific presence of the artist's own hand in the production of either paintings or prints: 'I always encourage people to reproduce my paintings because I find the representations much better than the originals.'"[37]

Radford's assertion is well founded though too confident, for Dalí also expresses an almost slavish fascination with an artist's aura. In particular, he is *impressed* by some of the previously mentioned masters, Millet and Vermeer foremost among them. That said, Dalí evinces a strong penchant for replication, reproduction (artistic, not biological), recurrence, and repetition; he even considers himself a replication of his dead brother, also named Salvador. On a less psychological register, Dalí's repetition does not rely on a grid but on the insistence of a masterful model and then, later in life, on the blankness of lithographic paper and the alluring fullness of a famous name. His repetition relies further, perhaps primarily, on an economic system that valorizes the unique and the original because of the ways that they, as model or prototype, fold into repetition and recurrence in general. *Mona Lisa* postcards, velvet versions of *The Last Supper*, signed lithographs, restorations, ready-mades, casts, and replicas, authorized or not: all, and much more, circulate in a system in which the original serves as a most effective lure.[38] Repetition can vary, of course. The case of the blank sheets does not depend on the duplication of an image that many take to be definitive of forgery; rather, it involves the *multiplication* of the signature, the very sign that commonly serves to underwrite the value of a work of art. The multiplication of the signature might be related to the multiplication of images that is the hallmark of many of Dalí's most celebrated pieces, including *The Metamorphosis of Narcissus* (1937), *The Endless Enigma* (1938), and *Slave Market with Invisible Bust of Voltaire* (1940).[39] But once again, there is a difference: the absence of an image, multiple or otherwise, the absence of any detail, passionate or patient, other than a name, a signature, or—once Parkinson's Disease makes it difficult for Dalí to sign at all—a thumbprint, imposes itself on our attention.

Obviously, even Dalí's thumbprint can be valuable. It is the mark, after all, of the artist's presence, enduring in his absence, the stamp of his unicity, the fetish that ever so touchingly avows and disavows his absence. The paradox is imposing: Dalí's unicity, his genius, his megalomania, narcissism, and exhibitionism involve a technical skill whose measure is the erasure of the self. Dalí's interest in a traditional, even academic, style means that his own style is the style of others, at once preceding and exceeding him. Various critics have noted, and criticized, how Dalí's work is identifiable by virtue of its content rather than its form. Dalí's supposedly highly personal obsessions are manifested, that is, in what many consider to be a highly impersonal style, one that he claimed to have learned from Vermeer and Velázquez, two great painters about whom, biographically speaking, much remains unknown. The homage that Dalí pays these masters of realism may thus be read as homage to the occlusion of the artist by the work of art, the triumph of technique and tradition over personality. Dalí could hardly have been unaware of the paradox. His ostentatious lust for celebrity, bringing to mind the trajectories of Andy Warhol and Madonna, points less to a cult of personality than to a cult of a persona, a mask. His cultivation of a meticulous, "realist" technique generates something remarkably similar. Both pictorially and extra-pictorially, then, Dalí suggests that semblance and being are intimately confused. The artist's life, any life, is in some sense always secret, perhaps never more so than when it makes a spectacle of itself. All of this casts a curiously long shadow not just on fame, but on forgery and fraud as well. Van Meegeren has become a curiosity, famous for doing a "bad thing," a daring affront to art and art history.[40] Dalí, also a curiosity, is famous for doing bad things and bad art, even intentionally so. The episode of the blank sheets is, for many, a "bad thing" because it enables the proliferation of "bad art" or, alternatively, of blank art, no art, at least no art of Dalí's making, whether good or bad.

The Fame of Other Artists

Dalí *is* famous, and though his frauds are not as studied as those of Han van Meegeren, they still bask in the reflected glow of fame and become famous in turns. The question of fame, of celebrity, personality, visibility, and recognition is critical to the status of Catalonia, whether regional, national, international or universal, whether some, all, or none of the above. Admittedly, such a subject is not purely aesthetic, for it engages money, power, identity, politics, and so on. But this is precisely the point. A place can gain recognition through the fame of someone that comes from it, returns to it, or somehow "belongs" to it. Fame may be related, in other words, to a place, and often a commonplace. Dalí's assertion that his madness is commercial because he is Catalan is, though likely tongue-in-cheek, part and parcel of a wider storehouse of stereotypes. The stereotypes, famous within Spain, depict Catalans as consummate capitalists, capable of making a profit out of next to nothing, for instance, a blank sheet of paper and a name. Catalans are stereotyped in more ethically and racially coded ways as Phoenicians, Jews, and Poles.[41] They are likened to Phoenicians and Jews because they presumably know how to trade and to make and keep money, the anti-Semitic tenor of the stereotype being part of its troubling force.[42] And they are likened to Poles not because they find themselves caught between two more powerful national groups—the Germans and Russians in one case, the French and the Spanish in the other—but because they speak a language that is not Spanish. Catalans themselves may resist such stereotypes, but they may also assume them and, as Judith Butler might put it, parodically inhabit them.

Catalan nationalist literature from the late nineteenth and early twentieth century is peppered with references to Jews and other people without a state or in the process of consolidating a state: Basques, the Irish, the Provençal, Norwegians, Czechs. For example, contacts between Catalans and Czechs, Barcelona and Prague, were such that certain Catalan intellectuals referred to a "Czech model" by which Catalonia might fashion effective linguistic, civic, and political policies. [43] Exchanges between the "Catalans of Austria" and the "Czechs of Spain" circulated in newspapers and reviews,[44] as today they circulate between Catalans and Corsicans, Bretons, Basques, Galicians, the Welsh, the Scottish, Quebecois, Puerto Ricans, and so on. The Czech Republic is now a matter of international fact, but the Republic of Catalonia is not. What is more, in an anxiously globalized culture industry, the Czech Republic arguably needs the names of such famous figures as Milan Kundera and Franz Kafka as much as Catalonia needs the name of Dalí. Yet despite Dalí's fame, perhaps even because of it, he remains something of an embarrassment to many a Catalan artist and cultural pundit. As Josep Miquel Sobrer so wittily puts it, the Catalan "intelligentsia dedicated itself *en masse* to a Bretonian rending of vestments, not so much because of Dalí's 'avid dollarism' . . . as because of his monarchical-Francoist-españolista cockiness in the 1950s and later."[45] Dalí may be famous; he may bring fame to Catalonia, but not all Catalans want fame at a Dalinian price.

Miquel Barceló, a friend of Hervé Guibert, who was a friend of Michel Foucault, who was in turn famous for not being the only one to write to have no face,[46] provides a concise, if oblique, lesson in established Catalan artistic culture, in fame and place. In a pictorial work from his 1989 *Carnet*, titled *L'art catalá* [sic],[47] Barceló, from Mallorca, presents a select genealogy of modern Catalan art. Three names, each accompanied by a geometric symbol (a star or asterisk, a cross, and a dark circle or dot), grace the surface of Barceló's work: Miró, Tàpies, Barceló. Dalí is conspicuously absent, though Barceló's chutzpah in including himself in such illustrious company ironically shadows forth something Dalinian, and one might even say that Barceló takes Dalí's place. True, Barceló, like Miró and Tàpies, does not cultivate a passion for precision; for all their differences, the works of these three artists do not pay *technically* visible homage to Vermeer, Velázquez, Raphael, Leonardo, Millet, and other less famous artists that Dalí places in his own personal pantheon.[48] In that sense, Barceló does "fit" more easily than Dalí. And yet, in an excerpt from the *Carnet,* Barceló does compare himself to Velázquez and, funny as it may sound, he does so in the context of what he calls "true modesty."[49] Barceló's "modesty" is bound to the "certainty of being absolutely modern, the feeling of being increasingly closer to something essential."[50] This self-evaluation is penned in 1994, not 1924, and is further indication that the language of high modernism endures even after being declared dead.[51] "Everything becomes painting," Barceló proclaims, "I imagine Giotto; I imagine myself as Giotto, and that works."[52] The hubris of the artist allows for yet more ties to the self-proclaimed genius, Dalí. As far as Barceló is concerned, the self insists in a whirlwind of self-promotion, in which every scrap of paper, snapshot, and scrawl is catalogued, exhibited, reproduced, and put on the market. Everything becomes painting, even when it is not particularly becoming to the grand notion of painting, even when it gives the lie to imaginings modest or not.

Barceló's work is obviously indebted to Tàpies's. Both incorporate sand, pebbles, plaster, clay, marble dust, and dirt in their art to signal something earthy and primeval. The physicality of their art is metaphysical in its thrust, shot through with all sorts of meditations on reality and mystery.[53] Dalí also meditates on reality and mystery, but he tends to do so in a more ironic, comical, and self-implicating manner. But Antoni Tàpies, to an even greater degree than Barceló, is rarely ironic, and even more rarely comical, however self-implicating he may be. A measure of his seriousness may be found in his numerous articles on art and culture. Tàpies positions himself as a defender of everything modern and progressive; and, to his eyes, mass culture, information technology, and Salvador Dalí, modern though they are, are definitely *not* progressive. Tàpies has excoriated Dalí as both an artist and a human being, claiming that Dalí did not create a school, which, for Tàpies, is "the saddest thing that can happen to an artist."[54] Without a school, Dalí is also supposedly without any real support among critics and historians. The fact that Dalí, after Franco, is both popular and well received by many government officials irks Tàpies and merely proves his point: a Francoist past, he complains, is still quite profitable. True as that may be, Tàpies is on incomparably shakier ground when he declares that "the slightest brush stroke is a reflection of the painter's human qualities in the same way that handwriting reveals the soul of the person who writes."[55] A reference to graphology might be in order, but Tàpies's mystico-scientific certainty, somewhere between that of a shaman and a forensic detective, affords him a privileged perspective indeed. Pitting the common people—"el vulgar de la gent"—against the "expert who knows perfectly well that a painting is or is not interesting according to the degree of humanity and intelligence of its author," Tàpies sides with the all-knowing expert.[56] Hubris again rears its head, proving that Dalí is by no means the only modern Catalan artist to suffer from it, and perhaps not even the one who suffers from it most.

Tàpies first published these comments in 1983 in the major Spanish daily, *El País*. What motivates his words is the "official reencounter with Dalí": King Juan Carlos grants Dalí the title of marquis in 1982, and the concession of nobility, along with the success of a retrospective of the artist's work, is too much for Tàpies to let pass. Yet Tàpies's commentary assumes an incisively binary form. Just as he pits the common people against the art experts (siding with the latter), so he pits Dalí against Miró (again, siding with the latter). Under Tàpies's pen, Miró's "human qualities"[57] stand in stark contrast to Dalí's lack of the same; Miró, in other words, plays the hero to Dalí's villain. Tàpies is not alone in his evaluation. Eduardo Arroyo, in *Portrait of the Dwarf Sebastián de Morra, Buffoon of the Court Born in Figueras in the First Half of the Twentieth Century* (1970), depicts Dalí as a lackey of power. Inspired by Velázquez, Arroyo's burlesque presents a little man, sporting Dalí's trademark moustache and looking blankly out at the spectator. The dwarf's costume is covered with badges whose images range from Donald Duck and a dollar sign to the Spanish flag and *ABC* (the name of a conservative newspaper) to a work by Miró, *La maternité* (1924). The diminutive presence of a Miró in the depiction of a diminutive Dalí raises questions about the relationship between the two artists. While few in the art world would employ Tàpies's shrill humanistic language,[58] few would place Dalí above Miró. And yet, significantly, there is little reason here, *outside of their Catalan heritage*, to pit them so decisively against each other in the first place.[59]

Whatever may recommend Miró to critics, one of the things that recommends Dalí is the way he imposes on critical attention the still strained relation between popularity, measured often as not in a demand to buy and own works, and criticism itself. That Dalí might be an unapologetic elitist with populist effects, and that his commercialism might be as sincere as it is sincerely validated by many a viewer and buyer, merely heightens the dilemma. The dilemma exists because, once upon a time, "those in the know" took Dalí seriously. The once generally positive appraisal stays with Dalí and undergirds calls for reappraisal. Even those who, like Brooks Adams, question the "traditional wisdom" according to which Dalí "was only at his best for a brief period from 1927–38, and that anything after 1940 in his oeuvre is really not worth looking at," know that traditional wisdom had once validated something.[60] Picasso and Miró also suffer from a similar chronological evaluation, and Picasso in particular came to be known for his own brand of Midas-like commercialism: more elegant perhaps (at least if one finds bulls and satyrs elegant), but extraordinarily lucrative nonetheless.[61] Miró himself was not the immaculate innocent that Tàpies makes him out to be; nor was he always so far removed from Dalí. According to Ruth Brandon, "the businesslike Miró" gave Dalí, recently arrived in Paris, "a swift lesson in social climbing," replete with sartorial advice (Miró insisted that Dalí buy a formal dinner jacket) and tips on everything from etiquette to how to woo wealthy patrons.[62] In fact, not one of these famous artists—Picasso, Miró, Dalí, Tàpies, and, more recently, Barceló—is anything remotely like a failure in the market. What interests me, however, is the way in which their works, and the works of others, are taken as *representative of the nation,* its achievements, genius, and *international* significance.

Both Miró and Tàpies have major foundations and outdoor sculptures in Barcelona, and Barceló has many of his works housed (though not always exhibited) in the new Museum of Contemporary Art. The other major international artist associated with the city, Pablo Picasso, is *not* Catalan. The Picasso Museum is in Barcelona's Gothic Quarter, not far from the Carrer d'Avignó, a street of former ill repute that inflects Picasso's famous *Demoiselles d'Avignon.* Dalí is Catalan, though, as noted, one must hop on a train to Figueres to see his works. Admittedly, this is primarily an effect of Dalí's own history, his desire to pay homage to his past. One could even argue that Dalí is *more* Catalan by locating his museum outside of Barcelona, capital and port city open to all sorts of foreign influence. But the relative absence of Dalí in Barcelona is overdetermined. The Francoist and Bourbon connections cast a shadow on Dalí's Catalan connections, rendering his references to Catalonia suspect for many, like Tàpies, serious about Catalan culture. Javier Tusell points out that Dalí shifted his loyalties from Barcelona to Madrid in the 1950s, more or less as the polemical arbiter of controlled civic Catalanism, Eugeni d'Ors, had shifted his loyalties in the 1920s.[63] The shift created such resentment that, as Tusell remarks, Dalí was excluded from an exposition on Barcelona organized in Madrid, by Catalans, in 1980.[64]

Of course, long before Franco, Dalí had lambasted established Catalan culture. In his "Yellow Manifesto" (so named for the color of paper on which it was printed), Dalí, along with Sebastià Gasch and Lluís Montanyà, had denounced "the racial commonplaces of [Àngel] Guimerà" and "the sickly sensibility served up by the Orfeó Català."[65] Shortly thereafter, he attacked the regional, typical, and local. After Franco, Dalí drew up a will that bequeathed much of his estate to the Spanish State. As Adams notes, the failure to mention Catalonia in his will "caused an enormous furor in Barcelona."[66] In fact, a number of Dalí's most recognizable works, including *The Great Masturbator*, are housed in the Reina Sofía Center for Modern Art in Madrid. That some of Dalí's most famous paintings are in Madrid instead of Barcelona is a result of a last will, though not necessarily a free will. Death and taxes combine to make Dalí's will the will of the state—the Spanish State, with Madrid as its capital. Some members of the press presented Dalí's will as a virtual disinheritance of Catalonia.[67] Even Jordi Pujol, long-time president of Catalonia, participated in the fray, accusing the central government of deception and manipulation. Amid all of the accusations, one thing is clear: Dalí is a subject of national concern; his works, the highly symbolic work of the nation. Regardless of the views of Tàpies and Barceló, in the view of others, Dalí's art is, or *should be*, Catalan. It belongs, for them, in Catalonia, its rightful "home."

Jordi Pujol, a politician, may claim Dalí for Catalonia, but Antoni Tàpies, an artist, is decidedly more reticent. Their differences notwithstanding, both the politician and the artist do agree, it seems, on the seriousness of Catalonia, its international projection. Nations, after all, are serious entities, demanding love, loyalty, obedience, and sacrifice. This is not to say that Tàpies's work slips into a nationalist project along the lines of Pujol's, but merely that it takes the nation seriously. The same cannot be said of Dalí without qualification. Dalí, even in his paintings that address or engage such momentous events as civil war, always seems to be tottering on the edge of frivolity. Breton and others considered Dalí's perception of Hitler to be frivolous and hence quite serious in its ramifications; Tàpies considered Dalí's perception of Franco to be, quite simply, serious. The blank sheets and other brushes with fraud and forgery, as if confirming an already established tendency, constitute, then, a serious manifestation of Dalí's lack of seriousness. What arises is a study in paradox: Dalí is seriously frivolous.

Such serious frivolity may help account for the absence of Dalí from Barceló's limited Catalan roster. Barceló seems serious too, and yet his *L'art català* [sic] bears a curious resemblance to the Valencian Javier Mariscal's ludic advertising campaign from 1979 in which the name of Barcelona is tellingly broken up: Bar, cel, ona: Bar, sky, wave; or, if you will, sex, sun, and surf. Catalan art may be all well and good, but what draws the crowds, what gives Catalonia its international name and fame, is Barcelona, city on the sea. Mariscal knows this because he knows what sells. Others know that he knows it, hiring him to design bars, nightclubs, and an array of knick-knacks. His creations include Mickey Mouse chairs, shopping bags that resemble Antoni Gaudí's Casa Milà, and a gigantic, smiling crustacean atop the Gambrinus Restaurant on the revamped waterfront in Barcelona.[68]

Mariscal is responsible for Cobi, the 1992 Olympic mascot that enjoyed the ubiquity once reserved to gods. Mariscal has also signed the second manifesto of the recently created *Babel Forum* that criticizes Catalan linguistic policy as being *too* Catalan.[69] That Mariscal's *Bar cel ona* should require knowledge of Catalan, and Barceló's *L'art català* [sic] knowledge of Catalan *and* Catalans, is not bereft of irony. What is at stake is nothing less than the arbitration of Catalan culture, in which authenticity and inauthenticity, veracity and fraud, seriousness and frivolity, are key terms of cogitation, criticism, and consumption. Mariscal is in many respects the commercially savvy heir of Dalí, who for his part worked briefly with Hitchcock, met Disney, endorsed Lavin chocolates, appeared on the cover of *Time* magazine, and partied with the jet set.

And yet, Mariscal appears even lighter and more innocuous than Dalí, less inclined to parade himself as a genius and to hitch his star to a grand artistic project. The differences and similarities are effects of history, not just quirks of individual talent. Like Dalí, Mariscal makes his way in an entrenched capitalist order; unlike Dalí, Mariscal comes into his own *after* the much-ballyhooed collapse of the *grand récit*, the death of Franco, the liquidation of revolution, and the exhaustion of the avant-garde. What both politicians and artists return to, over and again, is the image of Catalonia, its importance and attractiveness as a site of culture and, of course, as a site of investment and tourism. For this purpose, and quite curiously, Dalí appears to be of more dubious value than Miró and Tàpies. I do not mean that Dalí's works may not fetch higher prices than theirs do; I mean simply that the value of Dalí's works is questioned with greater intensity, and that he provokes, by way of frivolity, fraud, and falsifications, among other things, such questioning. Where the project and projection of Catalonia is concerned, it would appear that Miró and Tàpies—whose foundations do not receive as many visitors as Dalí's—do the job less suspiciously.

Joan Miró, after all, repeatedly cites Catalonia in his art. In *Catalan Landscape* (also known as *The Hunter*), from 1923, the first four letters of the Catalan national dance, *la sardana*—forged as such in the nineteenth century—are clearly visible in the lower right-hand corner. In *Head of a Catalan Peasant*, from 1925, a red cap, or *barretina*, allows for a local connection. These paintings are by no means devoid of ambiguity, but both explicitly name Catalonia and implicitly cite the traditional, landed values of the Catalan *Renaixença*. The *Renaixença* is generally taken as beginning in 1833 with the publication of Bonaventura Carles Aribau's poem "La pàtria" and continuing to the late nineteenth century when *modernisme*, with its emphasis on cosmopolitanism, national internationalism, and progress, comes to the fore. *Modernisme* shifts the values of the *Renaixença*, uprooting them and setting them in circulation, a circulation that becomes more

Figure 5.1 Joan Miró, *The Tilled Field*, 1923–24. Oil on canvas, 26 × 36½ inches. Solomon R. Guggenheim Museum.

frenetic with the avant-garde. Still, the shifts are accompanied by a drag. A rural locale is hurtled into the avant-garde in a manner that, as Griselda Pollock explains with respect to Van Gogh, is tied to a growing tourist industry that traffics in modern renderings of the non-modern.[70] For example, the form of the peasant's beard in Miró's painting recalls the Catalan flag, or *senyera*. Similar forms appear in *Garden with Donkey* (1918) and *The Tilled Field* (1923; fig. 5.1). In the latter painting the Catalan flag appears along with, and actually larger than, the French and Spanish flags attached to the same pole. And though the French flag appears twice, the Catalan flag—whose dotted contours evoke the v-shaped bird figures just above it—seems to reverberate as the tilled field. Then again, if the field can be taken as a variation on the Catalan flag, it can also be taken as "an undulating ornament," nothing more.[71] Obviously, these are not unequivocal allusions, and not just for those who do not know the Catalan flag; for the *senyera* has four red strips or bars—*quatre barres*—on a yellow background, whereas here, in both *Garden* and *Tilled Field*, the number of rows in the field is different.

Decidedly less equivocal is Tàpies's *Catalan Spirit* (1971), in which the four red bars are literally scratched into a surface itself scratched with bits and pieces of words (fig. 5.2). There is a trace of something violent here, a forced engraving, at once furtive and frontal, by which the symbol of Catalonia comes to view. Partaking of both expressionism and proto-narration, the painting is a study in unresolved tensions. The words "LLIB-ERTAT," "DEMOCRACIA," "VERITAT," and "CULTURA," all in capital letters, accompany two similarly inscribed phrases: "CATALUNYA VIU" ('Catalonia lives') and "VISCA CATALUNYA" ('long live Catalonia'). The painting is covered, moreover, with other Catalan words and phrases that range from "spirituality," "materialism," and "spontaneity" to "the right to disobey the law" and "the law does not create rights." Produced four years before Franco's death, the work is a challenge to the dictatorial order. For Pere Gimferrer, Catalan poet and member of the Real Academia Española, *Catalan Spirit* is central to Tàpies's artistic project. After declaring the distinctive note of modern art to be the disappearance of theme, and after warning against seeing Tàpies's work in terms of graffiti, chipped walls, and fragments, Gimferrer effectively thematizes Tàpies's incorporation of graffiti, traces, and "pseudo-paleographic" inscriptions in *Catalan Spirit*.[72] This is not surprising, for it is arduous to maintain that Tàpies's art is the very materialization of mystery and magic. The scratches, cuts, and traces almost inevitably lend themselves to a grand thematization of the disappearance of themes.

Graffiti, to be sure, can be found almost anywhere in Barcelona that is not diligently policed, but a work by Antoni Tàpies is another story: Its fragility, mystery, and evocation of resistance are relatively secure in well guarded, climate-controlled rooms. And when Tàpies's publicly exposed works—such as his tribute to Picasso—suffer from neglect, vandalism, and the ravages of age and weather more than one person worries about their conservation. The insistence with which mystery is bandied about cannot but bring me back to Dalí. For if Dalí spoke about the materialization of mystery and the concretization of irreality, he also spoke about what neither Gimferrer nor Tàpies seems inclined to mention: the "mysterious" materiality of money and the art of making it while appearing not to care. Gimferrer refers to the didacticism of Tàpies's *Catalan Spirit*, the way it materializes a "patriotic affirmation" and a "call," presumably to action.[73] Dalí's work rarely if ever makes such affirmations or emits such calls. In its seemingly obsessive reference to the artist's phobias and desires, it performs a solipsistic game that ironically may be its more socially committed message, turning on any grand notion of art as redemptive. Self-referentiality is not, in other words, always and everywhere self-evident or self-same. Dalí's self-referentiality typically refers to Dalí, to Dalí's self, or to his persona, while Tàpies's self-referentiality refers not to Tàpies but to his art or, better yet, to art: beyond all petty possessive adjectives.

I am tempted to say that Dalí is postmodern and Tàpies modern, but instead I might venture a rather vulgar assessment: The great masturbator of

Figure 5.2 Antoní Tàpies, *The Catalan Spirit,* 1971. Mixed media on wood, 78¾ × 106¼ inches (200 × 270 cm). Private collection, Madrid. Photograph from the Tàpies Foundation, Barcelona.

modern Catalan art might just be Tàpies, not Dalí. For masturbation is typically a furtive act, one performed in isolation, a supplement, as Derrida would say, to what passes as central, primary, and true. Dalí, laying bare his penchant for masturbation, displaying it in his art and playing with it, with himself, in various public venues, lays waste to a modest part of bourgeois ideology from the inside. Tàpies, laying claim to nothing less than the arcane nature of art itself, and professing to have never concerned himself with material success or fame, conceals his "self" in the works that bear his name. The *Fundació Tàpies* would accordingly have arisen as an almost natural effect of a mystically coded indifference to success and self. It would be of course improper to speculate as to the pleasure, or benefit, that Tàpies himself might derive from such a state of affairs. What appears more proper is to pronounce the truth, and Tàpies persistently presents himself as doing just that. As he tells Barbara Catoir, "I was attacked by all the people who regard Dalí, for example, as a Catalan nationalist."[74] Those who so regard Dalí are not as multitudinous as Tàpies would have us believe, for *internationally* Dalí's fame has arguably less—or at least no more—to do with Catalonia than Miró's. In fact, to many an outsider, Catalonia, its national status, is itself something of an enigma.

For all the talk of enigma, Tàpies emits a fairly explicit message in *Quatre barres i muntanyes* (1973) and *Catalunya endavant* (1988), where Catalan words are set against a backdrop of materials associated with *arte povera*. In *Quatre barres*, the Catalan flag is brought into play, as it has long been, with emblematic mountains whose names—Montseny, Montserrat, Canigó, and so on—are scribbled across the bottom red bar and just above an uneven line of white triangular forms suggesting mountains. The words "Catalunya" and "visca" ('long live') also appear, as if hurriedly written, partially erased, and written again. The base material is paper, not wood (as with *Catalan Spirit*) or canvas, and the overall effect is one of fragility and insistence. Here, and in *Catalunya endavant*, political graffiti—often indicative of a censorial apparatus and defiant expression—again punctuates Tàpies's work. An impoverished, if by now conventional, form is accordingly enriched, thematically, by the presence of discernible nationalist signs and, economically, by the presence of the art market. The result is a work that wavers between a resistant economy of signs and its dissolution.

On the level of form, *Catalunya endavant*, *Quatre barres*, and *Catalan Spirit* recall Robert Motherwell's *Elegies to the Spanish Republic*—though only if the words that cut the surface of Tàpies's painting are ignored. For unlike Tàpies, Motherwell conserves an abstraction in his *Elegies* that admits of no particular meaning *outside the presence of the title*, which at once anchors and keeps adrift the non-figurative images. What is conveyed is, perhaps, the *absence* of the Spanish Republic, its invisibility, indecipherability, and non-existence, except in memory. True, Motherwell employs shades of red, yellow, and blue or lilac that recall the colors of the Spanish Republic, but *these* colors with *that* meaning are likewise part of historical memory. Tàpies's incorporation of the colors and forms of the Catalan flag accomplishes something similar, but the continued use of the flag and the presence of letters, words, and phrases situate these works in a different register. Most of Tàpies's work, however, does not deploy words. The impression of a foot or a hand, relatively common in Tàpies, suggests a general humanity while the imprint of words in Catalan remits the viewer to more particular meanings. Whatever *Catalan Spirit* recalls on the level of form, it recalls, on the level of genre, Miró's *Aidez l'Espagne*, a political poster produced during the Spanish Civil War and associated, along with Picasso's *Guernica*, with the Spanish Pavilion in the 1937 Universal Exposition in Paris. The locality of universality and the universality of locality—no less than the nationality of internationality and the internationality of nationality—can bear on art and culture in decisive ways. Four red lines on a yellow background can mean more, or more particularly, than an arrangement of red, white, and brown, just as "llibertat" can mean more, or more particularly, than "A" or "T" (the artist's initials) and certainly "*" or "+".[75]

The Fame of a Nation (Without a State)

I will return to Universal Expositions and pavilions, but for the moment I want to stay with the *senyera*, which is derived from a violently expirational act. Guifré el Pelós, or Wilfred the Hairy, who allegedly unites Catalonia and makes Barcelona its capital toward the end of the ninth century, is wounded in battle by the Saracens. Victorious yet bleeding, Guifré receives the king, Louis the Pious who, finding the victor without a blazon, sticks his fingers into Wilfred's wound and traces them across a golden shield. "Obviously this stirring story cannot be true," Robert Hughes remarks, "since Louis died before Guifré was born, and Barcelona was conquered long before that."[76] As a result, the symbol of Catalonia, fraught with blood and gold, is, like so many symbols, something of a fiction, a fraud. Fraudulent, it nonetheless has some powerful effects, calling to mind the sacrifice by which Catalonia struggles into being. For more than one Catalan, Catalonia struggles still, taking poignant pride in having its national day, the 11th of September, commemorate defeat at the hands of the French in 1714. The French connection is as vexed as it is persistent. In the last century and a half, after the Bourbons had acquired Spanish credentials, France came to occupy an important place in the Catalan imaginary, a place of tolerance, creativity, and wealth. Of course, it is more than a little interesting that France, for all its allure, has been more effective in the suppression of Catalan language and culture than Spain.

Geography is critical, and Catalonia's location between Spain and France, *within* Spain and France, accounts for a monumental appearance of the *senyera* on the border, in La Junquera-Le Perthus. In Ricardo Bofill's *Pyramid*, the four bars are massive red bricks rising into the sky. Bofill recently designed the Barcelona International Airport and the National Theater of Catalonia, but he left his mark on Catalonia earlier, with the rehabilitation of a Cement Factory and the construction of a mammoth housing project named Walden Seven, just outside Barcelona, in the early nineteen seventies.[77] He came to fame, however, in France, where Valéry Giscard d'Estaing declared that he was the world's greatest living architect and where François Mitterand extolled his classically inspired housing projects, which Bofill called inhabitable monuments, in an obvious reworking of Le Corbusier's inhabitable machines.[78] The *Pyramid* is only one of the structures that led Charles Jencks to declare Bofill responsible for "[t]he most extraordinary invention of mass-produced ornament, or constructional ornament" in history.[79] The *Pyramid* is indeed an ornament,

Figure 5.3 Ricardo Bofill, The Marca Hispànica Pyramid, 1976. Le Perthus, France. Photograph by Serena Vergano.

more so even than the "palaces," "circuses," "theaters," and "arches" that function as mass housing in Montpellier, Marne-la-Vallée, and Saint-Quentin-en-Yvelines. Although the *Pyramid* recalls temples in Central America and thus signals other kinds of geopolitical contact, a Catalan national dimension clearly predominates.[80] (See fig. 5.3)

An even more inventive example of nationally inflected architecture is Antoni Gaudí's Casa Batlló, dating from 1904 to 1906, during the heyday of Catalanism. Gaudí is another international star, famous for an architecture that, unlike that of his compatriot Josep Maria Sert, appears to have little "international" about it. Drawing from established artisanship and reworking a preexisting structure, Gaudí scatters shards of broken tile across the façade of the Casa Batlló, appends wrought iron balconies to many of the windows, and crowns the whole thing off with an undulating roof. There is no *senyera* here, but there is perhaps something equally as powerful: the legend of St. George, patron saint of Barcelona, and the Dragon.[81] For the Casa Batlló is a building where tiles are scales; balconies, dragon jaws; and the roof, a dragon's back. St. George's lance, buried up to its cruciform hilt, signifies that the building, so alive with images, is also quite dead. Similar references to St. George, by way of the dragon, can be found at the entrance of Gaudí's Parc Güell and the Finca Güell. The Casa

Batlló, named after another capitalist (like Güell), is famous throughout Catalonia. It caught the eye of Charles Jencks, who, in his landmark *The Language of Post-Modern Architecture*, first published in 1977, takes the building as the measure of radical eclecticism or even critical regionalism. For Jencks, the Batlló house "pulls together different kinds of meaning, which appeal to opposite faculties of the mind and body, so that they interrelate and modify each other. The taste of the building, its smell and touch, engage the sensibility as much as the sight and contemplation. In a perfectly successful work of architecture—that of Gaudí—the meanings add up and work together in the deepest combination."[82] Geoffrey Broadbent takes Jencks to task for describing the Casa Batlló, as I have also done, as "an expression of Catalan nationalism" by which the building gestures to "the martyrs who have died in the cause."[83] According to Broadbent, "this represents a 'higher' level of meaning—shading towards illusionism—which is certainly not revealed by a direct reading of the simple, visual analogies."[84] Broadbent suggests that one thing is the evocation of bones and scales, and another the evocation of an entire national epic.

Broadbent has a point: Famous as the building is in Barcelona, not every inhabitant, let alone visitor, sees it for the text that Jencks reads. Even those who follow the red-tiled *Ruta Modernista* (something like an *art nouveau* version of Boston's Freedom Trail) do not necessarily see the Casa Batlló as a Catalanist hymn. They may see colors, lines, and shapes that have an organic charge, but they may not know, or even care to know, how it signifies locally, historically, nationally. Something similar goes for Bofill's *Pyramid* or, for that matter, Dalí's, Miró's, and Tàpies's paintings. Gimferrer remarks that Tàpies's *Catalan Spirit* has particular meaning for the Catalan spectator.[85] The remark can be spun generally, for any number of artworks, including Vermeer's *View of Delft*, Goya's *The Second of May*, and Grant Wood's *American Gothic*, can be seen as having particular national significance. As Pollock observes, even the work by an artist as ostensibly "uprooted" as Van Gogh can be invested with national signs, and that to attend to them is not perforce "an act of cultural nationalism."[86] The national can play internationally, of course, even through effacement and under erasure. Gaudí may be deeply rooted in Catalonia, but Catalonia does not saturate his constructions, which may be experienced in more transient, touristic ways.

Internationality in architecture and art is such that specific signs and symbols do not, in general, tend to be read in their specificity. Or to put it differently, they are read, in general, as signifying nothing so much as specificity, in general. Roland Barthes's "effect of the real" can be recast as the effect of the specific, the regional, and the local.[87] The problem is prickly, to be sure. In subsequent editions of his work, Jencks has toned down the celebratory references to Gaudí, though he does continue to claim that his work is "perfectly successful." He seems reluctant, under-standably enough, to take a specific work of Catalan *modernisme* to be the model of a postmodernism that somehow, in its regional particularities, covers the earth. Jencks might also have had second thoughts about de-scribing architecture as appealing to so many senses. After all, the idea of the taste, smell, and touch of Gaudí's buildings is not of Jenck's making, but rather of Dalí's, for whom Gaudí represented the *ne plus ultra* of delec-table architecture.[88] The opposite, the architecture Dalí simply could not stomach, belonged to the International Style, very broadly understood. Dalí's distaste for Mondrian was matched, that is, by his distaste for Le Corbusier, that "masochist and Protestant architect," as he so disdainfully quipped.[89] Against Mondrian, Dalí pits Vermeer, and against Le Corbusier, Gaudí, "whose name, in Catalan," Dalí writes, "means 'to enjoy' or 'to come,' just as Dalí's means 'desire.'"[90]

Gaudí does indeed resonate with the Catalan, *gaudir*, but also, as chance would have it, with the English "gaudy," which has the same Latin root: *gaudium*, meaning "joy" and *gaudere*, meaning "to rejoice." Dalí, playing with tongues, desired his name to come from the Catalan *delit*, meaning "delight," though related to "delicacy," "delectable," and, semantically, to "joy," "enjoyment," and "pleasure." Phonetically, the word *delit* is close to *delicte*, meaning "delinquency" or "crime," a similarity, where Dalí is con-cerned, too felicitous to leave unsaid. Gibson, suspicious of the signer of the blank sheets, does not quite take Dalí's word on his name and tracks it down, locates its origins, and corrects the artist's evaluation of one of his most prized possessions. According to Gibson, "Dalí" stems from "the Ara-bic for 'guide' or 'leader,'" which designated a kind of strong staff wielded by the *daliner*, or boss, of the men employed to tow boats from the river-bank."[91] Gibson further acknowledges the connections to the Catalan *adalil* and Spanish *adalid*, also meaning "leader." He then speculates that had Dalí "realized that his highly unusual surname coincided with the word for 'guide' or 'leader' in Arabic, he would no doubt have informed the world."[92] The name in which he took such pleasure survives, then, in Gib-son's reading, as something of a misnomer, a fabrication whose truth might have taken its bearer, had he only known it, down a different path. There is, however, no assurance that Dalí did *not* know all of this. It is just as reasonable to speculate that he did know and that he simply preferred to refer to himself, however falsely, through pleasure rather than through some obscure mode of leadership: as if to be happy he had to create a school.

Word play is seductive business, usually silly, but at times quite serious. As I move through so many visual images, I cannot but pause before the word, most notably, the English word "to forge," whose polyvocality is imposing. In Spanish, in Catalan, in so many other languages, the plays are not as imposing, the word "forge" fracturing into "forja," "fragua," and "falsear" in Spanish and into "forja," "farga," and "falsejar" in Catalan. The figurative possibilities are still there, more or less, but they are not melded into such a smooth, unified, or inclusive fabrication as in English. I pause before the word, in languages that are not English, because I am struck at how certain images—Gaudí's façades, Miró's murals, Dalí's mustache—presumably need no translation. I am struck, that is, at how certain images can work iconically, if not metaphorically, and at how they can call forth, in general, a specificity with which we presumably need not tarry. More than one, like Jencks, has written of the "language" of art and architecture, the "language" of the visual, and more than one has called this language not just postmodern, or modern, or even international, but universal as well. With respect to Catalan architects, in more recent editions of Jencks's work, Gaudí recedes and Bofill gains prominence.[93] Jencks explicitly links Bofill to Dalí and Buñuel, claiming that the architect's affection for fantastic realism is beholden to that of the artist and the filmmaker.[94] Bofill may just possibly come to the fore because, linked as he is to a locally inflected internationalism, he raises questions that concern Jencks, most significantly, the status of the universal.

Few events invoke the universal as strongly as the Olympics. In 1992, year of the Barcelona games, the city seemed to be all but governed by architects and urban planners.[95] In 1999, Barcelona was awarded the Royal Institute of British Architects gold medal, the first time a place and not a person or team of people had been so honored. The RIBA prize acknowledged, from the outside, the city's revitalization and internationalization. It was no accident that the Olympics provided the occasion to justify massive and generally much-needed urban reforms as well as extensive and ambitious cultural initiatives. With the site of the athletes' housing designated as the New Icaria, Barcelona launched an international publicity campaign that sought to make it, and Catalonia, famous.[96] It included a full two-page ad in the *New York Times* that cited Catalonia as the host country of the games. But it also included a nationally motivated international reconstruction: not of a building by Le Corbusier, Dalí might be happy to know, but of a building by Mies van der Rohe, Dalí might *not* be happy to know: the German Pavilion of Barcelona's second Universal Exposition, held in 1929. The pavilion, dwarfed by the monumental architecture of the Primo de Rivera dictatorship, was demolished shortly after the Exposition closed. Also demolished, but before the Exposition opened, were four red columns that, like Bofill's *Pyramid*, deliberately recalled the *senyera*; unlike the German Pavilion, the columns were not rebuilt.

The German Pavilion is cited in virtually every history of modern architecture.[97] In the words of Kenneth Frampton, it is "a horizontal centrifugal spatial arrangement . . . subdivided by free-standing planes and columns," recalling both Wright and De Stijl.[98] Frampton is probably referring to the original, though it is difficult to be sure. For the German Pavilion *does* exist and does admit visitors, drawing them in with the illusion of a masterpiece whose integrity is such that is seems to have never been demolished and hence to have never been reconstructed. As a meticulously faithful reconstruction undertaken in the 1980s, the German Pavilion is of the order of duplications. That does not mean that it is not as "good" as the original, for as Rudolph Arnheim observes, "the distinction between original and reproduction is anything but obvious."[99] As a case in point, Arnheim refers to the sacred Ise shrine of Japan, which has been demolished and rebuilt every twenty years since 478. "The faithful maintain," Arnheim continues, "that every one of these embodiments is *the* Ise shrine, thereby reminding us that no individual entity is under obligation to exist only once."[100] The analogy is flawed, of course, because the German Pavilion is not a religious shrine, but a structure that attests to the expanded secularization of the West, where "catholic" is refashioned and rearticulated as "cosmopolitan." And yet, the analogy *does* function because the Pavilion has become a shrine to secularization, modernization, and internationalization, a shrine, perhaps, to the secularization of shrines. Unlike the Ise shrine, the German Pavilion is a "shrine" whose aura is not imperiled by the use of "power tools and nails, regardless of whether or not the average visitor could tell the difference."[101] In fact, being built anew may actually reinforce the aura of the German Pavilion, steeped in the practices of modern power. Duplication, or multiplication, as we have seen, does not necessarily destroy the original, far from it. Put somewhat bluntly, seriality becomes the measure of international originality.

It is perhaps hazardous to assimilate the building to an international style, just as it is hazardous, Frampton remarks, to negate the "different climactic and cultural" marks of the international style, thanks to which, he declares, "it never became truly universal."[102] And yet, as Frampton continues, the international style nonetheless "implied a universality of approach which generally favored light-weight technique, synthetic modern material, and standard modular parts so as to facilitate fabrication and erection."[103] Fabrication is at the very root of forgery, *fragua, forja, farga: fabrica, fabricare*, and it gives me pause before I come, ever so generally, to my particular conclusion. For the German Pavilion, refabricated, stands as alluring testimony to the "universal" structure of a Universal Exposition by which, in comparison, the long-standing, nationally marked "theme park" known as the *Poble Espanyol* that lies close by the Pavilion, seems almost too absurd to be believed. What is absurd, or risible, or delectably kitsch about the Spanish Town—or Spanish People, as we might also translate it—is the condensation, if not miniaturization, of Spain, the location of all the regions of the Spanish nation in a little corner of the Catalan capital. Without the proper guide, the Spanish Town calls to mind not so much the megalomania of the military dictator Primo de Rivera as the kinder and gentler megalomania of an entertainer such as Walt Disney. Beside it, the socialist-inspired reconstruction of the German Pavilion shimmers in a sort of cultural self-sufficiency, a serious work of architecture that provides testimony to modernity, internationality, technical control, good taste, purity of form, and fame. Never mind that you do not need to know a word of Catalan, or Spanish, or German, to approach it, to enter it, to appreciate it. Never mind that it is an Olympic inflected refabrication of a nationally inflected Universal Exposition erected under a military regime. Never mind that Dalí, signing off on blankness, would never have swallowed it. Never mind that, like the Spanish Town, it too is, in a sense, a fraud.

In any case, a new project is under way: drawing on the success of *l'any Gaudí*, the year of Gaudi, in 2002, prominent Catalans will be promoting 2004 as *l'any Dalí*, the year of Dalí, not just in Catalonia but throughout the world.

Notes

1. All translations, unless otherwise indicated, are mine.
2. See Nicholas Capasso, "Salvador Dalí and the Barren Plain: A Phenomenological Analysis of a Surrealist Landscape Environment," *Arts Magazine* 60 (1986): 72–83, for a reading of the presence and absence of a Catalan landscape in Dalí.
3. The principal competitors of the Dalí museum are the Prado in Madrid and, more recently, the Guggenheim in Bilbao.
4. Dalí is, for Breton, a fraudulent surrealist, his paranoid-critical method notwithstanding. For Dalí, Breton is the fraud and he, Dalí, the true surrealist, perhaps because unconcerned with fraud or because more adept at dealing with, and in, fraud. In a radio interview from 1952, published in *Entretiens* (Paris: Gallimard, 1969), Breton says that Dalí's early paintings "were worth more than the utterly American fame that they currently enjoy," 158.
5. Dalí's tantrum and arrest are reported as high farce on the front page of *The New York Times* (17 March, 1939): "Art Changed, Dali [sic] Goes on Rampage in Store, Crashes Through Window Into Arms of Law." Dalí reaped considerable financial benefits from the brouhaha. Lee Catterall, *The Great Dalí Art Fraud and Other Deceptions* (Fort Lee, New Jersey: Barricade Books, 1992), reports that "[n]ews accounts of the incident created long lines at Julian Levy's gallery, and within two weeks, the twenty-one Dalí works exhibited there had been sold for more than $25,000 each," 35.
6. Salvador Dalí, *Diccionario privado* (Madrid: Altalena Editores, 1980), 26.
7. Dalí, *Diccionario*, 26.
8. See S. J. Woolf, "Doodles Come to Town," *The New York Times Magazine* (12 March, 1939). For a sample of the coverage of the blank sheets scandal in Spain, see Alfons Quintà, "Salvador Dalí ha firmado documentos y papeles en blanco que permiten la reproducción sin control de su obra," *El País* (13 March, 1981): 28–29.
9. For Màrius Carol, *Dalí: El final oculto de un exhibicionista* (Barcelona: Plaza & Janés, 1990), the best known painter to have admitted forging a "Dalí" is Manuel Pujol Baladas, 117.
10. Catterall, 37.
11. Karl Marx, *Capital*, Vol. 1, trans. Samuel Moore and Edward Aveling (New York: International Publishers, 1967), 73.

12. Marx, 74.

13. Ruth Brandon, *Surreal Lives: The Surrealists 1917–1945* (London: Papermac: 2000) notes that "laughter of any sort did not come easily to Breton," 154.

14. Dalí, *Diccionario*, 67.

15. For a detailed account of the politics of surrealism, see Helena Lewis, *The Politics of Surrealism* (New York: Paragon, 1988), who refers to Dalí's "aesthetic fascism," 152.

16. Ian Gibson, *The Shameful Life of Salvador Dalí* (London: Faber and Faber, 1997), 546–547. Dalí was certainly not the only one to profit from such activities. An array of secretaries, advisors, associates, and others profited as well. According to Carol, an agent of the FBI estimated that the traffic in fraudulent works by Dalí involved some 400 million dollars annually, while Dalí's lawyer put the figure at 625 million dollars, 117.

17. Thomas Kincaide, the king of cottage kitsch, also deploys a signatory assembly line to great personal profit.

18. Catterall, 43–44. Each of Dalí's signatures was worth $40, and with the help of assistants he could sign up to 1,800 an hour, 43–44.

19. Gibson, *Shameful Life*, 547.

20. Gibson, *Shameful Life*, 547.

21. I take the "descriptive" terms from the opening of Hope B. Werness's "Han van Meegeren *fecit*," in *The Forger's Art: Forgery and the Philosophy of Art*, ed. Denis Dutton (Berkeley: University of California Press, 1983): 1–57.

22. Rudolf Arnheim, "On Duplication" in *The Forger's Art: Forgery and the Philosophy of Art*, ed. Denis Dutton (Berkeley: University of California Press, 1983): 232–245.

23. See Salvador Dalí, "La conquista de lo irracional," in *¿Por qué se ataca a la Gioconda?*, ed. María J. Vera, trans. Edison Simons (Madrid: Ediciones Siruela, 1994): 178–188.

24. In *Un chien andalou*, *The Lacemaker* appears as a reproduction in a book that the female protagonist lets fall from her lap. In *Cet obscur objet du désir*, *The Lacemaker* is evoked in the final scene of the film, when the protagonists stop to contemplate a woman in a shop window mend a torn and bloodied garment, perhaps a wedding gown. The camera focuses on the thread as it enters and leaves the cloth. Among other things, it is a metaphor for the editing process.

25. Jean-Paul Sartre, in *What is Literature?*, trans. Bernard Frechtman (Northampton: Methuen & Co, 1967), also appreciated Vermeer for the sense of freedom he finds in his detailed "realism," 40.

26. For more on automatism and the connections between Dalí and Breton, see Laurent Jenny, "From Breton to Dalí: The Adventures of Automatism," *October* 51 (1989): 105–114.

27. Salvador Dalí, "Sant Sebastià," in *L'alliberament dels dits*, ed. Fèlix Fanés (Barcelona: Cuaderns Crema, 1995): 15–23. The essay was originally published in *L'Amic de les Arts* 16 (1927): 52–54. Rafael Santos Torroella, in "Sant Sebastià i el mite dalinià," in *Dalí Escriptor* (Barcelona: Fundació Caixa de Pensions, 1990): 33–47, links Dalí's interest in Saint Sebastian to the artist's relationship with Lorca.

28. Dalí, "Sant Sebastià," 15–16.

29. Werness, 29. In some respects, even the paintings by Vermeer whose authorship is beyond dispute have become their own reproductions. Such exquisite works as *View of Delft* and *The Girl with a Pearl Earring* have been carefully reviewed, retouched, and restored; Vermeer's brush strokes have been studiously imitated in order to preserve and revive the real thing, in all its original glory. For an account of the restoration of the paintings, see Jørgen Wadum, et al., *Vermeer Illuminated: Conservation, Restoration and Research* (The Hague: Mauritshuis/V+K Publishing, 1995). Restoration raises interesting questions about the authenticity of art, the role of science, and the "life" of a painting. What one now sees is not exclusively the work of Vermeer.

30. Alfred Lessing, "What is Wrong with a Forgery," in *The Forger's Art: Forgery and the Philosophy of Art*, ed. Denis Dutton (Berkeley: University of California Press, 1983): 58–76, 76.

31. Salvador Dalí, *The Secret Life of Salvador Dalí*, trans. Haakon M. Chevalier (New York: Dial Press, 1942), 68.

32. Dawn Ades, *Dalí* (London: Thames & Hudson, 1982), remarks how Dalí came to express a certain appreciation for abstraction, particularly for that of Willem de Kooning, later in his life.

33. Rosalind E. Krauss, *The Originality of the Avant-Garde and Other Modernist Myths* (Cambridge: MIT Press, 1986), 158.

34. Krauss, 158.
35. Brooks Adams, "Reassessing Dalí," *Art in America* 79 (1991): 56–59, 58.
36. Ralf Schiebler, *Dalí, Genius, Obsession and Lust*, trans. Fiona Elliot (Munich: Prestel Verlag, 1999), 7.
37. Robert Radford, *Dalí* (London: Phaidon Press, 1997), 283.
38. Duchamp authorized replicas of both his signed urinal and his large glass. He played with authorization, and it is telling that museums continue to announce the artist's authorization as the justification for the inclusion and display of a work of art. The play with authorization is, as Duchamp surely knew, itself a commodity of art and art history.
39. Ades gives an illuminating overview of Dalí's multiple imagery and its relation to the paranoid critical method, 119–149.
40. See Ben Broos, "Un celebre Peijntre nommé Verme[e]r," in *Johannes Vermeer*, ed. Arthur K. Wheelock, Jr. (Zwolle: Waanders Publishers/Royal Cabinet of Paintings Mauritshuis, The Hague/National Gallery of Art, Washington, 1996): 47–65. Broos waxes indignant on the subject of van Meegeren and forgery, 62.
41. See José-Carlos Mainer, "De ciutats a capitals: El diàleg difícil de dos nacionalismes," in *Barcelona/Madrid 1898–1998: Sintonies y distàncies* (Barcelona: Diputació de Barcelona/ Centre de Cultura Contemporània de Barcelona, 1997): 44–53.
42. The play of stereotypes was not always playful. Dalí's anti-Semitism, reinforced by his wife Gala's (though she was, it seems, of Jewish descent herself), seems too real to discount. Catterall discusses Dalí's particularly contemptuous attitude toward Jewish art dealers, 71.
43. Benet R. Barrios, "Txeques. D'instrucció," in *Els modernistes i el nacionalisme cultural*, ed. Vicente Cacho Viu (Barcelona: Edicions la Magrana/Diputació de Barcelona, 1984): 329–333.
44. Barrios, 330.
45. Josep Miquel Sobrer, "J. V. Foix, Salvador Dalí y la modernidad," in *El aeroplano y la estrella: El movimiento de vanguardia en los Países Catalanes (1904–1936)*, ed. Joan Ramon Resina (Amsterdam: Rodopi, 1997): 131–150.
46. See Michel Foucault, *The Archaeology of Knowledge*, trans. A. M. Sheridan Smith (New York: Pantheon, 1972), 17. Hervé Guibert is best known for his autobiographically inflected AIDS chronicle, *To the Friend Who Did Not Save My Life*, trans. Linda Coverdale (New York: Macmillan, 1991).
47. "Catalan" is spelled "Català" in Catalan and "Catalán" in Castilian. Barceló's use of the accent (though perhaps merely an indication of hurry) is intriguing, whether accidental or deliberate. Functioning as a bilingual hybrid, it conjures up the fusion of the two languages and calls forth a correspondingly hybrid national vision. It also upsets the play of accents among the names of the artists: Miró and Barceló both ending in an accented "o" and Tàpies and Català, both containing an accented "a." It is as if Barceló did not want to privilege Tàpies more than he already does; Tàpies already occupies the central and hence mediating position in the list, and, moreover, his name means "earthen walls" in Catalan. The geometric symbols that accompany the names allude to motifs used by each of the three artists in such works as Miró's *The Poetess* (1940), Tàpies's *Newspaper Cross* (1946–47), and Barceló's *Systole-Diastole* (1987). And yet, Miró, as Karl Ruhrberg notes, in *Painting*, vol. I. of *Art of the 20th Century*, 2 Vols., ed. Ingo F. Walther (Köln: Taschen, 1998), was especially fond of the circle, which "took a place of prominence, whether in pure of irregular form," 150. That Barceló assigns the circle to himself reinforces, as I see it, the connection with Miró over and above Tàpies. The accidental connection, already signaled in the "ó" that ends the name of both Miró and Barceló, is given support by means of Barceló's appropriation of the circle.
48. Miró pays homage to the Dutch masters in such works as *Dutch Interior* (1928), but Dalí is incomparably more insistent about reproducing their technique. Dalí presents a table of artistic mastery in *Les cocus de vieil art moderne* (Paris: Bernard Grasset & Fasquelle, 1956) and his *Dairy of a Genius Diary of a Genius*, trans. Richard Howard (London: Hutchinson, 1990). In it, Vermeer has the highest score and Mondrian lowest. Fascinated by Vermeer, Dalí produces *The Ghost of Vermeer of Delft, Which can be used as a Table* (1934) and confronts a rhinoceros with a copy of *The Lacemaker* in a zoo outside Paris in the mid–1950s. Still, Millet's *Angelus* is the work that has left the most spectacular traces in Dalí's production, inspiring an array of visual reminiscences; see Dalí's *El mito trágico del "Angelus" de Millet*, ed. Oscar Tusquets (Barcelona: Tusquets, 1989).

49. Miquel Barceló, *Miquel Barceló* (Paris: Éditions du Jeu de Paume/Réunion des musées nationaux, 1996), 133.

50. Barceló, 133.

51. Thomas McEvilley, "Barceló, entre modernisme et postmodernisme," in *Miquel Barceló* (Paris: Éditions du Jeu de Paume/Réunion des musées nationaux, 1996): 153–158, also sees Barceló as both modern and postmodern, 154. He likewise notes the national dimensions of internationalism, germane for Barceló, who has lived in Naples, New York, and Mali.

52. Barceló, 133.

53. For Ruhrberg, Tàpies's "are not metaphysical but tellurian landscapes, very much of the earth in that they point far back in time to forms of pre-existence of our planet," 261. But the tellurian is not perforce opposed to the metaphysical, especially not when it "points" to "forms of pre-existence." Even if the metaphysical is obscured in Tàpies's paintings—which I do not believe to be the case—it is definitely not obscured in his writings, where mysticism and the absolute are repeatedly invoked. Barceló presents a similar tension. In fact, the quest for true or ultimate reality sent Barceló, in typical ascetic fashion, to the desert.

54. Antoni Tàpies, *Per un art modern i progressista* (Barcelona: Empúries, 1985), 105.

55. Tàpies, 106.

56. Tàpies, 106.

57. Tàpies, 83.

58. Tàpies's language is reminiscent of George Orwell's in a 1944 essay on Dalí's *Secret Life*, with the difference that Orwell at least uses Dalí to make a case against censorship. For a study of Orwell's view of Dalí, see P. Vervoort, "'Benefit of Clergy': Opposition to Salvador Dalí," in *Orwell x 8*. (Winnipeg: Frye, 1986. 67–92). Tàpies's language is also reminiscent of Breton's, where moral indignation, seriousness, and ironclad integrity predominate.

59. Such a state of affairs in art criticism holds a paradoxical promise. For Brooks, commenting on a major showing of Dalí's work in Mexico City in 1991, "Dalí is, of course, ripe for reappraisal, since he is at once the most popular and least respected of the major 20th-century painters,"57. Adams generally praises the exhibit, noting with obvious approval that "there was not a trace of the trashy multiples, forgeries and scandalmongering that so besmirched Dalí's later years," 58. Reappraisal has its limits, it seems, and trashiness and fraud are two of them. Tàpies's use of worn-out material, of junk, is apparently not of the same order as Dalí's use of his past works and his name.

60. Adams, 57. In the afterword to *The Shameful Life*, Gibson encapsulates the chronological evaluation of Dalí: "Dalí's work after he moved to America in 1940, grows increasingly hackneyed and repetitious, whatever some people may have thought at the time," 627.

61. For more on fame and money in Picasso, see John Berger, *Success and Failure of Picasso* (Middlesex: Penguin, 1965).

62. Brandon, 326.

63. Javier Tusell, "Barcelona de Madrid estant," in *Barcelona/Madrid 1898–1998: Sintonies y distàncies* (Barcelona: Diputació de Barcelona/Centre de Cultura Contemporània de Barcelona, 1997): 31–41, 35.

64. Tusell, 35.

65. Salvador Dalí, "Manifest groc," in *L'alliberament dels dits*, ed. Fèlix Fanés (Barcelona: Cuaderns Crema, 1995): 99–105, 103.

66. Adams, 58.

67. Gibson, *Shameful Life*, 624.

68. For more on Mariscal, see Guy Julier, *Mariscal* (Köln: Taschen, 1992).

69. The Babel Forum is a controversial response to the controversial "Law of Catalan." For more, see Antonio Santamaría, ed, *Fòrum Babel: El nacionalisme i les llengües de Catalunya* (Barcelona: Áltera, 1999).

70. Griselda Pollock, "Van Gogh and Holland: Nationalism and Modernism," in *Avant-Gardes and Partisans Reviewed*, by Fred Orton and Griselda Pollock (Manchester: Manchester UP, 1996): 103–114, 109.

71. Ruhrberg, 150.

72. Pere Gimferrer, *Antoni Tàpies y el espíritu catalán* (Barcelona: Ediciones Polígrafa, 1974) 19, 23, 24.

73. Gimferrer, 24.

74. Barbara Catoir, *Conversations with Antoni Tàpies*, trans. John Ormrod (Munich: Prestel-Verlag, 1991), 70. As Catoir says, "Tàpies is no bohemian: He has always clung to the forms

of support offered by tradition, by his family and the familiar surroundings of his native city. Although his art is concerned with a quest for new spiritual horizons, it retains a firm sense of physical place," 36. So described, Tàpies is the very embodiment of "rooted" Catalan values.

75.   The "title" of a 1957 painting by Mark Rothko is *Red, White and Brown*. Many of Tàpies's works are similarly titled (i.e. *Fragile White on Grey and Brown*, 1961; *Grey Relief in Four Parts*, 1963; and *Rose Parentheses on Grey*, 1965).

76.   Robert Hughes, *Barcelona* (New York: Alfred A. Knopf, 1992), 80.

77.   Bofill's earliest works, largely apartment complexes in Ibiza and Barcelona, date from the early 1960s. Walden Seven has become notorious, however, for its shoddiness, which includes falling tiles and lack of light, and its arrogance. Juan Marsé lampoons the building in a polemical novel, *El amante bilingüe* (Barcelona: Planeta, 1990).

78.   Warren James, *Ricardo Bofill: Taller de Arquitectura: Buildings and Projects 1960–1985* (New York: Rizzoli, 1988), discusses Bofill's French fame, but not before noting the architect's early "unabashed Catalan flamboyance," 203, whatever that means.

79.   Charles Jencks, *The Language of Post-Modern Architecture* (London: Academy, 1991 ed.), 136.

80.   Catalan nationalism (like, though obviously unlike, Spanish nationalism) is suffused with regional and regionalist references. One of the most important is the *Lliga Regionalista*, a largely conservative political formation founded in 1901 and led by Enric Prat de la Riba, author of the influential *La nacionalitat catalana* (1906). After the parliament in Madrid passed bills aimed at preserving the unity of the Spanish nation, the conservative *Lliga* came together with Catalan working-class associations to form *Solidaritat Catalana*, a coalition that swept the elections in 1907. Class tensions subsequently tore *Solidaritat* apart, and Catalanism itself assumed various political guises, but regionalism, in many cases, clearly called forth nationalism.

81.   For Catterall, Dalí's rendition of Saint George and the Dragon is "cherished today as a truly 'original' print," 37.

82.   Charles A. Jencks, *The Language of Post-Modern Architecture* (New York: Rizzoli International Publications, 1977 ed.), 132.

83.   Geoffrey Broadbent, "A Plain Man's Guide to the Theory of Signs in Architecture," in *Theorizing A New Agenda for Architecture: An Anthology of Architectural theory 1965–1995* (New York: Princeton Architectural Press, 1996): 124–140, 137.

84.   Broadbent, 137.

85.   Gimferrer, 24.

86.   Pollock, 112.

87.   See Roland Barthes, "The Reality Effect," in *The Rustle of Language*, trans. Richard Howard (Berkeley: University of California Press, 1989): 141–148.

88.   See Salvador Dalí, "La visión de Gaudí," in *¿Por qué se ataca a la Gioconda?*, ed. María J. Vera, trans. Edison Simons (Madrid: Ediciones Siruela, 1994): 271–275. See also Daniel Abadie, "La Ripopée de Barceló" in *Miquel Barceló* (Paris: Éditions du Jeu de Paume/Réunion des musées nationaux, 1996): 9–10, who sees Barceló's art also in gastronomic terms, 9.

89.   Dalí, *Cocus*, 33.

90.   Dalí, *Cocus*, 35.

91.   Gibson, *Shameful Life*, 30.

92.   Gibson, *Shameful Life*, 31.

93.   According to Jencks, "[i]t seems the people who live in and visit these [inhabitable] monuments do prefer them to other mass-housing. They may be a trifle bombastic and overdense in certain places, they may suffer from too much architecture, they may not be perfect in detail, but like the Brighton Pavilion, it's nice to have them around," *Language*, 1991 ed., 137.

94.   Jencks, *Language*, 1991 ed., 137.

95.   Works by journalist and critic Llàtzer Moix, *La ciudad de los arquitectos* (Barcelona: Anagrama, 1994) and architect Ricardo Bofill, *La ciudad del arquitecto* (Barcelona: Galaxia Gutenberg, 1998) make the point abundantly clear.

96.   Icarus may have fallen for aspiring too high, but that is precisely his challenge and appeal. The Icarian project in Barcelona dates back to the urbanist Idelfons Cerdà and others influenced by utopian socialism and the ideas of Etienne Cabet, author of *Voyage en Icarie* (1842).

97.   See Ignasi de Solà-Morales, Cristian Cirici, and Fernando Ramos, *Mies van der Rohe Barcelona Pavilion* (Barcelona: Editorial Gustavo Gili, 1993), the architects who saw the

project to completion. They describe the reconstruction of the Pavilion as "a traumatic undertaking," 39. The trauma, for them, entails "entering into that Duchampesque perspective in which [they] had to accept, *helás!*, a certain inanity in [their] aesthetic operations," 39. Though they acknowledge the "distance that exists between the original and its replica," they urge their readers to move beyond "the closed circuit of paper architecture" and "to go there, to walk amidst [sic] and see the startling contrast between the building and its surroundings," 39.

98. Kenneth Frampton, *Modern Architecture: A Critical History* (London: Thames and Hudson, 1992), 164.
99. Arnheim, 237.
100. Arnheim, 237.
101. Arnheim, 237.
102. Frampton, 248.
103. Frampton, 248.

PART 2
Forging Selves

CHAPTER 6

The Art of Forging Music and Musicians

Of Lighthearted Musicologists, Ambitious Performers, Narrow-Minded Brothers, and Creative Aristocrats

REINHOLD BRINKMANN

Reflecting on the subtle art of forging in the fine art of music, I will not initiate a theoretical discussion or present an exemplary case study. Instead I will point a spotlight on a variety of individual cases and draw some hopefully illuminating conclusions. To avoid the impression that my narrative will be a potpourri only, that is, according to the *Concise Harvard Dictionary of Music,* a sequence of tunes from various repertories "which are played in succession connected by a few measures of introduction or modulation," I will try to make what I propose to present more or less coherent. Thus I will follow the subtitle of a work by Richard Strauss: "Nach alter Schelmenweise in Rondeauform" (after the old rogue's tale, in the form of a rondeau). That is, I will "perform" a piece with 3 ritornellos, 2 episodes, and a more substantial middle section. Here, then, is my little *Rondo burlesco sopra aliqui soggetti depravati.*

Introduzione in modo narrativo

Scholars seem to live a dangerous life these days. This is true not only of fieldworkers, those courageous anthropologists or ethnomusicologists who find the objects of their desired research in the jungle or desert or isolated mountain hamlet. Even within the closed walls of the academy it is possible to become trapped, stymied by a surprising discovery that undermines your confidence in the trustworthiness of your own discipline, of scholarship in general. Take the everyday case of the Harvard Online Library Information System, or HOLLIS for short. Let us assume that you conduct a keyword search, using—just at random—two German words, say *Duplizität* and *Dichotomie*, both in themselves innocent and harmless, *Fremdwörter* (foreign words) in German, representatives of "otherness" so to speak, but demonstrating, when used together, the author's command of modern scholarly language.

Indeed, a book with the title *Dichotomie und Duplizität* (Dichotomy and Duplicity) resides in the Harvard College Library, a book on basic methodology, as the subtitle "Grundfragen psychologischer Erkenntnis" (Fundamental Questions of Psychological Cognition) suggests. It is a memorial volume commemorating, it seems, an important scholar in the field of psychology: "Ernst August Dölle zum Gedächtnis." A credible professor of psychology, Theo W. Herrmann from Marburg University, is listed as the editor, and the publisher of the 1974 paperback volume is Hans Huber of Bern, Switzerland. The essays in this book display serious scholarship, as evidenced by the tone of the titles: "Dölle und der Positivismusstreit" (Dölle and the Positivism Debate) by Hans W. Albert may recall the dispute between Albert and Theodor W. Adorno; Jochen Moshaber's "Dölles Dualitätsprinzip in der Perspektive der materialistischen Dialektik" (Dölle's Principle of Duality from the Perspective of Materialist Dialectic) promises a methodological discussion with continued relevance to the present; Klaus M. Foppa's "Aporetisches in E. A. Dölle's Lerntheorie" (Aporetic Elements of E. A. Dölle's Theory of Learning) adds the important pedagogical perspective, and so on.

Even as a musicologist you may be intrigued by this scholarly work and want to know more about the erudite man who inspired his distinguished colleagues to such enterprising titles. But a computer search for books by Ernst August Dölle has a shocking result: It seems that this important figure has not published a single book! And when a search for essays or journal articles likewise renders no positive result, one grows rather suspicious. Ernst August Dölle no longer exists in any form of writing—except in the eulogies of his *Gedenkschrift* (memorial volume). Did he ever? Has he vanished? Or has the international scholarly community been fooled and Dölle simply invented? If so, what does it mean that a solid Swiss publisher supports such a frivolous undertaking?

This is a disturbing discovery, to say the least. In order to restore confidence in the scholarly system, your musicologist retreats from the obviously corrupt field of psychology and turns to the safety of medieval musical studies, a field viewed as the embodiment of methodological integrity and uprightness. In my Rondo performance I have thus entered the Hauptsatz.

Ritornello 1

Enjoying myself immensely, I am reading a Latin treatise edited by the eminent musicologist and music theorist Hugo Riemann, an industrious and serious author with an abundance of books listed in the Harvard library's computer catalogue, who lived from 1849 to 1919 and from 1895 taught at the University of Leipzig in Saxony. I turned to Riemann because his theories about rhythm, meter, and phrasing, as well as his ideas about a musical logic, have recently—in the form of a neo-Riemannian theory—gained new actuality for the field of music theory (after a period in which virtually all practitioners concentrated exclusively on Schenker and Schoenberg). Riemann's essay collection *Präludien und Studien,* published in three volumes between 1895 and 1901, is of special interest. The third volume, from 1901, contains the edition of a Latin treatise from the beginning of the fourteenth century, "De cantu fractibili brevis positio," with a translation into German and commentary. The original codex is said to be preserved in Leipzig and bears the signature "Cod. Lips. Thomas. 6 III."; the author, a Magister Ugolino de Maltero from Thuringia, dedicated this presentation of his theory of musical phrasing to his Polish colleague Franciscus Culacius. The content of this medieval text is quite remarkable, for it does no less than prove that Hugo Riemann's controversial theory of phrasing was not only practiced but also theoretically reflected upon and taught as early as in the fourteenth century. The discovery of this treatise was of particular importance to Riemann, the editor himself, whose own theory was heavily attacked during his lifetime by other theorists, prominent among them his Berlin colleague Franz Kullack, whose father was born in Krotoschin, Poland. Indeed, the rediscovery of Ugolino de Maltero would seem to add a strong historical argument for the plausibility of Hugo Riemann's theory and assign it an almost universal validity. As a musical example, the medieval author uses a melody, "Diex servasse" by a certain venerable Josephus, a fairly simple song that, according to Riemann, was immensely popular at the time the treatise was written. Humming the melody will help us to understand this popularity:

Figure 6.1 First music example. "Diex servasse" de primo modo ex omnibus perfectis (1. Modus mit lauter perfekten Longae).

But—something is strange here. Its incipit, "Diex servasse"—that is, "Gott erhalte"—alone evokes an allusion. Here it is again, in modern notation:

Figure 6.2 Second music example.

Doesn't a string quartet with many variations on this melodic idea come to mind? After the encounter with Ernst August Dölle, naive confidence in scholarly integrity has vanished. And now unsettling parallels become apparent: The phonetic identities of "Hugo" (Riemann) with "Ugolino" (de Maltero), and of "Franz Kullack" with the Riemann opponent "Franciscus Culacius." The musicologist who tried to escape scholarly anxieties caused by too close an examination of the modern psychological literature now encounters—with a sense of horror—similar machinations in his own field. Land mines everywhere! But now real scholarly curiosity demands careful investigation.

With that we are, in our little thematic Rondo, at Episode 1.

Episode 1

Who was Ugolino de Maltero? Unlike Dölle, he is listed in modern dictionaries: he is a lexical entity. The short biographical entry "Ugolinus de Maltero" on page 824 from the twelfth edition of the *Riemann Lexikon, Personenteil*, vol. 2, edited by Wilibald Gurlitt and published in 1961, is but one example. The bibliography for this entry also reveals that René Leibowitz —the underrated conductor, overrated composer, and influential writer on modern music whose books introduced many musicians from my generation into the world of the Second Viennese School—found the fourteenth-century treatise so important that, as late as 1950, he reedited and translated it into French as *Un Traité de la Variation (XIVme Siècle)*. What the bibliography does not list is a Berlin dissertation from 1935 by Margarethe Appel on the terminology in medieval musical treatises, a thesis supervised by Arnold Schering, that uses Ugolino's Latin text as a relevant source—without any reservation. And even in 1963 an essay published in an international musicological journal expresses astonishment about the advanced state of the technique of variation at this early point in history—the author believed in Leibowitz's edition (see Acta Musicologica 35, 1963, 124). The commentary on Ugolinus in the *Lexikon*

Ugolinus de Maltero, Magister; deutscher Musiktheoretiker, aus Thüringen stammend, verfaßte einen Traktat *De cantu fractibili,* den H. Riemann (der die Schrift zuerst herausgab) mit ›etwa 1320‹ datiert und der einige merkwürdige Aufschlüsse zum Stande der älteren und neueren Musikschriftstellerei bringt. Ausg.: De cantu fractibili, in: H. RIEMANN, Präludien u. Studien III, Lpz. (1900); dass., als Un traité inconnu ... hrsg. v. R. LEIBOWITZ, Lüttich 1950. Lit.: H. BESSELER, Bourdon u. Fauxbourdon, Lpz. 1950, S. 26, Anm. 3.

+**Ugolinus de Maltero,** 13./14. Jh. Die Diskussion um U. de M.s Traktat +*De cantu fractibili* wurde bis in die jüngere Zeit hinein fortgesetzt (vgl. H. Besseler in: AMI XLI, 1969, S. 107f.). Ausg.: +H. RIEMANN, Präludien u. Studien (III, 1901), Nachdr. Hildesheim 1967.

Figure 6.3a Riemann Dictionary 1961.

Figure 6.3b Riemann Dictionary Supplement 1975.

entry, however, reads, to uninformed eyes and ears, rather strangely: Ugolino's treatise, the entry states, "gives some curious disclosures about the state of ancient as well as present penmanship with regard to music." The *Riemann Lexikon* supplement, vol. 2 from 1975, contains an update of this Ugolino entry—with information which makes it clear that the discussion surrounding this author continues.

Giving up my introductory persona of the disturbed scholar—at least for the moment—let me narrate what in fact happened. Around the turn of the century Hugo Riemann wrote a fictitious Latin treatise against his critic Franz Kullack, a musicological joke. He included several identifying clues. First, his own name: Hugo/Ugolino; second, his birth town: *Malter* is a box to measure flour; *Mehl,* leading to "Maltero" as a Latinization of his hometown, "Gross-Mehlra"; and third, the signature "Codex Lips. Thomas. 6 III" refers to "Leipzig, Thomasiusstraße no. 6, 3d floor" (that is, 4th floor in the US), Riemann's private address before 1900 (the entry in the *Leipziger Adreß-Buch für 1898* reads: "Riemann Hugo, D. phil., Musiklehrer, Docent a. d. Univ., Thomasiusstr. 6 III"); and finally—the biggest hint—Joseph (venerable Josephus) Haydn's melody "Gott erhalte Franz den Kaiser" in mensural notation. Here any serious reader-hummer must figure out what in fact is going on. And similarly, the two Ugolino entries in the *Riemann Lexikon* and supplement both end with a citation of a footnote or a remark in the secondary literature where the Ugolino puzzle is solved, the case cleared up. But the musicological game continues at another page.

Ritornello 2

Obviously, Hugo Riemann had let loose a virus. The musicological community reacted like an infected body. The Ugolino articles in the twelfth edition of the *Riemann Lexikon* can be viewed as an attempt to inject a degree of Riemannian spirit and humor into the dry business of a dictionary authorship. But now the imitators began their work, making use of Riemann's "Ugolino method." There are other entries in the same edition of the *Lexikon* that could be similarly demystified; and even Stanley Sadie and his *New Grove Dictionary* play their secret part in this musicological game. (And the jest continues: as I was writing this essay, the first volume of the new *MGG: Die Musik in Geschichte und Gegenwart,* "Personenteil," edited by Ludwig Finscher, arrived and demonstrated that the Riemann virus affects German musicological seriousness still today.) I will not reveal, however, the Italian manifestations of "Riemannerei," nor will I call by name the northern phantom that roams the eighth volume of the British flagship of musical encyclopedias. I will only warn non-musicologists: Be aware that there are traps, abysses, everywhere. Musicology is a dangerous field, untrustworthy in the extreme.

But it gets more serious when reputation or money is involved, as it may have been in the two centerpieces of the next page of my little detective story—which, in my continuing Rondo, is the contrasting Episode 2.

Episode 2

This is designed as a sonata-like developmental discourse made up of two parts. Two well-known classical composers are subject as well as object of this section: Haydn first, then Schubert. And after the questioning summary, the voice of Fanny Hensel may be heard briefly, in her dispute with her beloved brother.

One or two years ago you could still buy a CD titled "Paul Badura-Skoda (Fortepiano) Plays Six Lost Piano Sonatas by Joseph Haydn." But there is a problem here. If the sonatas are "lost," surely they cannot be performed and thus cannot be recorded on a CD; if, on the other hand, they are performed, they are in fact not lost. Here is the background. In 1765 Haydn began to list his compositions in a catalog with brief titles and musical incipits. This catalog is known—somewhat misleadingly—as the "Entwurf-Katalog." Forty years later Haydn's copyist Eyssler, under the composer's supervision, put together a much more comprehensive catalog, referred to as the "Haydn-Verzeichnis," again with titles and thematic incipits. Both catalogs are organized by genre. Among the keyboard sonatas listed are seven that at present remain lost. Sonata no. 22 in A major appears in the 1765 catalog as "Divertimento per il cembalo solo"; the musical incipit notates, on two staves, right and left hand, the first four measures of the first movement. So far, so good. In 1993 the noted pianist Paul Badura-Skoda, a specialist in the Viennese classical repertory and historical performance practice, received photocopies of a manuscript comprising six of the then-lost seven Haydn sonatas, identifiable through the incipit entries in the two catalogs. The sender was a Mr. Winfried Michel from Münster. The manuscript itself was obviously not in Haydn's hand but written by a copyist. Based on the manuscript description provided by Mr. Michel (watermarks, paper, etc.), a musicologist dated the copy as from about 1805 and most likely of Italian provenance. Asked to reveal the whereabouts of the manuscript, Mr. Michel claimed that it was the property of "an elderly and infirm lady from somewhere outside Münster" whose identity he had promised never to disclose. Although Mr. Badura-Skoda remembered a basic rule about resurfacing authentic manuscripts formulated by the leading autograph dealer Albi Rosenthal—"Never believe in the provenance of a manuscript that comes from a little old lady living out in the country"—he immediately fell under the spell of the music. As he himself reports, the musical content of the works "swept aside" all his reservations. His judgment was reinforced when, at a London press conference, the leading Haydn scholar of our time, Mr. H. C. Robbins-Landon, announced that the rediscovery of the lost sonatas could well be the most important musical discovery of the twentieth century. Mr. Badura-Skoda agreed with Mr. Michel's suggestion that he should make a digital recording and give the first public performance of the sonatas. The concert premiere was scheduled for Sanders Theater on the Harvard campus.

A second look at the CD reveals some strange features. First, on the front cover, accompanying the title "Six Lost Piano Sonatas by Joseph Haydn," a diagonal line is added: "Unauthorized Version." Thus, here are six Haydn sonatas not authorized by Haydn—a rather euphemistic wording for quite a simple fact. And the back cover-side is even more explicit: Two question marks follow the composer's name! The reason lies in a dramatic turn in the evaluation of the manuscript. The sensational new manuscript was presented to scholars at the Haydn Institute in Cologne. And the Haydn experts turned everything upside down. In their judgment, based on investigations into eighteenth- and early-nineteenth-century script design, writing habits, and the materials used, the manuscript undoubtedly was a fake—an almost masterly forgery, to be sure, but a twentieth-century forgery nevertheless. (One issue was the use of a steel pen—an instrument that did not exist at the time the manuscript was supposedly written.) The Haydn Institute went public, journals such as *Der Spiegel* picked up on the story, and the scent of a nice little scandal wafted through the musical world. Finally, in early January 1994, the eminent Mr. H. C.

Robbins-Landon retracted his earlier enthusiastic statement and declared, using another superlative, that the sonatas were the work of the greatest musical forger of all time. (And I do not hesitate to mention that those of us who had already begun to organize a scholarly panel at Harvard to accompany this expected world premiere could—almost at the last minute— luckily escape the disaster of a de-authentication post festum.) Mr. Michel, meanwhile, the provider of the manuscript copy, stood by his assurance that it was no forgery, and Mr. Badura-Skoda, deprived of a rewarding, if not sensational, concert appearance, continued to believe in the authenticity of the six sonatas (though the hard evidence did in the end lead him to accept the verdict of an "unauthorized version"). As one would expect given its source of "a little old lady living out in the country," the manuscript itself never surfaced. Today the case is closed.

Why do such forgeries appear on the scene? Certainly money could be involved. Still, there is much less to be earned from the sale of a Haydn manuscript than from authenticating a Caravaggio. The seduction of forgery is far less intense for musicologists than for art historians. And Mr. Michel, at least during the early stage of this story (and an early stage is all there is), seemed uninterested in lucre, rejecting a substantial offer from a publishing house for the purchase of the manuscript. On the other hand, at that moment, before the concert, the peak of the possible sensation had not yet been reached. Someone who wanted to "make money" was better off to wait until the media had publicized and sensationalized the case. But there may simply be a personal background for Mr. Michel's completion mania. When in the Haydn case certain doubts were voiced regarding authenticity, Christoph Wolff searched the Harvard library's computerized catalogue for Winfried Michel. And indeed, Mr. Michel had twenty-three publications listed, exclusively music, mostly continuo realizations of baroque instrumental works. But there are also a few items that may be called suggestive for our case: completion of a fragmentary sonata by Wilhelm Friedemann Bach; pieces for flute and basso continuo by Johann Joachim Quantz (identified in the library catalogue as "works of uncertain authorship"); and a "Sonata a tre e Ciacona a tre flauti senza basso," op. 8, by Giovanni Paolo Simonetti, but published with the remark "composed [!] and edited by Winfried Michel." From here, the composing of the Haydn sonatas seems like an almost logical step.

Some intermediary, "summarizing," comments seem appropriate here. (In my Rondo performance they introduce some Ritornello elements into the central Episode . . .) A general force seems to be driving the Haydn case. I refer to the fascination with unfinished or "lost" works, or even sources, of major composers, the lost autographs of Beethoven's Third and Fourth

Symphonies being a typical example. Because their incipits are in fact known, Haydn's "lost" keyboard sonatas must excite particular longing in this respect. The desire to compose the fragments "whole" seems quite natural, especially for someone who is in the business, so to speak, of completing incomplete compositions. (The musician who did that for all the fragmentary keyboard sonatas by Schubert that are assembled in the third volume of the Henle edition, not insignificantly, was a certain Paul Badura-Skoda, yet he did it expertly, with considerable sensitivity to the form and character of Schubert's mature language—in small print and thus clearly distinguishable from Schubert's text. This is how it should be done.) Other famous examples that kept generations of scholars and arrangers busy are Franz Schubert's symphonic projects. The many proposals to finish the "Unfinished" belong here. And there are the debates over the so-called Gmunden and Gastein Symphony (or Symphonies), as well as the various presentations, in words and notes, of solutions for this problem, including Joseph Joachim's orchestration of the "Grand Duo" for piano four hands. And in our day, the music world is confronted with the marketing of CDs that claim to include all "10 Symphonies by Franz Schubert," though Schubert completed only seven symphonies and left five large symphonic fragments, of which only the first two movements of the "Unfinished" are actually completed, the remaining four are in different stages of incompleteness. Thus, the advertising of 10 Schubert symphonies is wrong in both directions: there are either seven or twelve. I am inclined, therefore, to call this selling of "10 Schubert Symphonies" a forgery that is in essence, if not in dimension, rather similar to the case of the six Haydn sonatas.

Schubert is also the focus of the second major case in this central section of my *Rondo burlesco*. It concerns a symphonic score and is directly related to the question of the lost, or not lost, or not existing, "Gmunden/Gastein Symphony" or "Symphonies" just mentioned. The work in question is a symphony in E major, comprising the traditional four movements and dated by its defenders at 1825. These defenders were confronted with two obstacles: First, they had to authenticate the score as Schubertian; and second, they had to disprove the recently revised dating of the C Major Symphony, the so-called Great C Major, as being from 1825–26 and restore the old assumption that that symphony was finished only in 1828. It is quite interesting to observe that the structure of this case is absolutely parallel to that of the Haydn sonatas—the one difference being that for Schubert no thematic catalog exists that could prove the prior existence of the work and give an initial thematic idea, in a sense setting the tone. First, there was a copy taken from a dubious manuscript; in this case the provider, a Mr. Elsholz from Kronberg near Frankfurt, claimed that he had written out the full score himself from an older set of parts. Second, these parts were not accessible; accòrding to Mr. Elsholz, they were in the possession of an old aunt in Berlin—the precise urban equivalent to Mr. Michel's "little old lady living out in the country." And third, there was the forcefully interested professional promoter, in this case an insistent Swiss musicologist from East Berlin (GDR), Prof. Harry Goldschmidt, a Schubert expert. Goldschmidt seemed possessed by his conviction that he had found the score of the "Gmunden Symphony," thus solving a Schubert riddle that was by then almost a century old. Such a discovery would certainly have adorned his name with an aura of immortality. The validity of Messrs. Elsholz's and Goldschmidt's claims was seriously hampered by a number of major discrepancies that the Schubert Research Institute in Tübingen immediately pointed out: At first the old full score from which the aunt's parts had been copied by an anonymous copyist was said to be unknown; later it was said to have been in the possession of an uncle (thus, not only "little old ladies" are involved!) who around 1930 copied the parts and then supposedly lost the score. Also, the material that accompanied the Elsholz score to support its authenticity could quite easily have been falsified. Indeed, a letter from Schubert to a friend dated 1826 that was presented with the parts and mentioned this symphony proved beyond doubt to be a fake: The handwriting was clearly from the twentieth century. A one-page photocopy of an "original" violin part, the only documentation of the source manuscript that Mr. Elsholz presented likewise did not pass a philological test but was shown to have been faked. And so on. Despite considerable verbal energy expended by Professor Goldschmidt over several years, and despite the fact that in 1982 and 1985 two publications of the full score appeared, today the vehemently debated case of an E major "Gmunden Symphony," as presented by Elsholz/Goldschmidt, has been definitively shelved.

Looking back to the various cases of willful falsification I have presented here, let me turn to a comparative evaluation—and to the question of morality. If I took proper care during my report, I presented the scholarly games faking the lexical existences of Dölles, Ugolino, Culacius, and others as innocent professional jokes and witnessed with a smile the expansion of Riemann's original idea into our day. The forging of manuscripts by Haydn and Schubert, however, I obviously consider a much more serious problem. Is my lenience on the one hand and my censure on the other justified? Are the faked entries in dictionaries as harmless as I take them to be? And are the forgeries à la Michel or Elsholz as detestable as I, in my heart of hearts, seem to believe?

It is interesting to view the role of musicology in these cases from another perspective. The same branch of the humanities that used dictionaries as the fields for their ball games intervened rigidly in the cases of Haydn and Schubert. It was, after all, the Haydn and Schubert Research Institutes that silenced both Badura-Skoda and Goldschmidt and acted as purifier—and not without pointing a moral forefinger. Could this uncompromising reaction have been due to a certain over-identification with the great masters of classical music, whose integrity and legacy musicologists feel has to be preserved? How would the profession react if a modern composer was involved? In addition, we must acknowledge one very important distinction: Whereas Riemann and his followers merely invented historical figures, Michel and Elsholz dared to add music, complete musical works, to the museum of masterpieces. There is another distinction. Riemann's original text and the entries in the *Lexikon* are designed in such a way that one can discern the author's wiles. As demonstrated, Riemann provided several clues that identify both Ugolino and his treatise as "musikalischer Spass" (musical fun). Indeed, one clue is quite blatant: In the twelfth edition of the dictionary, the last item in the bibliography for "Ugolino de Maltero" refers to a footnote in Heinrich Besseler's *Bourdon und Fauxbourdon* where the figure's fictitious character is expressly disclosed. (In the meantime, Besseler himself, who obviously did not understand why the reference to his book appeared in the *Lexikon*, published a note about the entire affair praising Riemann for his sense of humor . . . , see Acta musicologica 41, 1969, 107–8). In another case of musicological "Riemannerei," however, Italian scholars again and again searched for a certain Guglielmo Baldini, a Renaissance composer of madrigals from Pomposa mentioned in vol. 1 of the *Riemann Personenteil* from 1959—as one would expect not a single inquiry was successful. A final comment at this point: Obviously by continuing to forge Ugolino and to invent other fictitious figures, the lexicographers gained neither private nor professional advantage, not to speak of profit. On the contrary, they probably had to hide their actions from the senior editor to avoid professional penalties. The cases of both the providers and the promoters of the Haydn sonatas and the Schubert symphony, however, are definitely different, though the promoters, who were performers as well as scholars, were also clearly taking a professional risk: Their reputation as experts was at stake. As a partly subjective judgment, the exercise of expertise regarding a work's authenticity necessarily leaves its author vulnerable. In the case of the Haydn sonatas, however, the most telling verdict was the experience that no aesthetic judgment could match the power of the big name. If these sonatas were indeed such masterful forgeries, as both experts, Robbins-Landon and in the end also Badura-Skoda, believed, then they were certainly worth being performed, at least with the same right as the many sonatas by other minor composers that are flooding the music market. But plain aesthetic quality counts for little in this market: After a short period of sensation-generated interest, the sonatas—no longer by Haydn—fell into oblivion. (This case is quite similar to that of Rembrandt's famous *Man with the Golden Helmet* in the Berlin Gemäldegalerie: having been stripped of the authorship of Rembrandt, the picture is no longer considered a masterwork. Its only hope is a reversal: a re-authentication, which, I am convinced, will certainly come.) But let me now finish performing my Rondo. And there, before I come to my last *Ritornello,* our fictitious composer has inserted two cadenzas.

Two *Cadenzas*

Using passages that are not directly based on motifs or materials from the other cases—like true cadenzas, they go a bit astray. The first relates back to the question of how the musicological or critical profession would react if a modern composer was actively involved in forgery. I do not have a forgery in the classic sense at hand. But what about the case of Conte Giacinto Maria Scelsi, the Italian composer who died in 1988 at age eighty-four and only in his seventies became—at least outside Italy—an icon of avant-garde musical circles? Today it is known that Scelsi used a paid assistant to actually write the music that he was imagining and, due to professional deficiencies, could not put down on paper himself; he published the result under his name alone. In Germany and France, Scelsi's works are today perceived as the ultimate representations of modernist aesthetics; in his native Italy, by contrast, Scelsi is considered to be not a composer but a swindler, a crook. Is—as his followers believe—a distinction possible and valid between the "musical thought" that is present in, and therefore governs the work of music, and a quasi-external craftsmanship that is servant to the spirit of artistic creation? Is "idea" everything and "technique" of secondary importance? But even if such an aristocratic differentiation could be established, and if Scelsi's works could thus be vindicated, there remains something more. Why did the wealthy Conte not acknowledge the collaborative nature of his works? Why did he never publicly mention the name of Vieri Tosatti, who "assisted" him—to use a gentle euphemism. Certainly this can be called a solid case of forgery. But doesn't such a mixture of class structure, money, and self-centered mystification have a moral perspective as well? (Here I cannot but think of the famous story of Franz Count von Walsegg, who commissioned from Mozart a *Requiem* for his late wife and had it performed under his name in December 1793. But the first performance, as it turned out, had already been given in January 1793—most likely without the count's knowledge—arranged for by Baron Gottfried van Swieten to benefit Constanze Mozart and her children.) On the other hand, when Scelsi died, Tosatti's work on his own did not flourish, he did not live up to the originality of ideas and the level of compositional sophistication from the time of the collaboration. Obviously the two needed each other . . .

Another historical case seems at a first glance very similar to Scelsi's. Again a musician publishes the work of a colleague under his own name, without any acknowledgment whatsoever. I am speaking of none other than Felix Mendelssohn Bartholdy, then twenty-five years of age, who among his published song collections in 1830 included, under his name, Lieder by his highly talented and beloved sister Fanny—for example, her "Sehnsucht," after a text by Johann Gustav Droysen, a work we knew until recently only as no. 7 of Felix's twelve songs op. 9. Clearly Felix Mendelssohn adhered to a bourgeois view of the role a young woman had to fulfill in the male-dominated society of his time. In a letter of June 24, 1837, to his mother, Felix allows no doubt about this:

> You write about Fanny's new pieces and tell me that I should encourage her and provide an opportunity to publish them. You praise her new compositions, and to be sure, that is not necessary, for I should rejoice about them, and think of them as beautiful and excellent, in any case. I do know who composed them! Also, I do not need to say a word about the fact that, if she decides to publish something, I would provide her with such an opportunity as best as I can, and would relieve her of all pains one could possibly spare her. But encouraging her to publish—that I cannot, because it is against my opinion and conviction. Earlier on we have talked a lot about this and I still keep my view—for me, to publish is something very serious (at least, it should be), and I believe that one should do it only if one wants to expose oneself as an author during one's whole life. [..] As to being an author, Fanny, as I know her, has neither passion nor professionalism. She is too much a woman, as it should be; she educates little Sebastian and cares for her home, and does not think of an audience or of the musical world at large, nor even of music itself, except when the first vocation is fulfilled.

The letter needs no commentary: The ideological position is self-evident. But can we completely rule out an element of jealousy or, at least, professional competition? In any event, it is good to know that Fanny showed strength and later published her works under her own name. But that neither occurred as a matter of course, nor was it easily achieved. A letter written by Fanny on July 9, 1846, reveals that she had still to argue against the principles of her own education, the view that a bourgeois wife of her class and upbringing (reinforced by her status as an assimilated Jew) had no public role to play as a creative artist. Even at age forty she confesses a fear of her brother's reaction to her publication, as if she were once again a fourteen-year-old facing her father. And she continues with the startling remark: "I hope that I do not bring disgrace upon my family, because I am not a *femme libre* and to my sorrow I am not at all a 'young Germany.' " It is rather disturbing to see that Fanny's only point of reference to a woman as a public figure was the "femme libre"—the prostitute. Yet it is only within this context that the actual dimensions of Felix's self-pronounced brotherly care, his publication of the beloved sister's songs as his own, become clear. Fanny, through her mindset, paid the price. But the morality of form of my Rondo requires at the end a return to its serene beginning.

Thus: *Ritornello 3*

As a historian of the music of the twentieth century I am always interested in promoting modern composers and their works. Let me therefore introduce another twentieth-century artist, Otto Jägermeier, the prolific German composer from Munich who spent most of his life in exotic Madagascar. He has been discussed quite often ever since K. R. Nerval, in 1902 in the *Rheinische Musik- und Theater-Zeitung*, pointed to his existence. The most detailed information about Jägermeier is to be found in volume 1 of the *Riemann Lexikon* supplement, edited by Carl Dahlhaus in 1972—though Dahlhaus himself was not at all responsible for the entry—neither its content nor its inclusion in the volume. (Again, this could have been said in another way, using the figure of the uninformed senior editor . . .) Jägermeier's compositional output leans exclusively toward symphonic poems, and works such as *Psychosen* or *In den Tiefen des Meeres* have often been mentioned in connection with Richard Strauss. Thus when Dietmar Polaczek, in the *Frankfurter Allgemeine Zeitung* of August 10, 1979, reported on a concert performance of Franz Schmidt's *Fredigundis*, he discussed this revival in the light of works by Schreker, Strauss, and Jägermeier. Similarly, when the committee of friends who wanted to honor the Wagnerian Egon Voss on his fortieth birthday with a collection of essays, for presentation in a private ceremony during the 1976 Bayreuth Festival, they chose Jägermeier as the sole subject. The small Festschrift, which has the borrowed title *Gradus ad Parnassum*, contains essays by, among others, Ludwig Finscher, John Deathridge, Reinhart Strohm, Martin Geck, and Isolde Vetter. In 1979 the book was reviewed in *Die Musikforschung*, the journal of the German Musicological Society. The reviewer praised it for its innovative character, stressing in particular how it advanced new research methods: for example, the "vertexology" that Finscher seems to practice as he (quite successfully!) retraces Jägermeier's journeys through the Alpine landscapes. There was, however, an awkward moment when the reviewer ascribed to Gustav Jenner several lyrical piano pieces that Vetter discusses under the assumption that they were composed by Brahms. The reviewer's claim that signed sketches for these pianos pieces—signed by Jenner—were preserved in the Jenner

Nachlaß of the Marburg Staatsarchiv caused the director of the archive and the scholar in charge of the Jenner manuscripts, who both could not identify these sketches, a few nervous days . . . I could turn the pages of the review in *Die Musikforschung* for more details, including the name of the reviewer—but time has run out, and in any case, the next step might get me into personal, too personal, territory. As a true positivist in this case, I must therefore remove myself from the picture. Let me end, however, by saying that I highly recommend that everyone in this room should get to know Jägermeier and his music; it is a rewarding experience, for both heart and brain. The easiest way to begin this joyful adventure is to read about this remarkable but underrated historical figure and to join in the circle of his friends. You may even be able to find some of his works in a bookstore in the United States. Try it! And good luck. *Finis Rondo burlesco.*

CHAPTER 7

Jean-Etienne Liotard's Envelopes of Self

EWA LAJER-BURCHARTH

"[Liotard] has been in Paris for a while and he is very much in fashion despite the sincerity of his brush and the extravagance of his prices [. . .]. The furrowed foreheads, the baggy eyes, the not-quite-good-looking dread him like the rascals dread the penetrating look of an honest man; but the beauty, the youth, the naive graces and the reasonable people are all for him."[1]

The artist thus described by the Parisian journalist and critic, Pierre Clément, was Jean-Etienne Liotard, a much sought-after peripatetic portraitist of European aristocracy and other elite clients. Born in Geneva to a French Protestant family that had to emigrate from France after the revocation of the edict of Nantes, Liotard developed an international career working in Constantinople, Vienna, London, Amsterdam and, on repeated visits—including the one in 1748, at the time of Clément's writing—in Paris, where he had originally trained as a miniaturist. Along with Maurice-Quentin de La Tour and the Venetian artist Rosalba Carriera, Liotard was one of the leading practitioners of pastel, a technique then much in fashion. He enjoyed considerable success in Parisian society and his clientele included the royal family,[2] yet, as Clément hinted, his work was also quite controversial.

The controversy had to do with Liotard's unusual portrait style. The artist's consistent refusal to embellish and idealize, which gained him a sobriquet of "the painter of truth,"[3] his scrupulous and resolutely unflattering gaze as a portraitist was obviously objectionable to some of his clients.

Yet, it was not simply the lack of flattery but a matter of aesthetic difference in Liotard's likenesses. To put it briefly, Liotard's vision was at the antipodes of rococo, then the dominant stylistic idiom. Liotard's veracity, his insistence on the material appearance of things utterly shorn of pictorial flourish, his careful suppression of the painter's touch, his avoidance of all manifestation of the *faire*, including such accepted painterly procedures as shading, in sum, these aspects of his style that prompted a well-known international art connoisseur, Francesco Algarotti, to describe Liotard's *La belle Chocolatière*, as "a Holbein in pastel"[4] went against the grain of the pictorial manner prevailing then in the Parisian elite circles from which the artist's sitters came. At the same time, while opposed to or incompatible with rococo, Liotard's manner was not, as may be expected, embraced by the critical champions of the rising anti-rococo reaction, as was Greuze's later.[5] It was indeed work difficult to place in relation to Parisian pictorial production and the aesthetic values of Liotard's contemporaries.

If Liotard's style was, in a sense, estranged from the dominant (rococo) visuality, so was the artist himself, who deliberately cut a figure of a stranger in Paris, defining himself as a *peintre turc*. In the wake of his extensive travels Liotard carefully designed for himself a whole Turkish persona which he sustained through daily sartorial performance, appearing in public in an exotic attire that consisted of loose pantaloons, a fur-trimmed caftan, a fur toque or else a skullcap on his head, and a beard.

The artist first took to wearing Turkish clothes during his long sojourn in Constantinople, where he lived and worked for four years (1738–42) catering to European diplomats, expatriates, and members of the local community. He grew a beard and developed a penchant for fur toques in emulation of the noblemen of Moldavia, where he went subsequently on an invitation from a local prince. But it was only upon his return to western Europe that Liotard self-consciously made these newly acquired exotic dressing habits into key components of his professional identity, first presenting himself as the *peintre turc* at the imperial court in Vienna, and retaining this designation while he shuttled between Paris, London, Amsterdam, and Geneva.

It was also in the wake of his Ottoman sojourn that Liotard turned to self-portraiture as the means of both rehearsing and enforcing his at once sartorial and professional self-redefinition. The two self-portraits which the artist painted in Vienna in 1744–45 initiated a whole series of Liotard's self-images in which his exotic attire and his beard figure prominently as his major defining attributes.[6] (Fig. 7.1)

It is with the strangeness of Liotard's vision and with his artistic self-construction as a "stranger" that I want to engage. I shall focus, in particular, on Liotard's portraits of the sitters in exotic costume and settings and on the

J. E. Liotard
de Geneve Surnommé
le Peintre Turc peint
par lui même a
Vienne 1744

Figure 7.1 Jean-Etienne Liotard, *Self-portrait*, 1744. Pastel. Uffizi, Florence. Copyright: Scala / Art Resource, NY.

artist's own exoticized self-representations. My question is: What *kind* of self was envisioned in the art of this nomadic portraitist? What should we make of the sartorial exercises in cultural otherness envisioned by Liotard, and how are we to reconcile this French-Swiss "Turkish painter's" committment to visual "truth" with his penchant for exotic fabrications?

Both cultural cross-dressing by Liotard's sitters—as in his portrait of the British archeologist Richard Pococke—and the artist's own adoption of the Ottoman clothing are aspects of a broader cultural phenomenon of eighteenth-century exoticism, which, though it has been discussed extensively, is in dire need of a more nuanced assessment. Such a task obviously exceeds the scope of this paper, but, at the risk of stating the obvious, two points must be made briefly. First, the eighteenth-century mode of engagement with the "Orient" needs to be separated from the post-Napoleonic, nineteenth-century Orientalism as a form of cultural colonialism. The nature of power relations between Europe and the politically weakened but nevertheless still powerful Ottoman Empire could not be understood in colonial terms for obvious historical reasons.[7] It is in fact more accurate to speak of the eighteenth-century exoticism in terms of mutual East/West fascination, a bi-directional discourse of curiosity and wonder—not to deny the dimension of power in it, but to recast it as different from the colonial model.

Furthermore, we need a more nuanced account of the eighteenth-century exoticism understood as a cultural construction of the relation between the self and an other. As has been noted, the term "exotic" at that time referred exclusively to specific objects—flowers, plants, rare specimens, luxury commodities, and costumes—and by no means did it evoke a totalizing myth of otherness or some consistent Western attitude or psychological state, as it began to do later, in the nineteenth century.[8] Yet, this should not prevent us from examining the *subjective* dimension of the eighteenth-century fascination with things foreign, with due respect to its historical specificity. To do so, we must consider the vogue for the exotic in relation to a broader discursive concern with the relation between cultural difference and subjectivity, a notion which itself was undergoing a major conceptual recasting in this period. "How can one *be* Persian?" Montesquieu's ironic question summed up both the urgency behind the cultural effort to reimagine the self in relation to the cultural "other" and its inherent difficulty.[9] The question, reported by Rica, a fictional Persian on a visit to Paris, referred to a "terrible state of non-existence" into which he was plunged when, annoyed by the persistently curious and exoticizing gaze of the Parisians, he decided to renounce his Oriental attire in public. Though, shedding all foreign adornments, our Persian visitor only hoped to be "assessed more exactly," he found himself instead obliterated from the Parisians' screen of cultural and subjective recognition. "Oh! Oh! Is he Persian? What a most extraordinary thing! How can one be Persian?"[10]

Central to Rica's story is the appreciation of the fundamental role of clothing in cultural self-representation. The adoption of the exotic attires by the eighteenth-century elite Europeans may be seen in conjunction with such literary confrontations with (cultural) strangers as a mode of rehearsing a nascent imagination of the self *implicated* in an other. Playful or frivolous as they may have been, these self-exoticizing sartorial practices were nevertheless culturally significant experiments in being at once self-same and different, a Parisian *and* Persian, as the case may be, experiments that also put some pressure on the distinction between the (innate) interiority and the culturally contingent exterior. The question is how exactly did Liotard's portraits of these individuals contribute to this nascent imagination of a different self?

My argument is that Liotard's portraits of exotically clad sitters were not simply stylistically different from the Parisian *turqueries*, but they articulated a self altered by travel, as was Liotard himself. Liotard's way of seeing was, in my view, profoundly "othered" by his travel experience. The way in which he used it to forge a strategy of self-presentation as an autonomous professional, to position himself as an individual artist in the competitive business of portrait-making by defining himself as an exotic outsider, call for an approach that would account for the cross-cultural nature of this artist's vicissitudes and his vision. In short, Liotard's case invites us to consider the idea of a *cosmopolitan artist*.

To be sure, Liotard had been called a cosmopolitan artist before, but in a descriptive sense of the word—referring to his extensive travelling and the different nationality of his sitters. I want to consider the *aesthetic* dimension of such designation and, relating it to the personage Liotard developed for himself, to explore cosmopolitanism as a historically specific psycho-cultural ideal. It is not just a question of Liotard catering to clients from different countries, but of a vision of a cosmopolitan subject that his art offers in a complex, culturally situated and formally sustained sense.

Within the discourse of the Enlightenment, the term cosmopolitan referred to the *philosophes*' ideal of a "citizen of the world," an unprejudiced thinker who, according to the *Encylopédie*, "either had no fixed dwelling or did not feel foreign anywhere."[11] It was assumed, moreover, that such a person wished to be distinguished by a readiness to borrow from other lands and civilizations in the formation of his [or her] intellectual, cultural, and artistic patterns."[12] Hume defined a cosmopolite as "a creature, whose thoughts are not limited by any narrow bounds, either of place or time, who carries his research into the most distant regions of the globe and, beyond this globe, to the planets and heavenly bodies . . ."[13] I wouldn't want to make such big claims for Liotard. His case is at once much more modest and more earthly located—in Constantinople.

In the eighteenth century, Constantinople was a cosmopolitan city par excellence, not only because of its multi-ethnic inhabitants, but because of the international expatriate community that lived and thrived there. Liotard staked his artistic ambition precisely on the Franks, as the Europeans living in the Ottoman Empire were called, who often adopted the Ottoman costume either for the reasons of commodity or respect for the local customs. Seeking to provide these subjects complexly—both commercially and culturally—implicated in the Ottoman context, with an image, Liotard developed a subtly composite portrait formula, in which Western and local aesthetic traditions and modes of self-presentation were combined.

Look at the French consul to Smyrna, Gaspard de Péleran, a man in a perfect Parisian outfit—an *habit brodé Louis XV* complete with a wig—who is stretched out at once comfortably and somewhat incongruously on an Oriental *pafose*. (Fig. 7.2) The minutely rendered, elaborately decorated fabric covering its cushions reminds us of the chief reason for the French consul presence in Smyrna: textiles. An outlet of the vast territory of Anatolia, Smyrna was a crucial commercial outpost, and a stronghold of French commerce in the area, especially in cloth.[14]

It is, though, not just the elaborate pattern of the *pafose*'s exquisite fabric coming to life under Liotard's crayons, but the way in which Péleran's body inscribes itself onto it that at once hints at the sitter's ambassadorial mission and exceeds it—a body taking possession of this cushiony environment and *bending to fit it*, renouncing the standard portrait pose of a Western male sitter in favor of a quasi-feminine one. We are given to see someone who takes his place in a new environment with an air of self-possession, but who also stoops to the customs of the culture he is in, projecting a sense of ease with the very environment that alters his bodily and cultural axes, even showing his soles. As if to underscore his double French/Ottoman cultural definition, Péleran's body is fleshed out through the technique called *à deux crayons*. Combining sanguine and lead pencil, this technique articulates the interlaced duality of his sitter's commercial and cultural circumstances in Smyrna, producing a subtle representational web that catches the consul's corpus—and his self—in its "bi-cultural" pattern.

It is through such subtle mesh of patterns that Liotard brings forth the likenesses of Frank women living in Constantinople. These portraits constitute a major part of Liotard's Ottoman portfolio. Executed in drawing (again, mostly through the technique *à deux crayons*) or in pastel, these images present the sitter emerging from an abstract, unspecified space or in rudimentarily defined interiors, either at leisure or engaged in simple daily tasks.

The artist develops and reformulates in these portraits the format of ethnographic illustration popularized by Jean-Baptiste Van Moor, his predecessor working in Constantinople. In some—as in the image of the women playing a game of *mankala'h* on a sofa—Liotard lifts the iconographic formula verbatim from Van Moor's influential *Receuil de Cent Estampes représentant différents nations du Levant* (Collection of One Hundred Engravings Representing the Different Nations of the Levant), published in 1714. Yet, his images differ from Van Moor and, more broadly, from the tradition of travel illustration on which they draw, not only because of the physiognomic specificity of Liotard's models, in many cases dictated by their function as portraits, nor the far greater precision in the rendition of their costumes but, most important, in the distinct modality of the sitters' presence, at once aesthetic and subjective.

Figure 7.2 Jean-Etienne Liotard, *Gaspard de Péleran,* c. 1738. Black chalk. Department des arts graphiques, Musée du Louvre. Photo: Michel Bellot. Copyrights Réunion des Musées Nationaux/Art Resource, NY.

Liotard's subtle notations secure it without recourse to physiognomic codes, with minimal, if any, registration of feelings or states of mind. One modern commentator tried to capture these women's peculiar appeal stating that their faces "almost never lit up with an interior light."[15] It was precisely the artist's capacity to suggest such interior luminosity that was valued in portraiture at the time. The pastellist La Tour, for example, was seen to excel in subtly suggesting the invisible "beyond" behind the mask of face, something inside barely hinted at by a half-smile or a spark in the eye. As one critic from the period put it, it is "the soul that breathes in La Tour."[16]

Liotard, on the other hand, avoids any such indications of inwardness in favor of minutely observed and scrupulously registered external appearances. What his portraits share is an approach to representation—and to self—as a materially specific exteriority, more specifically, a surface. Thus, to begin with, note the relative absence of the body in these images: Not only are these women always rather thoroughly covered—you will find no nudes in Liotard's Ottoman oeuvre, no odalisques frolicking on the sofas, as in Boucher—it is also true that, except for face and hands and an occasional glimpse of the neckline, the body is mostly produced as clothing in such ornamental variety and richness so as to distract, if not to discourage, the viewer's perusal of flesh underneath.

Such is the *Frank Lady, Dressed in Turkish Style, and Her Servant*, which arrests us at the entry to a Turkish bath defined summarily by the carved stone basin with an ornate robinet. (Fig. 7.3) Telling is the very choice of the location: not the actual interior of a hammam but its antichamber, barring further visual access to the realm of feminine nudity. Bathing is evoked here not by a suggestive *déshabillé*—as in, say, Nattier's *Mme de Clermont as Sultana* (Fig. 7.4)—but by the details of dress and other accessories: The high heel shoes worn by both women, and the pot of dye and a comb held by the servant. There is no trace of exuberance, lassitude, and sensual pleasure typical of the imaginary constructions of Oriental bathing, epitomized by the Nattier. What we have instead is a quasi-documentary exactitude in registration of the details of clothing, a quiet confidence and sobriety of women's appearance with barely a hint of intimacy between them conveyed by their gestures and gazes.

Further, note the curious spaces these individuals occupy. Not only does Liotard refuse to render interiors with more than rudimentary specificity; frequently and, in my view, intentionally, he disregards perspective in favor of an aesthetic promotion of flatness, in all the richness of its possible patterns. There is hardly more than a corner—itself nothing more than a meeting point of two flat surfaces—that Liotard customarily uses to suggest spatial depth, and sofas are almost the only furniture he ever depicts, their painstakingly rendered ornamented fabrics engaging in a formal dialogue with the varied textures of the woman's costume. The *Servant offering a teapot to a Levantine lady* seated on an elaborately patterned *pafose* lining the naked walls of an interior is the case in point. It is not simply the more authentic setting that differentiates Liotard's work from Van Loo's contemporary rendition of a similar scene for Marquise de Pompadour's château of Bellevue, but its resolutely planar emphasis, the shift of aes-

Figure 7.3 Jean-Etienne Liotard, *Frank Lady, Dressed in the Turkish Style, and Her Servant* 1742–43. Pastel on parchment, 71 × 53 cm. Geneva, Musée d'art et d'histoire.

Figure 7.4 Jean-Marc Nattier, *Mme de Clermont as Sultana*. Canvas, relined, 109 × 104.5 cm. London, the Wallace Collection. By kind permission of the trustees of the Wallace Collection.

thetic attention from space and volume to surface and pattern. (While in Van Loo's *Sultana taking coffee* it is the flow of the sumptuous draperies with their proliferating folds that secures the connection between bodies and objects, in the *Levantine Lady* it is ornament and texture that produces the distinct morphology of the image.)

This pronounced planarity is enhanced by Liotard's unusual technique. The standard artistic procedure to produce the illusion of three-dimensionality was hatching—and Liotard's densely cross-hatched likeness of the *Young Roman Woman* of 1737, a highly elaborate profile portrait produced by the artist in Italy, at the very outset of his peregrinations, proves that he was perfectly capable of such procedure. Yet, in his Ottoman works, the artist developed a different approach, perhaps inspired by the local miniatures but also reaching back to his own early training as a miniaturist. Using the pointillist technique of a miniaturist in a standard-scale drawing, Liotard obtains an uncannily naturalistic effect of traceless tactility, of skin that seems co-extensive with the material support on which the drawing was executed.

Another example of technical privilege of the surface is Liotard's practice of underpainting both drawings and pastels on their reverse side for emphasis, as in his *Jeune Romaine* Liotard brushed the verso of the image with watercolor to obtain on the recto side a delicate blush effect for flesh and lighter areas and adding depth to the darker ones, and thus achieving a relief-like haptic illusion of a three-dimensional body.[17]

These technical procedures reflected the artist's aesthetic beliefs. Liotard's pronounced hostility to the *touche* was the leitmotif of his *Traité des principes et des règles de la peinture*, a painting manual he wrote in the 1770s.[18] In it, Liotard advocated the suppression of the painterly touch not only as the means to achieve naturalistic effects, but also as one of the principal rules of painting: "In the sublime picture of nature, he wrote, everything is admirably connected; all the parts, even the most disparate ones, are imperceptibly united; one does not see traces in the works of nature, a strong enough reason not to put it in painting. One should never paint what one does not see."[19]

Liotard's notion of representation was, then, essentially, perhaps also somewhat naively mimetic, but it is not his postulate of faithful imitation per se but rather his abdication of the artistic trace in favor of the (seemingly) unmediated eloquence of the material support—the unmarked yet signifying surface—that is most intriguing.

What, then, was the function and meaning of such consistently and multifariously displayed, aesthetic and technical investment in the surface, indeed the production of visual representation *as* surface? And, to come back to our original question, what kind of self was being thus envisioned?

I would like to suggest that it is a certain *fantasy* of the self that Liotard fleshes out in his consistently superficial likenesses. In a psychoanalytic sense fantasy is a setting in which the subject appears caught up in the sequence of images.[20] In Liotard, though, the subject of representation is captured by the sequence of surfaces, a latticework of patterns rather than images. These likenesses formulate the task of the portraitist as the artisan of the surface, a kind of embroiderer—and Liotard's propensity to represent embroidering women may have something to do with such scenes' capacity to metaphorize the artist's own procedure.[21] His figures materialize as surface-formations emerging into existence through the gossamer, veil-like texture of Liotard's vision, indeed a kind of screen.

Tempting as it may be to recognize it in psychoanalytic terms, as the Lacanian screen—that symbolic filter of culture on which the subject becomes visible and thus intelligible to itself and to others—this is actually not the case. Rather, I would say that Liotard's epidermic formations formulate a fantasy of the self that harks back to a much earlier, *pre-visual* stage of psychic development, when the subject first begins to recognize itself merely as an envelope of sound and touch produced through interaction with the mother. Defining the earliest subjective boundaries of the self—what Didier Anzieu has called the Skin-Ego[22]—this sonorous and tactile sheath, at once physical and imaginary, acts as a surface that both protects the subject and enables its communication with an other.

It is precisely that kind of tactile sheath that Liotard's work evokes, not only in its surface-bound aesthetics, but also in the way in which the artist employed his portraits as a kind of ready-made, a reusable envelope, slipping different subjects into his previous studies from the model and redeploying the same image to portray different individuals by simply altering his or her physiognomy. Such is the case of the presumed likeness of the *Countess of Coventry* which may have originated in a portrait of Mimica, a Greek woman Liotard knew in Constantinople, and which exists in several versions, each featuring a different sitter.[23] (Fig. 7.5)

This mode of cannibalizing one's own portrait practice—using likeness as if it were costume to be put on and off by different sitters—resembles the way in which Liotard's contemporaries used printed imagery, notably the luxury edition of Van Moor's engravings, in a popular parlor game called *gravure dressée*. This amusement, practiced in eighteenth-century homes by men and women alike, consisted of cutting out the costume part of the engravings and replacing it with the actual fabric or fur pasted over. The dressed picture thus produced was used as decoration, to make wall panels, screens, and fireboards.[24] But, beyond its immediate decorative purpose, this popular pastime may be seen as an everyday-life practice of sartorial negotiation of cultural difference and, as such, to be symptomatic of deeper cultural concern of an eighteenth-century self with an other.

If *gravure dressée* consisted of grafting the self (one's own piece of fabric) to an image of an other, Liotard's practice was the opposite: It was the touch of the other that it brought to the image of the self. How else are we to interpret Liotard's abdication of his own trace? Through such devices as underpainting the portraits on reverse side, or reworking the surface through *frottage*, which he used obsessively to copy his own work (as in the counter-copy of his *Countess of Coventry* [Fig. 7.6]), the artist lent his own

Figure 7.5 Jean-Etienne Liotard, *Young Woman in a Turkish Costume Seated on a Divan*, 1749. Pastel on parchment, 23.5 × 19 cm. Property of the Eidgenössiche Kommission der Gottfried Keller-Stiftung, deposed at the Musée d'art et d'histoire, Geneva. Photo: MAH.

hand to register the presence of another—not as a trace but as an internal *pressure* on representation. Materialized by the morphology of his portraits are the semi-porous walls of the nascent self, behind which a diffuse, not-yet-objectified presence of the other—as mother—may still be sensed. Liotard's reversal of his own signature scripted backward on the edge of his sitter's dress as if from the *other* side of representation epitomizes this submission of the authorial trace to this maternal pressure from within.[25]

And it is as such that Liotard's work may be seen to offer a counter-fantasy to the Parisian *turqueries*, notably Van Loo's and Nattier's, that constituted the prevalent mode of engagement with Ottoman culture in mid-eighteenth-century France. For Liotard's vision, articulated as an inclusive yet not appropriatory *interface*, was in its very logic informed by a kind of doubleness that forfeited the binary, positioning distinction between the self and the other. Reciprocity rather than appropriation was at stake in this psychosexually-specific fantasy featuring the exotically-clad sitters: not reversal of control over but avowal of dependence on the cultural other—as mother.

It was, then, in a particular sense that Liotard envisioned a cosmopolitan subject: a self emerging into formal existence by a diffused, maternal pressure of difference. As if responding to the doubt articulated by Montesquieu's fictional character Rica—"How can one be Persian?"—Liotard's strangers formulate another cultural doubt of the century haunted by the cultural specter of an other: "How can one be oneself?"

And it is, in a sense, as a subject of doubt that Liotard defines *himself* as a cosmopolitan artist—in his exotic sartorial masquerades as well as in his numerous self-portraits. It is not just that Liotard was obsessed with painting himself; it is also that he copied each of his self-portraits many times over. Such is the case of his Parisian *Self-portrait* of 1749, now in Geneva, replicated three times, each time more close-up.[26]

This quasi-obsession with his own self-image has been seen as a function of Liotard's penchant for introspection. Yet, in my view, these numerous self-portraits point in a different direction—again, not depth but surface. As an artistic task, self-portrait was for Liotard bound to a serial function, not a matter of plunging into the well of self, of capturing the "soul," but of a lateral movement of endless, quasi-mechanical replication. Products of a persistent yet unfulfilled narcissistic desire to inhabit one's own body, these relentless self-replications represent thus a specific kind of cosmopolitan subject: not the wise *philosophe* of the *Encyclopédie*, floating serenely above cultural borders, but another, anxious aspect of the Enlightenment self: someone who has no fixed abode except for the elusive envelope of his own body. A stranger to himself.

Figure 7.6 Jean-Etienne Liotard, *Young Woman in a Turkish Costume Seated on a Divan*, 1740–42. Counterproof, black and red chalk. Musée du Louvre. Photo: J. G. Berizzi. Copyright Réunion des Musées Nationaux/Art Resource, NY.

Notes

1. "Il est à Paris depuis quelques tems, & fort à la mode, malgré la sincérité de son pinceau, et *l'extravagance* de son prix . . . . Les fronts sillonnés, les yeux battus, et les mines équivoques le craignent comme les fripons redoutent le coup d'oeil d'un honnête homme; mais la beauté, la jeunesse, les graces naïves, et les gens raisonnables sont pour lui." Pierre Clément, *Les Cinq Années Littéraires*, 30 November 1748 (La Haye, 1754), as cited in Anne de Herdt, *Dessins de Liotard: suivi du catalogue de l'oeuvre dessiné* (Geneva and Paris: Réunion des musées nationaux and Musée d'art et d'histoire, 1992), p. 18.

2. Which prompted him to use the title of *peintre ordinaire du roi*, a clever entrepreneurial gesture.

3. Clément, ibid.

4. Algarotti showered praise on such characteristic aspects of Liotard's vision as the near-total absence of shadows, the use of a light background enhancing the effect of high relief (and thus the material presence of the body), and its utterly un-mannered quality. Letter to Mariette, 3 February 1751. Cited in François Fosca, *La Vie, les Voyages, et les Oeuvres de Jean-Etienne Liotard, Citoyen de Genève, dit Le Peintre Turc* (Lausanne-Paris: La Bibliothèque des Arts, 1956), p. 30. Rosalba Carriera declared *La Belle Chocolatière* to be the most beautiful pastel ever seen.

5. Liotard's position within Enlightenment culture requires a more nuanced assessment than we have been offered so far. He knew Fontenelle, Voltaire, and Rousseau, though we do not know how intimately, and his relation to the Parisian milieu of the *philosophes* remains to be clarified. For preliminary suggestions see Herdt, *Dessins*.

6. See N. S. Trivas, "Les portraits de J.-E. Liotard par lui-même," *La Revue de l'art ancien et moderne* LXX/372 (July 1936), 153–162.

7. Though weakened by internal economic and political problems, the Ottoman Empire was a power that European countries still had to reckon with in the eighteenth century. Moreover, due to an extended period of peace, we witness in this period a rise of reciprocal cultural curiosity between the West and the Ottoman "Orient." While Louis XV sent a succession of diplomatic and scientific missions to Constantinople, the sultans sent their representatives to Vienna and Paris. The arrival of the Ambassador Mehmed Effendi in Paris in 1721 was a major political and cultural event and his presence in the French capital generated a true vogue for things Turkish. At the same time, Mehmed Effendi's report on the life and culture of Paris contributed to the vogue for things French in Constantinople, such as leisure architecture, and a new garden style, both at the court of Sultan Ahmed and in the elite circles. See, among others, Robert Mantran, *L'Empire ottoman du XVIe au XVIIIe siècle* (London: Variorum Reprints, 1984); Fatma Müge Göçek, *East Encounters West: France and the Ottoman Empire in the Eighteenth Century* (New York and Oxford: Oxford University Press, 1987); Hélène Desmet-Grégoire, *Le Divan Magique: L'Orient turc en France au XVIIIe siècle* (Paris: Editions L'Harmattan, 1994); and *Europa und der Orient, 800–1900* (Berlin: Bertelsmann Lexikon Verlag, 1989).

8. See the entry "exotique" in Diderot and d'Alembert, *Encyclopédie ou Dictionnaire raisonné des sciences, des arts et des métiers* (1751–1780), facsimile edition (Stuttgart-Bad Cannstatt: Frommann, 1966), and Suzanne Rodin Pucci, "The Discreet Charms of the Exotic," in *Exoticism in the Enlightenment*, eds. G. S. Rousseau and Roy Porter (Manchester: Manchester University Press, 1990), pp. 145–174.

9. Montesquieu, *Persian Letters*, trans. C. J. Betts (London: Penguin, 1993), Letter 30, p. 83.

10. Ibid.

11. The first definition is from Samuel Johnson's *Dictionary of the English Language* (London: J. F. and C. Rivington, 6th ed., 1785); the second one is from Diderot and d'Alembert, *Encyclopédie ou dictionnaire raisonné des sciences, des arts, et des métiers* ("*un homme qui n'a point de demeure fixe, ou bien un homme qui n'est étranger nulle part*"). See also Thomas J. Schlereth, *The Cosmopolitan Ideal in Enlightenment Thought, its Form and Function in the Ideals of Franklin, Hume, and Voltaire, 1694–1790* (Notre Dame, Ind.: University of Notre Dame Press, 1977).

12. Schlereth, ibid., p. xi.

13. As cited in ibid, p. xiii.

n important theater of commercial rivalry between France and other Eur...
or the conquest of the Levantine markets. Péleran regularly filed his repor...
h, Dutch, and Venetian commercial activities to the Ministry of Foreign Affai...
e Paul Masson, *Histoire du commerce français dans le Levant au XVIIIe siècle* (Pa...
e & cie., 1911), pp. 474–75, pp. 553–55.

sage ne s'éclairait presque jamais de cette translucidité que la culture de l'espri...
le prêter au masque humain, que jamais il ne s'illuminait du feu d'une lampe in-
te.eure . . . ." Léandre Vaillait, "J. E. Liotard," *Les Arts* 118 (October 1911): pp. 2–32, 4.

16. Jacques Lacombe, "The Salon," Paris 1753, quoted in Geneviève Monnier, *Pastels: From the 16th to the 20th Century* (New York and Geneva: Rizzoli, Skira, 1984), p. 118. And, describing his approach to portraiture, La Tour himself declared: "I descend to the very bottom of [my sitters'] selves, without their knowledge, and I bring them forth as they really are." ("Je descends au fond d'eux-mêmes, à leur insu et je les remporte tout entiers.") Christine Debrie, *Maurice-Quentin de La Tour: "peintre de portraits au pastel," 1704–1788* (Thonon-les-Bains, Haute-Savoie: L'Albaron-Société Présence du Livre, 1991), p. 80.

17. Liotard also experimented with the materialization of the image as, literally, a film or a coating, in so-called transparencies (oil painting on translucent porcelain support), or portraits that had to be viewed against the light.

18. See Liotard, *Traité des Principes et Règles de la Peinture* (Geneva, 1781).

19. "Tout, dans le sublime tableau de la nature, est admirablement lié; toutes les parties, même les plus disparates, sont imperceptiblement unies; on ne voit point de *touches* dans les ouvrages de la nature, raison très forte pour n'en point mettre sur la peinture. On ne doit jamais peindre ce que l'on ne voit pas." *Traité*, règle VII, as cited in Baldine Saint-Girons, *Esthetiques du XVIII siècle: le modèle français* (Paris: P. Sers, 1990), pp. 356–7.

20. Jean Laplanche et Jean-Bertrand Pontalis, "Fantasy and the Origins of Sexuality," in *Formations of Fantasy*, eds. Victor Burgin et al. (London and New York: Routledge, 1989), pp. 5–34, 26.

21. See Herdt, *Dessins*, nos. 24–6.

22. Didier Anzieu, *The Skin Ego*, trans. Chris Turner (New Haven, Conn.: Yale University Press, 1989).

23. Another is the case of Liotard's double portrait of *Mlle Glavani and Mr. Levett*, for which he used a previous drawing representing *Young Tartar woman playing tamboura and man smoking*. In the former, the portrait head of Mlle Glavani—a daughter of the French consul in Antioch—has been inserted in the figure of the young Tartar woman, while the latter's male companion in Crimean costume has been transformed into Mr. Levett, a British merchant who settled in Constantinople. Moreover, the artist owned a trunk full of Ottoman attires which he continued to use in his itinerant portrait practice throughout his career, thus having different sitters pose in the same costume. See Herdt, *Dessins*, nos. 57 and 58.

24. Thus one female observer reported to her Swiss friend from Paris: "We are here in the height of a new passion for cutting up . . . engravings, just as we were last year for cup and ball. Every lady, great and small, is cutting away. These cuttings are pasted on sheets of pasteboard and then varnished. We make wall panels, screens, and fireboards of them. There are books of engravings which cost up to a hundred livres a-piece. If the fashion continues, they will cut up Raphaels." And in another letter she described the Duc de Gevres who received in bed while doing *découpage*. See Jerome Irving Smith, "An eighteenth-century Turkish Delight," *The Connoisseur* 156/629 (July 1964): pp. 214–19, 219.

25. *A Lady of Constantinople*, a drawing of the Cabinet des dessins, Musée du Louvre, Paris.

26. His 1744 Dresden *Self-portrait* exists in two replicas. Numerous pastels and drawings of himself in the Moldavian fur hat exist. Four replicas of different sizes exist of his *Self portrait in a red hat* of 1768, and two of the later one of c. 1770, with his hand on his throat. See Renée Loche and Marcel Roethlisberger, *L'Opera completa di Liotard* (Milan: Rizzoli Editore, 1978).

CHAPTER 8

Wrestling with Representation

*Reforging Images of the Artist and Art
in the Russian Avant-Garde*

JOHN E. MALMSTAD

The history of the self-portrait is almost as venerable as that of the portrait itself. Artists have been embedding images of themselves in their works since at least the time of the ancient Egyptians.[1] But the genre of the independent self-portrait really dates from no earlier than the Renaissance, if, indeed, the moment of self-portraiture can be dated with precision.[2] It first finds notable expression in the genre's foundational series by Albrecht Dürer the younger at the end of the fifteenth century and then, a century and a half later, in those that Rembrandt painted throughout his life.[3]

Picasso was a compulsive maker of images of himself, but we have no self-portraits from his Cubist period. This is so, I have elsewhere argued, because the very notion of a self-portrait "runs counter to the perceptual and conceptual act implicit in Cubist art." Yet in another sense "all Cubist canvases are portraits of the self in their registering of an individual perception of the visual chaos of reality."[4] This kind of ambiguity distressed Mikhail Bakhtin: "We find the author (perceive, understand, sense, and feel him) in any work of art. For example, in a painting we always feel its author (artist), but we never *see* him in the way that we see the images he has depicted. We feel him in everything as a pure depicting origin (depicting subject), but not as a depicted (visible) image. Even in a self-portrait, of course, we do not see its depicting author, but only the artist's depiction. Strictly speaking, the author's image is *contradictio in adjecto*."[5]

The statement reflects Bakhtin's anxiety about questions of "authorship" in general and his suspicions about the "Ich-Dichtung" of the lyric in particular. What concerns me here, however, is not the problem of "veracity" of likeness, but rather, convention, which in a sense makes any image of self or other a "forgery" by aligning it not so much with "reality" as with canonic models. Portraits have typically been employed to embody a community's specific ideals of appearance and demeanor, and conventions particular to a period, each fitting into the visual and social culture in which it originated, abound in such representations. They do so as well in self-(re)presentations which share this exemplary role, but do so to provide not only an image of the artist but on occasion of art itself. And it is a moment in the early history of the Russian avant-garde when a new generation, impatient with the pictorial pieties of its elders, challenged a regnant image and forged a new image of the artist and art through an unconventional self-portrait that I want to examine. As we are dealing with a Russian subject, some context is useful.

The beginnings of portraiture among the East Slavs go back to the icon, with representations of local saints, and then of metropolitans, tsars, and donors to the church. But as with so much in the history of early (and later) modern culture on the territory of the Russian Empire, the genre received its most powerful stimulus not from the Byzantine East, from which had come the art of the icon, but from the West, in this instance the Ukraine, which was joined to Muscovy in the mid-seventeenth century. There indigenous Eastern traditions of the icon met the tradition of miniatures from Persia and Armenia and of portraits from the thoroughly Western art of Poland (which controlled Ukrainian territory for centuries) to develop the *parsuna* (from the Latin *persona*), the representation of a perfectly ordinary mortal.

When the *parsuna* began to make itself felt in Muscovite schools of painting, they had already also begun to feel the impact of the Polish and German artists who had been brought to the capital in the seventeenth century by the first two Romanovs to provide images for their greater glory. Peter the First quickened the tempo of the Westernizing processes begun by his father and grandfather; and the heightened need of the newly-styled Emperor and his successors for visual symbols and rituals with which to forge an imperial identity and a new national consciousness certainly provided the decisive impetus for the development of secular portraiture as an independent genre in Russian art in the eighteenth century.[6]

The earliest portraits, like those of Iakov Turgenev or Aleksei Vasilkov, from the series portraying members of *Peter's Drunken Synod of Fools and Jesters* (a blasphemous parody of the church hierarchy), were executed in the *parsuna* style by anonymous artists at the very end of the seventeenth century. The conventions of that style left their mark on much of the work painted by Russian (and some foreign) painters in Moscow and the new capital of St. Petersburg in the early decades of the eighteenth century (and on works painted in the provinces until well into the nineteenth), as the secular portrait began to emerge and along with it painters with names— insofar as scholars can attribute individual works to decidedly shadowy figures like the Nikitin brothers, Roman (c. 1680–1753) and Ivan (c. 1690–1742), or Ivan Vishniakov (1699–1761). They were followed by talented portraitists like Aleksei Antropov (1716–95) and Ivan Argunov (1729–1802), in whose works we see the new influence of the baroque and rococo, but the age found its finest image makers only later, in truly distinguished painters like Fedor Rokotov (1735?–1808), Dmitrii Levitsky (c. 1735–1822), and the Ukrainian-born; Vladimir Borovikovsky (1757–1825) who left a formal portrait gallery of the eminent and aristocratic of their day, but not images of the self. (A rare exception is Levitsky's fine *Self-Portrait* of 1783–1785 [Cheliabinsk Picture Gallery].)

As early as 1729 Andrei Matveev (1701/4–39) painted *Self-Portrait of the Artist with his Wife* (Russian Museum). Although unfinished, it seems to be the first self-portrait in modern Russian art. The circumstances of his aristocratic birth (the other painters I have mentioned were all of non-gentry origins) and his study in Holland and Rome, where he was exposed not only to Western styles of portraiture but Western attitudes toward the artist, may account for the painting's creation and virtual uniqueness. For no consistent tradition of self-portraiture was to develop in Russian painting, drawing, or sculpture over the course of the eighteenth century, no doubt in large part because the painters depended solely on commissions from the monarch and court and were, if admired, still regarded as functionaries.[7] But as new sentimentalist and early romantic breezes from Western Europe began to waft through the rather dusty attics of Russian culture in a period in which various schools—baroque, rococo, neoclassical—coexisted and often comingled, important changes began to occur in the visual and verbal arts.

In 1802 Vasilii Zhukovsky published "A Country Churchyard" ("Sel'skoe kladbishche"), his reshaping of Thomas Gray's "Elegy Written in a Country Churchyard," which provided an enormously influential model for the elegy, a new language for poetry, and a new persona of the poet. The Russian poet changed Gray's ending to "shape the topos of the poet's untimely death, which would become definitive in Russian poetic culture."[8] That topos helped shape Zhukovsky's own no less influential elegy "Evening" ("Vecher") of 1806, in which he explored and developed the language and persona of the earlier text. In the two decades that followed, the elegy, with its preference for introspection and individual, private subject matter, reflected as did no other genre the period's shifts in modes of "self-fashion-ing," to borrow Stephen Greenblatt's formulation, by at least two genera-tions of Russian poets.[9] Other forms would come to the fore in succeeding years, as new generations shaped the modern lyrical subject in Russian verse,[10] and not until the 1840s drew to a close did prose begin to mount a successful challenge to the dominance of the introspection, emotional and metaphysical, of lyric poetry in Russian letters.

At about the same time that Zhukovsky was at work on his "Evening," Orest Kiprensky (1782–1836), like Zhukovsky the illegitimate offspring of a nobleman and one of his serfs (in the poet's case a captive Turkish woman), began two oil paintings: *Self-Portrait with Pink Kerchief* and *Self-Portrait with Brushes behind the Ear*.[11] (Scholars disagree about the dating, some arguing for 1806/09, others for "about 1808.") The nervous intensity of the first image contrasts sharply with the almost placid assurance of the second. They differ as much from each other as from the later *Self-Portrait* of 1819, the first such Russian work commissioned by the Florence Acad-emy of Arts for the famous collection of self-portraits begun in the middle of the seventeenth century by Pietro Leopoldo Medici for the Uffizi, the 1822 *Self-Portrait with Album in Hand* and the *Self-Portrait in Striped Dressing Gown* of 1828.[12] As one critic asked with some exasperation: "But which of all these Kiprenskys is the 'real' one? Which one can we believe?"[13] The answer, of course, is all and none in any "absolute" sense, for the pic-tures provide a narrative of self as subtle and protean as we find in the works of his contemporary and acquaintance, Aleksandr Pushkin, whom he memorably painted in 1827. (Kiprensky did a highly romanticized por-trait of Zhukovsky in 1816, and left equally "iconic" images of other writer friends like Batiushkov, Gnedich, Krylov, and Viazemsky.) Each answered (and fashioned) his shifting sense of self (and style) and the changing ideals of representation in Russian art at a time of rapid development.

No other painter of Kiprensky's time (he died, not long before Pushkin, in Italy in 1836) made so many images of the self as did he, but Russian vi-sual art, like the literature contemporary to it, demonstrated in the first half of the nineteenth century a degree of self-consciousness and self-assertion without precedent in its history in an explosion of self-portrai-ture.[14] Even writers like Zhukovsky himself, Batiushkov, Baratynsky, A. S. Khomiakov, Lermontov, and Gogol, to name but the most famous, felt im-pelled to leave visual as well as verbal portraits of the self, as did Pushkin of course, over and over again, on the margins of his manuscripts.[15] The dis-course of self initiated by Kiprensky reached brilliant culmination near the end of the colorful careeer of Karl Briullov (1799–1852): the *Self-Portrait* of 1848 (Russian Museum), in which the dramatic contrast of black smock and red upholstery highlights the ashen pallor of the face and hand of the world-weary tubercular artist. Painters did not, of course, either abandon or ignore the genre in the decades that followed, but their numbers declined sharply.

The so-called "Itinerants" (Peredvizhniki), whose "critical realism" effectively determined the character and appearance of Russian art in the last four decades of the century, provide a case in point. They left the best portraits of their time, including ones of each other as well as most of their contemporary cultural luminaries, but, perhaps because of their suspicion of the subjective and private, many fewer images of the self by comparison. None is particularly memorable, with the exception of the remarkable *Self-Portrait* (1892–93, Museum of Russian Art, Kiev) by Nikolai Ge (1831–94), in which light can barely hold the gloom of imminent death at bay. When they did address the genre, however, their self-image as rebels yielded to the conventions of pictorial decorum that they had inherited from predecessors, both native and foreign, which were unremarkable at the time. Discounting a few medallion-like works, the great majority of the self-portraits painted and drawn in the first half of the nineteenth century and later decades adhere, for all their stylistic diversity, to a conventional compositional structure that the Russians learned from study abroad, or at the Academy in St. Petersburg, or from observing the collections of aristocratic families or the Hermitage. Here the upper body, with the occasional half-length pose to take in a hand, is centered against a neutral background with the head either confronting the viewer directly or angled in three-quarter profile.

At the turn of the century, the realist manner still dominated in Russian painting, as in literature, but its former vitality had dissipated into routine. The group of young painters who banded together under the name the "World of Art" (Mir iskusstva) mounted a successful challenge to it and to the smug temper of a xenophobic intellectual climate in thrall to a crudely utilitarian aesthetic that fiercely disapproved of private experience. Nonetheless, the World of Art did little to shake the remarkably stable compositional canon of the self-portrait and the image of art and the artist that it projected.

There is in Léon Bakst's (pseudonym of Lev Rozenberg; 1866–1924) 1893 *Self-Portrait* (Russian Museum) none of the riotous color and opulent sensuality we associate with the costume and set designs with which he conquered Paris and then the world less than two decades later in the "saisons russes" of the Ballets Russes. Those flamboyant productions would change conceptions of stage design forever. But in 1893 the revolutionary designer to come, who would help found the World of Art movement with Sergei Diaghilev and others in 1898, still gazes at the viewer in his archetypical black beret and white smock from well within the conventions of Russian (and Western) self-portraiture, even if he does so from over his shoulder. Almost twenty years later, Zinaida Serebriakova (1884–1967), one of the galaxy of great modern women painters in Russia (and one of the most overlooked in our attraction to her more radical sisters in the avant-garde), echoed Bakst in *Study of A Young Girl (Self-Portrait)* (1911, Russian Museum), which she showed under the modest title *Study* at the 1912 World of Art exhibit in Petersburg.

Valentin Serov (1865–1911) rekindled appreciation for the large-scale formal portrait in his psychologically penetrating images of Russia's elite, often posed in ways that shocked viewers in their unconventionality, but in his several self-portraits he did nothing to upset the conventions. The same can be said of his friend Aleksandr Golovin (1863–1930), who helped revive the moribund art of stage design in the Imperial theaters in Petersburg, usually in collaboration with the revolutionary director Vsevolod Meyerhold (Meierkhol'd). Even Mikhail Vrubel' (1856–1910), who exhibited with the World of Art, but whose maverick brilliance could be contained by no group, muted the prismatic distortions of form and the "terrifying pulverization of the material body,"[16] with which he splintered realism in his mature period and inspired the nascent avant-garde, in his 1905 *Self-Portrait with Mother-of-Pearl Shell* (Russian Museum). While the pose remains within the convention, the painter, who averts his haunted eyes from the viewer, rejected the traditional neutral background. He instead alluded to several of his own most famous works by including within the picture's view of the sitting room of his Petersburg apartment a porcelain swan (the 1900 painting *Swan Princess* [Tret'iakov Gallery] and the 1901 *Swan* [Tret'iakov]) and the shell itself (the 1904 *Pearl* [Tret'iakov]). He also reminded us of what we often forget: The self-portrait records the artist's confrontation with self and mirror, in whose position we as viewers stand. Diaghilev immediately gauged the importance (and greatness) of the picture in the Russian pictorial tradition, and he begged the artist to lend it for a forthcoming exhibit of the World of Art. Vrubel' refused with some heat and even rubbed some of the color from one cheek in an odd gesture of protest, as his sister later recalled in her memoirs.[17] Shortly afterward, in March, when signs of the mental illness which had plagued him in the immediate past again manifested themselves, his doctor confined him to a mental hospital.

I must leave unremarked the numerous other instances of the convention of self-portraiture that I have been surveying by artists associated with other early modernist groupings in Russia, as well as the occasional foray by Russian painters into the "self-portrait with member of family" or "artist in studio" category, of which there are surprisingly few.[18] Two pictures, however, demand mention for the subtle challenge that they presented to the convention which we have been examining and to the image of the artist which it projected. In 1898, Konstantin Somov (1869–1939), a founding member of the World of Art and, like so many of its associates, gay, painted himself in a way that made it clear that the "Itinerant" manner that had ruled Russia for decades was coming under question. The bold cropping of the right margin of his *Self-Portrait* (Russian Museum; fig. 8.1) and the daring expanse of space on the left, which is dominated by the droop of the artist's hand—the means, of course, by which he practices his profession—have lost none of their power to startle. But it was the casual elegance and languid narcissism of the pose which announced that a time of unashamed enjoyment of the private sphere and a celebration of its pleasures, guilty no more, had come to Russian art and culture and that no more would the artist live artlessly in the world.

Even more remarkable is the painting of 1909 that Serebriakova exhibited under the title *At the Dressing Table* (Tret'iakov Gallery; fig. 8.2). The Russian of that title is ambiguous, and, I believe, deliberately so. "Za tualetom" can mean and be translated with the neutral "at the dressing table" or with the more personal "at *my* dressing table" or "at *her* dressing table." A viewer like her friend in the World of Art, the painter and critic Alexandre Benois (Aleksandr Benua, 1870–1960), one of its founding fathers, recognized it as a self-portrait and discussed it as such in his review of the seventh exhibit of the Union of Russian Artists in 1910.[19] But Serebriakova never identified it in that way, perhaps (and this is pure speculation) because she knew how radical it was. Here to be sure is the pose we can observe in hundreds of self-portraits, but the mirror is not some abstraction, but the very "real" mirror of her dressing table (we can clearly see the frame and both the candlestick on the table and its reflection in the mirror). It reflects the artist's bedroom, the objects on the vanity—hairpins, perfume bottles, jewelry, makeup—and the artist herself, shoulder seductively bared, with comb, not brush, in hand. We see not the palette and brushes with which the painter "makes up" her image on the canvas, but the makeup she uses every day to present herself to the world, a clever "baring of the device" of the self-portrait, to borrow Shklovsky's famous formulation. I cannot, with one exception, imagine a male artist of the time with the self-confidence to portray himself in such an intimate moment. For in Serebriakova's self-portrait the traditional social and professional roles that the artist's self-portrait projected for centuries have receded and sexual identity—the artist as woman who captivates and seduces the viewer with her glance—asserts itself.[20] (It was, of course, her Austrian contemporary, Egon Schiele, who presented far more radically intimate images of the sexual self in self-portraits which fascinate and repel.) We can recognize and appreciate the challenge these self-portraits by Somov and Serebriakova posed to reigning conventions of self-portraiture, but

Figure 8.1 Konstantin Somov, *Self-Portrait*, 1898. Watercolor, pastel, pencil on cardboard, 46 × 32.6 cm. State Russian Museum, St. Petersburg.

they projected an image of the artist and of art that was antithetical to the program of the emerging avant-garde.

The exhibiting history of that avant-garde may properly be said to date from the "Jack [or Knave] of Diamonds" ("Bubnovyi valet") exhibition which opened in Moscow on December 10, 1910. The nucleus of the young Muscovites who organized the show and formalized their association as

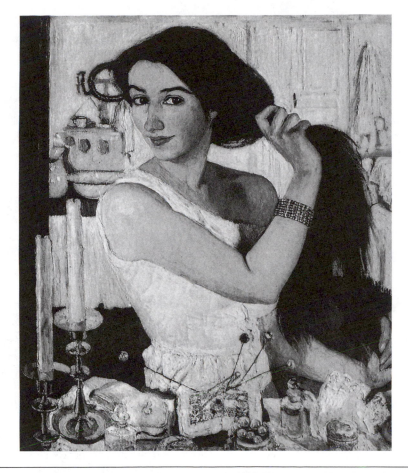

Figure 8.2 Zinaida Serebriakova, *At the Dressing Table*, 1909. Oil on canvas, 75 × 65 cm. State Tret'iakov Gallery, Moscow.

an exhibiting society after it closed in January 1911 consisted of Mikhail Larionov (1881–1964), Natal'ia Goncharova (1881–1962), David Burliuk (1882–1967), Aristarkh Lentulov (1882–1943), Il'ia Mashkov (1881–1944), Petr Konchalovsky (1876–1956), Robert Fal'k (1886–1958), Aleksandr Kuprin (1880–1960), and Vasilii Rozhdestvensky (1884–1963).[21] (It did not take long for the contentious Larionov and Goncharova to quarrel with the others and leave to form the rival "Donkey's Tail" ["Oslinyi khvost"] in 1912 and the "Target" ["Mishen' "] a year later.) They exhibited works by other Russians, among them Vasilii Kandinsky (four *Improvisations*), Vladimir Burliuk, Kazimir Malevich, Aleksandra Ekster, Aleksei Iavlensky (i.e., Alexei von Jawlensky), as well as a few paintings by Henri Le

Fauconnier, Albert Gleizes, and Gabriele Münter.[22] But the organizers themselves were the scandalous stars of the show which everywhere demonstrated their adversarial stance and interest in indigenous Russian folk culture, whether rural or urban (shop signs, toys, decorated trays, ceramics, the *lubok* [popular print], etc.), and its impact on their "neo-primitive" and thoroughly modern aesthetic. The vibrant, often clashing intensity of vivid primary colors and the deliberate simplification of form, both of which the Russians had learned from looking carefully at native folk art and at the post-impressionist masterpieces in the Moscow collections of Ivan Morozov and Sergei Shchukin, particularly riled critics and viewers.[23]

Lentulov, as adept a prankster as any of the "Jacks," belittled one of the pictures, Mashkov's *Self-Portrait and Portrait of the Painter Petr Konchalovsky* (Russian Museum; fig. 8.3), as nothing more than an "unserious" attempt to "flabbergast" viewers, so radically did it depart from the compositional convention of the self-portrait and the image that convention projected of the artist as serious and respectable.[24] (Other exhibitors were simply irritated, some to the point of fury, when Mashkov brought the painting to the show only hours before it opened and put it in the most prominent position in the central hall.) This bravura performance, for all its comic bravado, was anything but: Here is the painting as manifesto, with every detail making a polemical point.[25]

The sheer scale of the work (it measures 208 x 270 cm.) made a statement, as it recalls not the modest size of traditional self-portraits, but full-scale formal portraits, even as the semi-nude sitters, lounging on a sofa in red and blue gym shorts, subvert the pretensions and aesthetic of those formal emblems of social standing. They sit for all the world like two bulls in the china shop of a decorously bourgeois drawing room, wedged in the picture's shallow pictorial space between a table set with coffee and a bottle of liquor (not a genteel tea service), and an upright piano, the very symbol of middle-class respectability and as such a favorite object of defenestration by marauding Red Guards after the Bolshevik coup.

A sign hanging in Mashkov's studio stated, "In my studio there is room only for the healthy and strong," and he kept bodybuilding equipment in it.[26] Dumbbells and weights, like carefully placed stage props, sit at the feet of the barrel-chested painter and his friend in the drawing room on the canvas. Like the exaggerated muscularity of the biceps and thighs, they aggressively proclaim a masculinized sense of self and a vigorous new art, sharply at odds with what these painters viewed as the effeteness of the World of Art and the pallid twilight vaporousness of Symbolist-oriented groups like the "Blue Rose" and the "Golden Fleece." The oval picture frames behind the artists, like the numerous other circular forms throughout the canvas, echo the painters' muscles. They originally contained por-

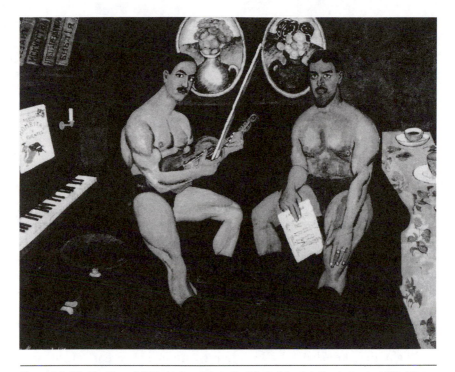

Figure 8.3 Il'ia Mashkov, *Self-Portrait and Portrait of the Painter Petr Konchalovsky,* 1910. Oil on canvas, 208 × 270 cm. State Russian Museum, St. Petersburg.

traits of their wives, but those images would have muted the gender image that Mashkov wanted to project. At the last minute he painted over the upper bodies with outsized vases and the faces with the kind of colorful flowers that he and Konchalovsky liked to include in their garish still lifes, some of which were executed on oval-shaped canvases. Sometimes those works even contained images of the Russian painted trays which, with French post-impressionst canvases, had inspired their intensification and chromatic tension of pure color.[27] The pictures, like the highly decorative treatment of the tablecloth itself, acknowledge the artists' debt both to folk culture and admired contemporaries like Matisse, whose style Mashkov had mirrored with such success a year earlier in the Fauvist *Boy in an Embroidered Shirt* (1909, Russian Museum).

The books on the shelf above the piano function as signifiers, not props, providing other details which, unlike most self-portraits, both temporalize and localize the image. Standing next to the first volume, a Bible (symbolic, perhaps, of commitment to the spiritual traditions of art), is a folio titled "Egypt. Greece. Italy." It may point to the foundational sources of Western (and their) art, but could also be read as a dig at the pictorial obsessions of Bakst, although the irony would be rather more subtle than the broad mockery usually favored by the "Jacks." (The folio size also recalls the large format volumes on the arts, like Igor Grabar's history of Russian art, which had started to appear in 1909, the period's equivalent of coffee-table books.) The adjacent volume, "Arts" (*Iskusstva*), affirms the profession of the sitters and their interest in the plurality of culture, while the titles of the next volumes, "Cézanne" (*Sezan*) and "Giotto" (*Dzhotto*—only the final four letters of the Russian are fully visible; the cropping of the picture's left margin removed the tops of the Russian letters *Dzh*) proclaimed the pictorial allegiance of the painters to the fountainheads of Western European art since the Renaissance and then modern times.[28]

The violin and bow held in Mashkov's hands provide ironic contrast to the picture's hyperbolic masculinity, for they look more capable of crushing than playing the delicate instrument (the painter was in fact an amateur violinist). The sheet music on the piano ("Marcha del Paseo. À. Ricardo Torres. Bombita II y Fuentes") and the fandango in Konchalovsky's fist, however, capture a Russian mania at the time for popular Spanish art forms. The bullfighter and bull on the cover of the sheet music serve a similar "citational" function: They echo in miniature the works on the bullfight that Konchalovsky had painted upon his recent return from Spain, three of which were hanging nearby at the exhibition.

In the years that followed, both Mashkov and Konchalovsky cemented their reputations as Russian "Cézannists" (although "Matissists" would be as apt), but as they checked the wildness of their temperaments and the extravagances of their styles, further self-portraits became more conventional. Mashkov's 1911 *Self-Portrait* (Tret'iakov Gallery) still has a blunt and simple directness and deliberate humor, with the artist, looking for all the world like some prosperous ship owner, incongruously posed against a background of the sea with a steamship and sailboat, which are painted in the crude manner of a carnival poster or the backdrops before which provincial photographers liked to place their sitters. Konchalovsky's 1912 *Self-Portrait in Spanish Hat* (collection of M. P. Konchalovsky) and *Self-Portrait with Tray* (Tret'iakov Gallery) from the same year have a similar neo-primitivist strength and monumentality, even if Mashkov's ironic deflation of the traditional image is missing.[29] All three of them do project the same image of exaggerated masculinity as the 1910 self-portrait, but none of the ones they painted thereafter was as bold as the 1915 *Self-Portrait* (Tret'iakov Gallery) of their fellow "Jack," Aristarkh Lentulov, which for size alone (142 x 104 cm.) justifies its subtitle: "Le Grand peintre."[30] The heroic image of supreme self-confidence "quotes" the long tapered fingers that are the signature of Van Dyck's portraits and the mark of his sitters' aristocracy, but by painting the fingernails green Lentulov slyly asserts that these fingers have shaped a rival modernist tradition.

In the seven years that followed the first "Jack of Diamonds" exhibition, when "ism" after "ism" rocked the Russian art world, we find few other self-portraits which went so much against the traditional grain of the genre as Mashkov's had done.[31] One young "left artist" after another now made a commitment to the most radical new "ism" to follow on the heels of Neo-primitivism, Cubo-Futurism. It left little room for the self-portrait. The style made a rather timid mark on Liubov' Popova's Picassoesque *Self-Portrait* of 1915,[32] which is nowhere near so innovative as her Cubo-Futurist master-pieces of the same year, *Portrait of a Philosopher* (Tret'iakov Gallery) and *Travelling Woman* (one in the Norton Simon Museum, Pasadena, California, and another in the Costakis Collection, Athens Greece). Ivan Kliun's 1914 image of himself is more thoroughly in the Cubo-Futurist manner,[33] but it pales beside its obvious source, Malevich's great *Finished Portrait of Ivan Kliun* (1913, Russian Museum). Malevich's career, in fact, is symptomatic of the fate of the self-portrait in radical art between 1910 and 1917. He made at least three self-portraits before 1910. In one, the gouache and varnish *Self-Portrait* of 1909 (Tret'iakov Gallery), he gave a decidedly demonic twist to the traditional pose, aligning himself with the Symbolist view of the artist as a seer and magus with superhuman powers, but he painted no more until the tragic 1933 *The Artist (Self-Portrait)* (Russian Museum). There the painter, savaged in the Soviet press and hounded by the authorities, insisted on his stature and achievement (he signed it with a tiny Suprematist black square, not his name) and proclaimed the permanence of his place in the history of art by deliberately aligning his image with self-portraits by German Renais-sance masters like Cranach, Holbein, and Dürer (the Christ-like *Self-Portrait* of 1500).[34] For Malevich, followed by most others of the innovative younger generation, had moved in the years after 1910 from Neo-Primitivism and Cubo-Futurism to the even more radical non-figurative realm, a journey that culminated in the Suprematism he first showed to the world in Decem-ber 1915 at the "O.10" show in Petrograd, the "Last Futurist Exhibition."

Mashkov's *Self-Portrait and Portrait of Petr Konchalovsky* may not have sparked a series of radical reimaginings of the conventions of the self-por-trait, but its new image of the artist struck a responsive chord that had been sounded by others as well at the 1910 "Jack of Diamonds" exhibition. In his neo-primitivist *Self-Portrait*, Larionov showed himself wearing an open-necked shirt against a garish yellow background, his face a comic mask brazenly leering at the viewer. The inscription on the painting iden-tifying the subject very consciously recalls the practice of icons and the *parsuna*.[35] (Note, however, that Larionov does strictly observe the com-positional canon of the genre.) And he exhibited *Portrait of an Athlete*,

Figure 8.4 Natalia Goncharova, *Wrestlers*, 1908–09. Oil on canvas, 100 × 122 cm. State Russian Museum, St. Petersburg.

actually a portrait of the painter Vladimir Burliuk, depicted holding a bar-bell in one hand while his long shirt covers enough for decency's sake but leaves massive neck, swarthy chest, and hugely muscular thighs exposed.[36] Nothing, however, better expressed the decidedly unpoetic cult of strength and athleticism that ran like an undercurrent through the exhibition than Goncharova's large oil *Wrestlers* (1908–09, Russian Museum, fig. 8.4).[37] Its two monstrous hooded colossi, who are coarsely painted in a violently contrasting red and lurid green, are the very incarnation of a menacing brute force barely contained by the circus arena, a deliberately anti-aesthetic image which, coming as it did from the brush of a woman, particularly offended "propriety."[38]

Wrestling was a consuming passion in Russian cities in these years and remained so for over a decade in a country that was, like those in Europe and the Americas, discovering in the sports of wrestling, boxing, soccer, and aviation and cycling races new forms of popular entertainment. (In 1918–19 Aleksandr Rodchenko made a series of drawings depicting wrestlers and wrestling champions from around the world.)³⁹ On February 7, 1909, the young scholar and critic Aleksandr Smirnov, an intimate of the World of Art circle who was to become the founder of Russian Celtology and a leading Soviet specialist and translator of Romance literatures, wrote from Petersburg to his close friend Sonia Terk, now resident in Paris where she would soon achieve fame under the name Sonia Delaunay. He informed her about major events of the capital's cultural life and took care to include in his listing of ballets, plays, and new books the outcomes of wrestling matches in the circus and details of the exploits of Russian and foreign wrestlers in the city.⁴⁰ (Russian daily newspapers carried accounts of wrestling matches in their theater, not sports, section.)

In his memoirs Lentulov noted a similar obsession in Moscow and recalled that he and his high-spirited friends from among the "Jacks" were as likely to organize a mock "parade of wrestlers in the circus" in his Moscow apartment as "living pictures" that poked fun at cultural icons like Raphael's *Sistine Madonna*, Il'ia Repin's *Ivan the Terrible and his Son Ivan* (1885), or Viktor Vasnetsov's popular painting of legendary Russian strongmen, *Bogatyrs* (1898): "The people imitating the wrestlers took off their jackets and shirts, and it was quite enough, of course, to see them in such a state to die from laughter—Konchalovsky with his hairy chest as wide as a cupboard, Mashkov's gorilla-like build, Rozhdestvensky, thin as a reed, like an emaciated cart horse, and the even funnier Fal'k with his glasses and sunken chest. But when I, at my witty best, announced their names and titles—'Petr Konchalovsky, the champion of Western-European painting oriented on Cézanne' or 'I[l']ia] Mashkov, the champion of Nizhnii-Novgorod-French painting'—everyone simply fell on the floor in laughter. Sometimes these comic turns ended in actual wrestling matches."⁴¹

In his assessment of the year 1911 in the preface to his uncompleted long poem *Retribution* (*Vozmezdie*), the poet Aleksandr Blok juxtaposed a series of seemingly unrelated facts in the most thoroughgoing Symbolist fashion, "hearing" in them a "single musical chord." He remembered his discovery of Strindberg; the "smell of burning, iron, and blood"; Pavel Miliukov's lecture "The Armed Peace and Armaments Reduction"; the appearance in a Moscow newspaper of a "prophetic article" titled "The Nearness of a Great War"; the stirrings of the Beilis Affair in Kiev; a terribly hot summer that scorched the grass to the roots; a naval incident in the Mediterranean between France and Germany, as well as between England and Germany; the murder of Stolypin; popular fascination with aviation; and the "flowering of wrestling [*frantsuzskaia bor'ba*] in Petersburg circuses; crowds numbering in the thousands showed an exceptional interest in it; there were real artists among the wrestlers; I will never forget the match of an ugly Russian heavyweight with a Dutchman, whose muscle system constituted a most perfect musical instrument of rare beauty."[42] (Blok himself took up bodybuilding at the time.)

More than a simple fascination with popular culture underlay the games of the "Jacks," in which play made them wrestlers or the *bogatyrs* of Russian folklore. By incorporating images drawn from that culture in paintings like Goncharova's wrestlers, a mighty icon of power, they broke down age-old distinctions between "high" and "low" subject matter in art, while Mashkov and Larionov's identification of the artist with the athlete challenged critics to find anything "decadent" about these virile specimens of manhood and art. There is, of course, more than an echo of the "Superman" ("Übermensch") here, for Nietzsche's call for new values based on strength and creativity appealed to many in Russian artistic circles no less than abroad. But the combative, even aggressive stance of some of the pictures exhibited in 1910 by the "Jack of Diamonds," which is similar to the violent tone sounded by the Hylaeans (who would take the name Cubo-Futurists) in manifestoes like *A Slap in the Face of Public Taste* (1912), dramatizes one of the avant-garde's favorite assertive credos: art as the struggle for the new and the artist, defiant of all conventions and opposition, as antagonist of the old.

The Russian avant-garde presents no monolith, either in theory or practice, but rather offers the spectacle of a whirlwind of ideas, isms, and counterisms. This is too often forgotten by critics who make generalizations about the period and the decades that followed. The notion of the artist as sportsman, and the association of art itself with physical strength, left no trace in works by many, perhaps, in fact, by the majority of the artists associated with what they themselves preferred to call "left art." But we find it in some of the most memorable works made in the years immediately preceding 1917, works that aligned themselves with the masculinized image that Mashkov had been so instrumental in fashioning. In Larionov's 1913 *Portrait of Tatlin* (Musée national d'art moderne, Paris), the muscular, barechested painter emerges from a web of cross-hatching that recalls Larionov's "rayist" manner.[43] Three years later David Burliuk painted a more vigorously crude (and humorous) *Portrait of the Futurist and Singer Warrior Vasilii Kamensky* (1916, Tret'iakov Gallery; fig. 8.5). Above the barechested figure of the poet, one of Russia's first aviators, flies a trumpet-carrying nude muse, while a train (another popular symbol of the speed of the new age) chugs heavenward.[44]

Kamensky's exploits inspired his fellow Cubo-Futurist friends—the poet Velimir Khlebnikov, the poet and theoretician Aleksei Kruchenykh, Malevich, and the painter and composer Mikhail Matiushin—to include an aviator, another new sports hero of the popular imagination, among the athlete-heroes of their 1913 collaborative theater piece, the opera *Victory*

Figure 8.5 David Burliuk, *Portrait of the Futurist and Singer-Warrior Vasilii Kamensky*, 1916. Oil on canvas, 97 × 65.5 cm. State Tret'iakov Gallery, Moscow.

over the Sun (*Pobeda nad solntsem*). Khlebnikov's great "beyondsense" (*zaum'*) "Prologue" immediately sets the violent agonistic tone of a work in which the sun, symbol of the traditional, now exhausted outer illumination of nature and the old art, is captured, imprisoned in a concrete chamber, and finally buried. It is as though by conquering nature, time, too, could be mastered and the superior inner creative powers of the new man (there are no women in the work) be set free to build an age in which the "Strongun will replace the Sicklan" ("Sileben zamenit khileben"—*sileben* and *khileben* are masculine noun-neologisms formed from the adjectives *sil'nyi*, "strong," "powerful," and *khilyi*, "sickly," "puny").[45] In the opera that follows, two "Futurian Strongmen" ("budetlianskie silachi"), costumed by Malevich to allow the performers to flex their arms upward only, begin the action by tearing apart the curtain. They then promise to "rout the universe" and "organize the bloody carnage of the timid" in their struggle for the future, while a chorus of "Sportsmen" sing "We are free, the sun smashed, hail darkness! . . . Our light is within."

In *Explodity* (*Vzorval'*, 1913), Kruchenykh, author of the opera's main text, had gone so far as to write "because of a despicable contempt for women and children, there will be only the masculine gender in our language."[46] He applied the principle in *Victory over the Sun*, in which the Traveler sings "Everything has become masculine" (or "male"—"Vse stalo muzhskim"), while all the nouns in his Song, no matter what their gender in Russian, are treated as though masculine. Similarly, the Futurian Strongmen's first song derides sentimentality and passion, which they associate with the "fat women beauties," already locked up, and the sun, their next target. The misogyny of Kruchenykh's text, as of several of the Futurist manifestoes, is striking considering his collaboration with and promotion of the careers of several women, his brilliant wife Ol'ga Rozanova among them. But then the line between promotion and patronizing can be slender.[47]

Strongmen, sportsmen, the aviator—none are identified as artists, but all are agents for change and new vision in the opera. A year later, Malevich painted the "alogical" masterpiece *Aviator* (Russian Museum), in which violent images of cutting and slicing accompany those of illumination and transcendence. When he introduced his severely non-figurative style of painting to the public in December 1915, he titled one work *Airplane Flying* (*Suprematist Painting*) (Museum of Modern Art, New York) and another *Suprematism. Painterly Realism of a Football Player* [*futbolist*]. *Color Masses in the Fourth Dimension* (Stedelijk Museum, Amsterdam). For the speed of the game and the constant movement, especially that of the player whose position is called "forward," represented a perfect metaphor for the Suprematist artist, whose art is ever expanding into the infinity of time and space.

Malevich remained loyal to the Cubo-Futurist vision of the athlete as icon of modernity and the "heroic man of the future, powerful, and in perfect control of mind and body," an image of "transfigured perfection"[48] and to the related belief, shared by some others in the avant-garde, that the human body is inseparable from the human identity and that both can be forged and perfected. Athletes are the subject of one of his last major paintings: *Sportsmen* (or *Athletes—Sportsmeny*; Russian Museum), c. 1930–1932. Mashkov, for his part, insisted in the late 1910s that his students at Moscow's Second Free State Art Studios (II Svomas) keep themselves fit and trim with vigorous physical exercise.[49] Malevich cannot have been pleased by the appropriation and "despiritualization" of this visionary figure in the new Soviet state, whose materialist ethos called down his wrath in the polemical *God is Not Cast Down* (1922). Throughout the 1920s, the athlete, in particular the speed and agility of the soccer player, became a favorite symbol in works of art and literature for the youthful vitality and the dynamic energy that the new society wished to project to its citizens and the world.[50] (El Lissitzky's *Football Player* [*Futbolist*], a 1922 photomontage of a player impelled into a futuristic space of overlapping suprematist-inspired planes, provides a fine instance.)[51] The image was quite one-dimensional in most works (athletes were among the most popular subjects for the artists who in 1925 banded together as the Society of Easel Painters [OST]) and became even more so in the decades that followed. Then, as in Fascist states in Western Europe, the athlete, both male and female, athletic competitions, and mass athletic demonstrations entered the ritual of the Soviet state, becoming propagandistic signs of its health, the unity of its cheerful and cheering peoples, and the unstoppable lockstep march of its "Great Family" into the end of history. We might be tempted to see in that a simple continuity with the previous valorization of the athlete by some in the avant-garde in Russia (and abroad). Here, however, was a true forgery of the celebration by Mashkov, Larionov, Goncharova, Malevich and other avant-gardists of the artist-athlete as a free-spirited, at times anarchic, Promethean "antagonist," wrestling with the static and stultifying in the name of ever new and perpetual creativity. As the Futurian strongmen intone at the conclusion of that avant-garde romance *Victory over the Sun*: "All's well that begins well and has no end, the world will perish but we have no end!"

Notes

1. See Ludwig Goldscheider, *Five Hundred Self-Portraits from Antique Times to the Present Day in Sculpture, Painting, Drawing and Engraving*, trans. J. Byam Shaw (London: George Allen and Unwin Ltd., 1937).
2. Jean Fouquet made a tiny enamel and gold likeness of himself c. 1450 (Louvre), while in 1484 Albrecht Dürer the younger did a silverprint drawing of himself as a boy (Albertina)

and c. 1485 Filippino Lippi inscribed a fresco self-portrait on a flat tile (Uffizi). See Pascal Bonafoux, *Portraits of the Artist: The Self-Portrait in Painting* (New York: Rizzoli, 1985).

3. See the masterful studies of Joseph Leo Koerner, *The Moment of Self-Portraiture in German Renaissance Art* (Chicago: University of Chicago Press, 1993), and H. Perry Chapman, *Rembrandt's Self-Portraits: A Study in Seventeenth-Century Identity* (Princeton: Princeton University Press, 1990).

4. John E. Malmstad, "Boris Pasternak—The Painter's Eye," *The Russian Review*, 51: 3 (July 1992), p. 318. Joseph Koerner has made a similar point: "Every picture becomes a self-portrait to the extent that we experience and interpret it as the unique product of a particular person" (Koerner, *op. cit.*, p. xvii).

5. M. M. Bakhtin, "The Problem of the Text in Linguistics, Philology, and the Human Sciences: An Experiment in Philosophical Analysis," in *Speech Genres and Other Later Essays*, trans. Vern W. McGee, ed. Caryl Emerson and Michael Holquist, (Austin, TX: University of Texas Press, 1986), Slavic Series 8, p. 109. What Lyotard calls the *figural*, implying a relationship "between the mind and something intrinsically exterior and unassimilable to itself" could also be noted. See Michael Sheringham, *French Autobiography: Devices and Desires* (Oxford: Clarendon Press, 1993), p. 94. Bakhtin ignored yet another problematizing "distance": All writing about visual art (and the performing arts as well) entails an act of substitution—of word for image—that displaces the object with another kind of narrative.

6. James Cracraft in *The Petrine Revolution in Russian Imagery* (Chicago: University of Chicago Press, 1997) and Richard S. Wortman in *Scenarios of Power: Myth and Ceremony in Russian Monarchy* (Princeton: Princeton University Press, 1995) discuss this "image making" in detail.

7. There were, of course, a few self-portraits other than that by Levitsky which I have not mentioned in my very summary account. Mention might be made of those by the minor painters S. S. Shchukin and F. I. Ianenko (done in the 1790s), but they neither created nor represent a tradition.

8. V. N. Toporov as discussed by Catherine Ciepiela, "Reading Russian Pastoral: Zhukovsky's Translation of Gray's Elegy," in *Rereading Russian Poetry*, ed. Stephanie Sandler (New Haven: Yale University Press, 1999), p. 31.

9. Stephen Greenblatt, *Renaissance Self-Fashioning: From More to Shakespeare* (Chicago: University of Chicago Press, 1980).

10. See the classic study by Lidiia Ginzburg, *O lirike* (Moscow-Leningrad: Sovetskii pisatel', 1964; second, revised edition 1974), especially her treatment of the "lyrical hero" (a concept originated by her teacher, Iurii Tynianov), the autobiographical persona that shapes an author's work.

11. *Self-Portrait with Pink Kerchief* is in the collection of the State Russian Museum (St. Petersburg), while *Self-Portrait with Brushes behind the Ear* is in that of the Tret'iakov Gallery (Moscow).

12. Both *Self-Portrait with Album in Hand* and *Self-Portrait in Striped Dressing Gown* belong to the Tret'iakov Gallery. All the self-portraits are reproduced and discussed in the second chapter of V. S. Turchin, *Orest Kiprensky* (Moscow: Izobrazitel'noe iskusstvo, 1975), pp. 44–53. See too D. V. Sarab'ianov, "Avtoportrety Kiprenskogo," in his *Obrazy veka* (Moscow: Molodaia gvardiia, 1967), pp. 6–14. Critics have never remarked the connection between the rise of the self-portrait in Russian art and the "time of the elegy" in Russian verse.

13. E[rikh] Gollerbakh, *Portretnaia zhivopis' v Rossii. XVIII vek* (Moscow-Petrograd: Gosudarstvennoe izdatel'stvo, 1923), p. 14.

14. Sarab'ianov has noted the "unprecedented number of early nineteenth-century self-portraits" in his *Russian Art from Neoclassicism to the Avant-Garde: 1800–1917* (New York: Harry Abrams, Inc., 1990), p. 31. See also Turchin, *op. cit.*, p. 45.

15. A dramatic rise in small-scale portraits and portrait drawing accompanied the flowering of self-portraiture in this period. See G. G. Pospelov, *Russkii portretnyi risunok nachala XIX veka* (Moscow: Iskusstvo, 1967).

16. Nikolai Berdiaev, as quoted in Aleksei Grishchenko, *Krizis iskusstva i sovremennaia zhivopis'* (Moscow, 1917), p. 16.

17. A. A. Vrubel', "Vospominaniia," in *Vrubel'. Perepiska. Vospominaniia o khudozhnike* (Leningrad: Iskusstvo, 1976), p. 152.

18. Mention might be made of Pavel Kuznetsov's unusual self-portrait drawing of 1907–08 (Tret'iakov Gallery), in which images familiar from his paintings (an infant, the face of a

woman with closed eyes, whose hand rests on the painter's shoulder, a sun-like shape) surround the head of the "Blue Rose" master, whose Symbolist-inspired works were obsessed with mysterious origins and birth. It recalls a self-portrait like James Ensor's *Ensor with Masks* (1899), in which images from his own works crowd around the artist's head.

19. Aleksandr Benua [Benois], "Khudozhestvennye pis'ma. Vystavka Soiuza. III," *Rech'* (St. Petersburg), no. 70, March 13 (26), 1910, p. 3. The critic wrote that "Serebriakova's self-portrait is without doubt the most pleasant, most joyous work" that he had seen exhibited that year.

20. Frances Borzello mentions the picture in her *Seeing Ourselves: Women's Self-Portraits* (New York: Harry N. Abrams, 1998). She misidentifies the picture as *Self-Portrait at the Dressing Table*, and writes only that it "crackles with the confidence, energy and pleasure in her femininity that earned her admiration in the World of Art group in pre-revolutionary Russia" (p. 137).

21. For an excellent history of the group see G. G. Pospelov, *Karo-bube: Aus der Geschichte der Moskauer Malerei zu Beginn des 20. Jahrhunderts*, trans. Irene Faix (Dresden: VEB Verlag der Kunst, 1985) and G. G. Pospelov, *Bubnovyi valet: Primitiv i gorodskoi fol'klor v moskovskoi zhivopisi 1910–kh godov* (Moscow: Sovetskii khudozhnik, 1990). Scholars still debate the origin of the anti-aesthetic exhibition title "bubnovyi valet." Pospelov links it to the French conversational expression for a rogue or swindler, "valet de carreau," as well as to the diamond-shaped emblem on convicts' uniforms (*Bubnovyi valet*, pp. 98–101). The group could thus have suggested to the traditionalists of art that they were outcasts and criminals. Larionov's collecting of hand-colored playing cards suggests another explanation. Petr Ashevsky, in a satirical feuilleton about the group's December 1910 exhibition, picked up on the suggestion of criminality in the name and literalized it. His piece presents the group being brought to imaginary trial in a Moscow court charged with having "insulted public common sense and the most elementary aesthetic feelings" for having exhibited "pieces of crudely smeared canvas." The verdict: "guilty, but deserving only of the deepest sympathy." See "Bubnovoe delo" in the newspaper *Russkoe slovo* (Moscow), no. 287, December 12 (25), 1910, p. 6.

22. The complete list of exhibitors and their paintings can be found in Pospelov, *Bubnovyi valet*, pp. 242–245, and in Valentine Marcadé, *Le Renouveau de l'art pictural russe 1863–1914* (Lausanne: L'Age d'Homme, 1971), pp. 314–16. Examples of the "isms" that came to be called "Russian Cézannism" (Fal'k, Mashkov, Konchalovsky, Kuprin, and others), "Neo-Primitivism" (Burliuk, Larionov, Goncharova, Malevich), "Symbolist Expressionism" (Kandinsky, Jawlensky), and the "pre-Cubism" of Gleizes and Le Fauconnier all confronted each other on the walls of the show, with many of the "isms," especially Cézannism and Neo-Primitivism, overlapping and mingling in many of the canvases.

23. Maksimilian Voloshin, the only writer associated with the Symbolists in Russia who was also an accomplished painter (he was friendly with many of the French Symbolist artists, like Redon, whom he championed in Russia, and with members of the "Nabis"), gave the only serious critical response to the exhibition. He noted the influence of shop signs and popular folk prints [the *lubok*] in the paintings on show, and expressed guarded admiration for the youthful vigor and talent of some of the artists, but he rejected the "hooliganism" that had been designed "pour épater" and to "drive the visitor's eye to a frenzy." See M. Voloshin, "Bubnovyi valet," in the section "Moskovskaia khronika. Vystavki," *Russkaia khudozhestvennaia letopis'*, 1 (January 1911), p. 12. Sergei Mamontov wearily dismissed the exhibit as yet another of the "regular yearly scandalous incidents" [*skandaly*] with which the "uncompromising" artists of the "extreme left" tried to create a "sensation" and nothing else. The exhibit, he added, resembled nothing so much as a "hospital for the mentally disturbed" ("Bubnovyi valet," *Russkoe slovo*, no. 289, December 15 (28), 1910, p. 6). See also a satirical "Little Feuilleton" about the exhibit signed "Arlekin" ["Harlequin"] and a highly critical review by S. Volzhanin in *Moskovskaia gazeta-kopeika*, no. 194 (549), December 12 (25), 1910, p. 3–4, 5; a review by A. Koiransky in *Utro Rossii*, no. 323, December 11 (24), 1910, p. 6, and another by Sergei Garin in the same Moscow newspaper, no. 324, December 12 (25), 1910, p. 5 (this review also picked up on the "criminality" implicit in the group's name); and a review signed Sergei Glagol' [S. S. Gouloushev], "Bubnovyi valet," *Stolichnaia molva*, no. 156, December 13 (26), 1910, p. 4.

24. See Lentulov's memoirs ("Vospominaniia") as cited in E. B. Murina and S. G. Dzhafarova, *Aristarkh Lentulov* (Moscow: Sovetskii khudozhnik, 1990), p. 189.

25. Voloshin recognized, but did not explore this dimension of the painting in his review of the exhibit: He called it "programmatic" ("Bubnovyi valet," *op. cit.*, p. 10). As late as 1916, Benois still remembered the picture when he wrote: "Here are two healthy, strong, simple painters. . . . They now have only to paint, paint, paint" since they have put their early days of "playing eccentrics" behind them. See his "Mashkov i Konchalovsky," *Rech'*, no. 102, April 15 (28) 1916, p. 2. Pospelov discusses the picture in his article "Portret v iskusstve rannego 'Bubnovogo valeta'," *Problemy portreta. Materialy nauchnoi konferentsii (1972)* (Moscow: Sovetskii khudozhnik, 1974), pp. 263–266.

26. See I. S. Bolotina, *Il'ia Mashkov* (Moscow: Sovetskii khudozhnik, 1977), p. 424. Another sign stated: "Those working in my studio are strictly forbidden to be sick." Photos of his studio taken in 1919–1920 show a set of weights, dumbbells, and gymnastic apparatus like rings that hang from the ceiling (pp. 403, 405). Bolotina also includes a photograph from the second half of the 1910s showing Mashkov in his studio. He is posed full length in profile, naked except for wrestling shorts (exactly like those in the 1910 picture) and shoes (p. 410).

27. I have in mind pictures like Mashkov's *Still Life. Berries with Red Tray in the Background* (1910–11, Russian Museum) or Konchalovsky's *Still Life. Tray and Vegetables* (1910, Russian Museum). Both are reproduced in the catalogue of the exhibition *Avangard i ego russkie istochniki* (Baden-Baden, 1993), pp. 89 and 91 (photos of three nineteenth-century trays are on p. 88). John Bowlt takes the floral pictures in the Mashkov we are discussing to be trays, although pictures seem more likely, given the positioning of the flowers within the borders, which is quite unlike the manner of trays. See his "Body Beautiful: The Artistic Search for the Perfect Physique," *Laboratory of Dreams: The Russian Avant-Garde and Cultural Experiment*, ed. John E. Bowlt and Olga Matich (Stanford: Stanford University Press, 1996), p. 46. The article raises several of the points on "athleticism" that I explore here.

28. In a 1908 letter to Konchalovsky from Italy, Mashkov wrote: "Giotto and his students (the frescoes in Padua) particularly delighted and enraptured me near the end of my trip" (cited in Bolotina, p. 16). In other letters he called Giotto "my god" and a "super-genius" (Bolotina, p. 17). He was no less enthusiastic about the paintings of Cézanne, Van Gogh, Matisse, and others that he saw that year in Paris, where he for a time stayed with Konchalovsky.

29. Both Mashkov's 1911 *Self-Portrait* and Konchalovsky's *Self-Portrait in Spanish Hat* are reproduced in Pospelov, *Bubnovyi valet*, p. 104 and 109, while Konchalovsky's *Self-Portrait with Tray*, can be found in Pospelov's *Karo-bube*, p. 114. For a color reproduction of the Mashkov, see G. S. Arbuzov and V. A. Pushkarev, *Il'ia Mashkov* (Leningrad: Aurora, 1973), no. 23.

30. The painting, in oil with the paper cut-outs that Lentulov liked to apply to his paintings at the time, is reproduced in color in Murina and Dzhafarova, *Aristarkh Lentulov*, p. 52.

31. The 1910 self-portrait of Vladimir Baranov-Rossiné or the 1912 self-portrait of Ivan Puni (Pougny), to give but two instances, are uncompromisingly "modern" in manner, but well within the compositional canon of the genre. Both are reproduced in Jean-Claude Marcadé, *L'Avant-garde russe 1907–1927* (Paris: Flammarion, 1995), p. 68. Vladimir Tatlin, who had served for a time in the merchant marine, painted himself as a *Sailor* in 1911 (private collection), while Aleksandr Shevchenko, the theoretician of Neo-primitivism, depicted himself in the equally masculine role of a soldier in partial uniform grooming a horse (1915–16, Russian Museum). Ol'ga Rozanova, with vividly colored flowers to her right and left, confronts the viewer full face in her 1912 *Self-Portrait*, but despite its radically simplified treatment of the human figure, the picture does not depart from the compositional canon. It is reproduced in black and white in Nina Gurianova, *Exploring Color: Olga Rozanova and the Early Russian Avant-Garde, 1910–1918*, trans. Charles Rougle (G + B Arts International, 2000), p. 23. For a discussion of the poet Vladimir Maiakovsky's *Self-Portrait* (c. 1915), the most audacious instance of self-portraiture by a figure aligned with "left art" (in it fragments of the modern city replace and, as it were, stand in, for any human element), see my article "Boris Pasternak—The Painter's Eye," *op. cit.*, pp. 307–308.

32. The picture, in a private collection in the United States, is reproduced in color in Dmitri V. Sarabianov and Natalia L. Adaskina, *Popova*, trans. Marian Schwarz (New York: Harry N. Abrams, 1990), p. 101. Nadezhda Udal'tsova's Cubist-inspired *Self-Portrait with Palette* (1915, Tret'iakov Gallery) is no more radical than the Popova; it is reproduced in color in Ekaterina Drevina's *Nadezhda Udal'tsova* (Moscow: Trilistnik, 1997), p. 4.

33. *Self-Portrait with Saw* (1914) is in the B. M. Kustodiev Gallery in Astrakhan, and is reproduced on p. 137 of the exhibition catalogue *Chagall, Kandinsky, Malewitsch und die rus-*

sische Avantgarde (Ostfildern-Ruit: Verlag Gerd Hatje, 1998). A photograph of another version from the same year can be found in the exhibition catalogue *I. V. Kliun v Tret'iakovskoi galeree* (Moscow, 1999), p. 63.

34. Both the 1909 gouache and the 1933 oil are reproduced and discussed in Charlotte Douglas, *Kazimir Malevich* (New York: Harry N. Abrams, 1994), pp. 50–51 and 126–27.

35. The self-portrait is reproduced in color in Waldemar George, *Larionov* (Paris: La Bibliothèque des arts, 1966), p. 80. See my discussion of Larionov's use of such inscriptions in "The Sacred Profaned: Image and Word in the Paintings of Mikhail Larionov," *Laboratory of Dreams: The Russian Avant-Garde and Cultural Experiment, op. cit.,* pp. 153–173, 307–319.

36. *Portrait of an Athlete,* now called simply *Portrait of Vladimir Burliuk,* is in the collection of the Musée des Beaux-Arts, Lyon. For a color reproduction, see George, *Larionov,* p. 57, and an article about the painting by Jessica Boissel: "Une exposition nommée 'Valet de carreau', Moscou 1910–1911. A propos du 'Portrait d'un athlète' de Larionov," *Bulletin des Musées et monuments lyonnais,* 3 (1997), pp. 40–49.

37. Viktor Bart exhibited *Boy and Discuss Thrower* at the 1910 show, Konchalovsky three bullfighting paintings, and Vladimir Bekhteev *Battle of Amazons.*

38. A color reproduction of the painting (100 x 122 cm.) can be found in the catalogue *Chagall, Kandinsky, Malewitsch und die Russische AvantGarde,* p. 107. Another version of the same subject, painted in 1909–10 and measuring 118.5 × 103.5 cm., is in the collection of the Museée national d'art moderne in the Paris Centre Georges Pompidou. This *Les lutteurs* is reproduced in color on p. 31 of *Nathalie Gontcharova. Michel Larionov* (Paris: Éditions du Centre Pompidou, 1995), a catalogue raisonné of their works held by the Musée national d'art moderne, Paris.

39. See German Karginov, *Rodchenko* (London: Thames and Hudson, 1979), pp. 48–49 (the 1919 *Wrestler* on p. 48 strongly recalls Goncharova's image); the catalogue *Aleksandr Rodchenko. Varvara Stepanova. Budushchee—edinstvennaia nasha tsel'* . . . (Vienna: Prestel, 1991), p. 156 (images of the champions of India, Japan, and the RSFSR from the series "Wrestling" ["Frantsuzskaia bor'ba"]); Selim O. Khan-Magomedov, *Rodchenko. The Complete [sic!] Work* (Cambridge, Mass.: MIT Press, 1987), p. 33 (the colorful *Champions of England and France*) and p. 89 (the champion of Canada holding barbells).

40. Jean-Claude Marcadé and I have prepared Smirnov's more than 200 letters to Sonia Terk-Delaunay (private archive, France) for publication (in press).

41. Murina and Dzhafarova, *Aristarkh Lentulov,* p. 188. Pospelov sees a connection between the Mashkov self-portrait with Konchalovsky and another form of popular entertainment, the cinema (*Bubnovyi valet,* p. 105), but the comparison seems strained.

42. Aleksandr Blok, *Sobranie sochinenii v 8 tomakh,* vol. 3 (Moscow-Leningrad: Khudozhestvennaia literatura, 1960), p. 296–297.

43. *Portrait of V. E. Tatlin* is reproduced in color in the catalogue raisonné *Nathalie Gontcharova. Michel Larionov,* p. 59.

44. For a color reproduction, see the catalogue *Russian and Soviet Paintings 1900–1930* (Washington, D. C., 1988), p. 65, or the catalogue *Kandinsky et la Russie,* Fondation Pierre Gianadda (Martigny, Suisse, 2000), p. 213.

45. See *Poeziia russkogo futurizma,* "Novaia biblioteka poeta" (St. Petersburg: Gumanitarnoe agenstvo "Akademicheskii proekt," 1999), p. 213.

46. *Manifesty i programmy russkikh simvolistov,* ed. Vladimir Markov (München: Wilhelm Fink Verlag, 1967), p. 62; slightly different translation in *Russian Futurism through its Manifestoes, 1912–1928,* trans. Anna Lawton and Herbert Eagle, ed. Anna Lawton (Ithaca: Cornell University Press, 1988), p. 66.

47. While it would be tempting to conjecture that male artists forged aggressive masculine images of the creative spirit as a reaction against the emergence in Russia of a series of important women painters and sculptors, there is no evidence to suggest that. For one, the first masculinized constructions of the painter-athlete were exhibited in 1910, before women artists, with the exception of Goncharova, were at all a presence, much less prominent, in the nascent avant-garde. (Recall too that both Mashkov and Goncharova exhibited their athlete paintings at the same "Jack of Diamonds" 1910 exhibition.) Benedikt Livshits dubbed Goncharova, Ekster, and Rozanova, three of the leading female painters of Russian "left art," "real Amazons" in his memoirs. "Amazons" suggests a forceful, even violent femininity, or at least a strong consciousness of gender, but we can see no interest in gender

politics or commitment to even the mildest form of feminism in their letters, diaries, and memoirs or in those of the other major pre–1917 women avant-gardists. They instead project a strong image of self-confidence without the slightest hint of inferiority *vis-à-vis* their male colleagues. Those looking for a painterly equivalent of "écriture féminine" in their works will be similarly disappointed. See the "Documents" section, as well as essays and reproductions of paintings, in the exhibition catalogue *Amazons of the Avant-Garde: Alexandra Exter, Natalia Goncharova, Liubov Popova, Olga Rozanova, Varvara Stepanova, and Nadezhda Udaltsova*, ed. John E. Bowlt and Matthew Drutt (Guggenheim Museum, 2000), and the "Chronology of the Life and Works of Olga Rozanova" in Gurianova, *Exploring Color, op. cit.*, pp. 135–182.

48. Douglas, *Malevich*, p. 120. Mandel'shtam's three poems of 1913 on football ("Sport," "Futbol," "Vtoroi futbol") have nothing of the almost metaphysical dimension of Malevich's conception of the athlete, football player. Nor does Iurii Olesha's portrait of the young football player hero in his 1927 novel *Envy* (*Zavist'*). The whole matter of football (and rugby) as a subject for modern Western art (think only of well-known paintings by Henri-Julien Rousseau [le Douanier] or Robert Delaunay in France) remains to be explored. In 1913, the Ballets Russes staged Nijinsky's "poème danse" *Jeux*, the first "sports ballet." (It was never seen in Russia, only abroad.) Typical of an enterprise that was inspired and directed by associates of the elitist World of Art, the sport in question was tennis, not "mass" sports like wrestling or weight lifting.

49. See I. S. Bolotina, *Il'ia Mashkov, op. cit.*, p. 68, for the program of Mashkov's classes. "Gymnastics" was point number one in the program for "strengthening the body," which also included weightlifting, wrestling, boxing, the rings, running, etc. There is a photograph of the rules hanging in his studio on p. 422.

50. Katerina Clark has noted that both the sports hero and the aviation pilot served as "symbolic" heroes and "paradigmatic new men" in Soviet literature; see *The Soviet Novel: History as Ritual* (Chicago: University of Chicago Press, 1981), pp. 124–29.

51. The picture, an illustration for Il'ia Erenburg's "Six Stories about Easy Ends" ("Shest' povestei o legkikh kontsakh"), is reproduced in the catalogue of the Tret'iakov Gallery's 1990 exhibit *Lazar' Markovich Lisitsky. 1890–1941*, p. 61.

CHAPTER 9

After the "Death of the Author"

The Fabrication of Helen Demidenko

JUDITH RYAN

In 1994, an Australian writer using the name Helen Demidenko published a novel that she allowed to be read as a thinly disguised version of her immigrant family's history. *The Hand that Signed the Paper* is narrated by a fictional Australian university student named Fiona Kovalenko, whose uncle, a postwar immigrant to Australia from Ukraine, has just been charged with war crimes during the Nazi period. The relation of this story to the Ivan Polyukhovich case of 1991, in which a 73-year-old Australian was accused of aiding a massacre in Nazi-occupied Ukraine in 1942/3, would have been evident to anyone who spent time in Australia during the early 1990s.[1] Fiona's story is told partly in her own voice and partly through "oral histories" gleaned from her uncle Vitaly and her aunts Kateryna and Magda. Given the similarity between the last name of the author, Demidenko, and that of the framing narrator, Kovalenko,[2] most of the novel's early readers saw it as a courageous venture in which a young Australian overcame understandable reticence in order to wash her family's dirty laundry—their collaboration with the Nazis—in public. In the narrative itself, the fictional Fiona underscores this point several times. "It's hard to own things when they're bad," she writes. "To admit they belong to you" (p. 41). Later she comments that the sheer act of writing about her uncle's participation in Nazi atrocities gives his history a character it did not have for her before: "It has permanence, now. I must own it"

(p. 84). The underlying notion, that Australia needs to "own"—and own up to—the shame and guilt of some of its citizens' pasts, gave *The Hand that Signed the Paper* an allure of boldness that commended it to many of its first reviewers.

When *The Hand that Signed the Paper* won a distinguished Australian prize for a first novel manuscript, most critics were happy enough with the decision, though one reviewer did have the good sense to say that the novel's author was "admittedly [. . .] no Dostoevksy."[3] The worthiness of the novel was put more severely to the test when it received two other important prizes.[4] The public now became convinced that the prize committees had been either pandering to modish multiculturalism or—quite the opposite—blinded by their own unavowed cultural prejudices into bestowing a prize on what had widely come to be perceived as an anti-Semitic book.

At this point in the debate about *The Hand that Signed the Paper*, its author, the Helen Demidenko of the title page, was discovered to be Helen Darville, daughter of British immigrants to Australia with no known Ukrainian heritage. With the aid of an embroidered Ukrainian peasant blouse and a pair of high leather boots, which she wore for public appearances regardless of the weather, Helen Darville had succeeded in persuading most of those who encountered her that she was in fact the first-generation Australian daughter of Ukrainian immigrants. Seemingly sealing her public identification as Ukrainian, Helen made frequent references to her tall stature, and drew attention to her long blond hair by constantly brushing it while on stage. At one public event, she even did a Ukrainian dance. When she was unmasked, one of her "friends"wrote an entire book about how disappointed she was in Helen: Why, even Helen's hair had been so drastically bleached that it "nearly broke off in the hands" of her hairdresser![5] Soon after this revelation of Helen's real identity, the scandal took a new turning when several critics claimed to have detected plagiarism in her novel. Like many historical novelists, Helen Darville had "researched" her topic by reading several accounts of Ukrainian and European history. But none of her flagrant borrowings from these sources, however "stolen" in the popular understanding of the word,[6] proved to be plagiarism in the legally actionable sense.

More troubling was the fact that Helen Darville had spent almost two years as an impostor. Various theories have been advanced about her extraordinary act of self-disguise, ranging from the notion that it was her way of "getting inside the heads" of her characters[7] to the charge that her own head was seriously disturbed.[8] That leaves us with the book itself, which had been presented as a novel, and not as an autobiography. The "author's note" clearly states, even in its first version: "What follows is a work of fiction. The

Kovalenko family as depicted in this novel has no counterpart in reality." (p. vi). Still, the Demidenko/Kovalenko similarity led many readers to conclude that the novel was an autobiographical fiction. Why did the book deliberately encourage identification between its author and its narrator?

Significantly, Helen's pseudonym "Demidenko" is not randomly chosen. Demidenko, as one early commentator pointed out, is the name of a Ukrainian murderer mentioned in Anatoli Kuznetsov's *Babi Yar. A Documentary in the Form of a Novel* (1967).[9] Helen Darville's use of material from Kuznetsov's *Babi Yar* was one of the reasons she was charged with plagiarism; her predecessor D. M. Thomas, who used the same material from Kuznetsov's *Babi Yar* in his 1981 novel *The White Hotel*, was also accused of plagiarism on account of his use of this material.[10] Is Darville's adoption of the name Demidenko an illegitimate theft or a clue that begs reflection on the relationship between *Babi Yar*, *The White Hotel*, and *The Hand that Signed the Paper*?

Those who saw Helen Demidenko as telling lies—and on one level, of course, that is what she was doing—might take note of another novel by D. M. Thomas's, *Lying Together* (1990), a profoundly self-reflexive postmodernist book in which Thomas explores at length the question of fact and fiction, including the nature of his own writing. In this novel, he tells the story of an editor who claims, falsely, to be dying and requests his publishing house's authors to "write something for him" (p. 73). The narrator sends in "some lines from 'And Death Shall Have No Dominion.' " "That was very suitable," comments his interlocutor (p. 73). One cannot help thinking that Darville and Thomas were both, in their own way, lying together. And in choosing the name Demidenko as her pseudonym, Helen Darville clearly chose to cast her lot with the D. M. Thomas of *The White Hotel*.

In addition to the name Demidenko, there are several other similarities between *The White Hotel* and *The Hand that Signed the Paper*. Both novels acknowledge some (though not all) of their sources in their frontmatter, and both novels have a strange dual apparatus of acknowledgements and "author's note." D. M. Thomas prefaces his novel with an excerpt from Yeats's poem, "Meditations in Time of Civil War" (1923), and Helen Darville uses two stanzas from Dylan Thomas's poem "The Hand that Signed the Paper" (1933). A quotation from Hobbes's *Leviathan* forms Darville's second epigraph. All three epigraphs have to do with brutality and violence: Yeats deplores the way in which idealism has turned into brutality during the Irish Civil War; Dylan Thomas argues that even the seemingly peaceful act of signing a treaty can sometimes lead to further bloodshed; and Hobbes describes the natural condition of man as one of general warfare. Both novels, *The White Hotel* and *The Hand that Signed the Paper*, explore the nature of violence and the ways in which it is motivated and reproduced.

Still, there were significant differences between the treatment of violence in the two novels. The opening sections of *The White Hotel* are predicated on the idea of a connection between sex and violence that owes its origin to Freud's link between libido and the death wish. *The Hand that Signed the Paper* is not a Freudian novel, not even one which, like *The White Hotel*, proposes some crucial revisions of Freudian doctrine. Rather, Darville's novel adopts today's concept of a "cycle of violence" by means of which violence is handed down from one generation to the next. By applying this notion to the motivation of Ukrainian collaborators with the Nazis, the novel suggested what Alan Dershowitz has called the "abuse excuse"[11]: that the Ukrainians' suffering under Communism during the famine of the 1930s is passed on as violence against the Jews. The idea that the Ukrainians were perpetuating a cycle of violence was shocking to many readers, who saw the novel as condoning the behavior of the Ukrainian collaborators. Although the novel claims to be exploring power structures, the hands that "signed the paper" are not those of an autocratic ruler, but those of peasants signing on to the Nazi cause in whose name they will commit mass murders.

In addition to these problems in *The Hand that Signed the Paper*, the moral positions taken by its various narrators are not always sharply differentiated. The primary narrator, Fiona, tends to accept what her aunt and uncle tell her; at least, she does not seriously question their belief in the cycle of violence theory. To be sure, at the end of the novel she takes a step beyond her uncle Vitaly, who shortly before his death is still "trying" to "be sorry" for his deeds as a prison guard at Treblinka (p. 154). Fiona, by contrast, does declare in the final sentences of the book that she is sorry for what her uncle did (p. 157).

Still, in the novel's penultimate section, Fiona tells us: "The war crimes trials came and went, came and went. I wrote letters to various Australian newspapers and magazines, protesting against the trials." (p. 156). We never find out how closely she accords with the opinion expressed by her friend, Cathe, at the beginning of the novel, that "trying people for what they did in a war legitimises other wartime activities that are left untried. War is a crime, of itself." (p. 4). This naïve and misinformed idea suggests that the actions of the Nazis and those who collaborated with them were part of a war, rather than a sweeping social program that had begun long before World War II. There probably are Australians of Cathe's and Fiona's generation who share this misapprehension; but we may rightly ask whether it was wise for Darville to allow this view to go unquestioned in her novel.

Linked with the portrayal of the younger generation is the motif of Fiona's brother, Bret, who served in Vietnam and returned half-crazed from his experiences, dreaming about "little gook children pocked with bullets and Vietnamese girls raped by both Americans and Vietcong" (p. 5). It is characteristic of Fiona's tendency to adopt other people's way of thinking that this passage simultaneously contains a racist epithet and an expression of outrage about rape. She also unreflectingly assimilates the Vietnam war to the Holocaust, implying that in both instances "people slaughtered without compunction" (ibid.). She goes on to contrast Bret with her parents' generation: "My father is sane. So are Vitaly and aunt Kateryna. None of them mad. Not now. Not one." (ibid.) In his last conversation with Fiona, however, Vitaly explains that bad memories can be either internalized or projected outward, but that in both cases they make one "sick": He sees himself as no less "sick" than Bret (p. 153). Here we do find a corrective to Fiona's unreflecting acceptance of popular conflations between different political situations, but the terms in which the corrective is offered are not differentiated in themselves.

One of the book's most sophisticated readers repeatedly describes *The Hand that Signed the Paper* as "imperfect and uneven"; he comments on its "uncertainty" and "miscalculations of tone."[12] When I first read the novel I, too, was troubled by these unevennesses; but then I began to suspect that the sheer number of obvious, even ludicrous, incongruities in the text might be more than accidental.

To be sure, many lapses can be put down to inadequate historical and cultural knowledge. When hungry Ukrainian children steal the lunches of Russians smaller than themselves, they not only find "blood sausage and tasty oatcakes," but also "sandwiches cut into four tidy squares" (p. 86). It is unlikely that any kind of bread in Eastern Europe during the 1930s had the shape of Wonder Bread. Vitaly's idea that being "six feet six" tall "has a nice ring to it" (p. 104) elides the fact that, at this point in the plot, Vitaly is still thinking and speaking in Ukrainian, and hence would not be using British measurements at all. Authorial ignorance may also account for the fact that the young man Fiona meets at the end describes his aunt, who died at Treblinka, as a "Quaker" (p. 157). And the reference to Fiona's supposedly Ukrainian father as resembling and acting like John Cleese in "Fawlty Towers" (p. 36) is almost certainly a slip. Still, other incongruities and anachronisms may be more deliberate. Candidates for intentional slippage may be the notion that the Ukrainian peasants live in "fibro shanties" (p. 20), where fibro refers to fibrous cement, a product frequently used for cheap housing in Australia, and the description of their children's hair as "filthy, matted" (ibid.), epithets that implicitly link the poor Ukrainians with the Australian aborigines mentioned elsewhere in the novel. Similarly, the idea that members of the German *Einsatztruppen* take "mental health days" (p. 67) is so patently ludicrous that it sounds more like an intentional discrepancy. Another such deliberate "plant," surely, is the description of the young Ukrainian who "had the SS runes excised into the short hair on the back of his head, about three inches high" (p. 112). The neo-Nazi look is an all too obvious anachronism in the historical setting of the Ukrainian episodes. The reader can hardly help but take these and other such incongruities in *The Hand That Signed the Paper* as clues pointing to the novel's status as pastiche.

One of the most peculiar moments in *The Hand that Signed the Paper* is a passage where the SS encourage their Ukrainian collaborators to sing while helping to maintain the security of the Treblinka death camp. A strangely flat narrative voice informs us that "soon, every morning, the killing fields rang with lively peasant aubades" (p. 98). The novel's opening paragraph takes a cynical view of Fiona's question "if Eichmann had a daughter and if she felt the same way as I do now" (p. 1). "It is an idle question," Fiona continues, "but I toy with it as the light and darkness at sunset plays over the glittering Ampol sign. This is one petrol station where they still serve you while you sit in your car" (p. 1). Fiona's pleasure at the privilege of being served, her aesthetic appreciation of a gas station sign (a knowing wink, perhaps, that alludes to Barthes's "empire of signs"), her designation of a crucial moral and psychological question as an "idle" one, and her use of traditional light and darkness imagery in a context she sees as mere "toying" or "play" (possibly a covert allusion to the concept of "free play" in Derrida) with an ethical issue—all these things speak volumes about Fiona's moral sensibility.[13]

At the end of the novel, after Fiona's uncle Vitaly has escaped trial through his death from a heart attack, Fiona admits she has given up protesting against the Australian war crimes trials. "My father was never charged," she writes, "and I concentrated on other things. I took a Russian subject [= course] in second semester. It seemed sensible." (p. 156). The novel ends on a note of deep ambiguity, since although Fiona claims she feels "sorry" about her uncle's past as a guard in the death camp, it is still not clear whether Vitaly himself ever came to feel "sorry" for his deeds at Treblinka before his untimely death.

This brings me, if somewhat indirectly, to the topic announced in the title of this essay: the "death of the author." Helen Darville's questionable friend Natalie Jane Prior writes, in 1996: "Already assessments of the situation are appearing which blame post-colonialism, multiculturalism, postmodernism (or whichever other '-ism' the writer happens to disagree with), the moral vacuum inhabited by 'today's youth' and even, bizarrely, the poor standard of contemporary English teaching at secondary and tertiary levels."[14] More humorously, a letter-writer to the newspaper *The Australian* makes the following points:[15]

> The controversy betrays the lamentable ignorance on the part of Australians of the central truths of post-modernism. As Roland Barthes has taught us, 'the author is dead.' So, that there is no Helen Demidenko is as it should be. (Helen Darville is a slight anomaly, but deconstruction can take care of this.)
>
> The text of 'The Hand' is said to contain portions of other texts: so must all! As is now well known, there is only the Intertext, of which all texts are fragments, and appropriation (the essence of post-modernism) is, and can be, only what the Intertext already 'owns'!
>
> Texts—again, this is well known—write themselves: French ones in the basement of Bibliothèque Nationale in Paris, Australian ones in the tea-room of the National Library in Canberra.

Critics have pointed out that Helen Darville would have been exposed to Roland Barthes and other postmodern theorists during her studies at the University of Queensland (the years, in fact, when she wrote the manuscript).[16]

Indeed, *The Hand that Signed the Paper* explores a number of theoretical concerns proper to postmodernism. One dominant theme is the concept of relativity, often criticized by opponents of postmodernism as "anything goes." The use of multiple narrators and hence multiple points of view withdraws the text from the kind of firm guidance that can be offered by an omniscient narrator. Even the "unreliable narrator" technique requires the presence of some kind of measure that can unmask the narrator's unreliability; but in the case of *The Hand that Signed the Paper*, it never becomes clear how its various narrators stack up along the reliability line.[17] The novel clearly also engages with the notion of "political correctness," as in a passage where a Ukrainian objects to the fact that some of the Nazi collaborators at Babi Yar are still wearing Soviet uniforms: "If there's one thing I cannot stand," he says, "it's politically incorrect dress" (p. 63). Not surprisingly, given this humorous travesty of the concept, the novel's conservative supporters claimed that it was being unfairly denigrated by the "thought police."[18]

As for the public's original supposition that Fiona Kovalenko was simply a flimsy stand-in for the novel's author, this can be seen as their unwitting fall into a postmodern trap. Barthes' essay, "The Death of the Author," however tongue-in-cheek, had already argued in 1968 for a distinction between the Romantic notion of the "Author" and the modern notion of the "scriptor." For the modern scriptor, Barthes wrote, "the hand, cut off from any voice, borne by a pure gesture of inscription (and not of expression), traces a field without origin—or which, at least, has no other origin than language itself, language which ceaselessly calls into question all origins."[19]

If we look at the first of the stanzas Helen Darville omits—and current theory tells us *always* to look at what's omitted—in her quotation of Dylan Thomas's poem "The Hand that Signed the Paper," we can see how post-modernity has acted upon the conception of the writing hand between Thomas's 1933 poem and Darville's 1994 novel:[20]

> The mighty hand leads to a sloping shoulder,
> The finger joints are cramped with chalk;
> A goose's quill has put an end to murder
> That put an end to talk.

The "hand" that writes Helen Darville's novel is clearly cut off from the shoulder, sloping or otherwise. By the same token, the "coldness" with which many readers charged the novel could be ascribed to the same disconnection between author and text. Or, as Foucault put it in his "What is an Author?": "The essential basis of this writing is not the exalted emotions related to the act of composition or the insertion of the subject into language. Rather, it is primarily concerned with creating an opening where the writing subject endlessly disappears."[21] In the case of "Helen Demidenko," the scriptor seemed continually to appear at prize-giving ceremonies, speaking engagements, and on talk shows, while the author literally—though not exactly endlessly—disappeared. In many ways Darville's enactment of the disappearing author can be seen as a prank played by an informed student of contemporary literary theory.[22]

The novel itself, finally, hints at this problem when it refers to "authenticity" in a seemingly insignificant passage. Here, a fair young man at Treblinka tells about a paper he wrote for Martin Heidegger. "In my paper [. . .], I argued that authenticity must be attained in the face of technologisation. And Martin argues that resoluteness and authenticity are inextricably linked" (p. 99). So he does. Heidegger argues, furthermore, that authenticity emerges out of a basic condition of inauthenticity. From this perspective, the Helen Demidenko episode is an amusing case in point. Darville certainly pursued with great resoluteness her claim to the "authenticity" of Helen Demidenko, a role in actuality based in inauthenticity. At a prize award ceremony, one of the judges, unaware at that point of Darville's deception, spoke eloquently of the "authenticity" of *The Hand that Signed the Paper*.[23] Yet few contemporary theorists regard "authenticity" as anything more than an effect.

Curiously enough, this theory contradicts another widely-held contemporary view: that texts treating particular ethnic groups should be written by members of these groups themselves. This is the problem that Cynthia Ozick refers to in her 1998 *New Yorker* article "Who Owns Anne Frank?" Are there any circumstances when it might be permissible for others to put themselves into the shoes of a Holocaust victim? In *The Hand that Signed the Paper*, Fiona Kovalenko answers this question quite unequivocally: "When I was cast as Anne Frank in the school play, I declined the role, then went home and threw up" (p. 39). Why does Fiona find it repugnant to represent Anne Frank on the school stage? And why did Helen Darville actually seem to find it amusing to spend two years acting her Ukrainian role in numerous public performances?

But this is not all. In implying that her book was in some sense autobiographical,[24] Helen Darville put to the test yet another contemporary theory: Philippe Lejeune's concept of the "autobiographical pact." However much the autobiographer—and presumably, by extension, the autobiographical novelist—may seem to retain central features in common with the narrator of his or her text, the basic premise of autobiography is, in fact, that "je suis un autre." In *The Hand that Signed the Paper*, Fiona Kovalenko has precisely this relationship of connection with and displacement from the supposed author of the novel, Helen Demidenko. And the hand that signed the publisher's contract was different from them both. Compounding this problem in a quite amusing—if also shocking—way was the fact that Helen Darville had made her own "I" into an "other" in recasting herself as a Ukrainian-Australian.

* * *

In order to understand the Demidenko Affair fully, it is essential to contrast it with the renowned Australian literary hoax, Ern Malley and his spurious poems, *The Darkening Ecliptic*. Not accidentally, the two scandals were separated by approximately fifty years: The Ern Malley poems were conceived and published in 1943, and Helen Darville began her novel project in 1993. Furthermore, a major book on the Ern Malley hoax had appeared to great acclaim in 1993.[25] World War II forms a backdrop for both *The Darkening Ecliptic* and *The Hand that Signed the Paper*.

The Darkening Ecliptic claimed to be the work of an Australian garage mechanic whose poetry had been discovered by his sister, Ethel Malley, after his death. Ern's quality of being Earnest was intensified by his untimely demise as a result of Grave's disease. Surrounded by volumes of modern verse and an army manual on mosquito-borne illness, James McAuley and Harold Stewart, two poets with established reputations, had set about creating a collection of poetry designed to expose what they regarded as the fraud of modernism. McAuley and Stewart, like many of their contemporaries, were disturbed by the difficulty and obscurity of modernist poetry, as well as by its appeal to an elite readership. Believing that modernism was essentially a lot of high-sounding nonsense, they decided to test whether "real" modernist poetry could be distinguished from fake. "The distinctive feature of the fashion [= modernism], it seemed to us," they subsequently explained, "was that it rendered its devotees insensible of absurdity and incapable of ordinary discrimination."[26] They thought of their effort as an "experiment."[27] The letter of inquiry they sent to the editor of a little magazine named *Angry Penguins* was signed by their invented poet's equally invented sister, and it was a brilliant imitation of someone who admires high culture without fully understanding what it is all about. The editor of *Angry Penguins* fell into the trap and published *The Darkening Ecliptic*. Once the hoax was exposed, the scandal resounded well beyond Australia to England and the United States. As one critic puts it, "The Ern Malley affair was, without question, *the* literary hoax of the twentieth century."[28]

McAuley and Stewart's poem-sequence was full of clues to the status of its alleged author, Ern Malley, as an imposter. These range from remarks about the poet's ontological position ("It is necessary to understand that a poet may not exist . . . ," p. 29) to comical adaptations of well-known lines ("In the twenty-fifth year of my age I find myself to be a dromedary," p. 39).[29] At times the poet doth protest too much: "There's damned deceit/ In these wounds, thrusts, shell-holes, of the cause/ And I'm no cheat" (p. 28). The final line of the sequence cannot be read otherwise than with a chuckle: "I have split the infinitive. Beyond is anything." (p. 40).

This essay is not the place to narrate in detail the complicated twists and turns of the Ern Malley affair, which among other things included a trial on charges of pornography. For writers of Helen Darville's generation, there were two important aspects to the affair: first, the public furor created by the poems themselves, and second, the myth of Ern Malley that remained in the cultural imagination. Malley became, in fact, a kind of folk hero. In 1952, a new literary magazine created by the former editor of *Angry Penguins* appeared under the title *Ern Malley's Journal*, a gesture intended as a sign of "faith in this 'Australian' poet."[30] In the inaugural issue, the German writer Wolfgang Borchert testified to his continued faith in Ern Malley, even though he knew that Malley was not a real person. He claimed that "Ern Malley embodies the true sorrow and pathos of our time."[31] Later, in a 1974 painting titled *Ern Malley*,[32] the legendary figure was brilliantly depicted by the Australian artist Sidney Nolan, known for his portrayals of another Australian folk hero, the convict outlaw Ned Kelly. Both figures embody the Australian admiration for those who rebel against convention and mock the establishment. But younger generations of Australians began to think of the poems as more than merely an experiment to expose the sham of modernism: They now discerned poetic merit in *The Darkening Ecliptic*, and thought of the hoaxers as having written good verse in spite of themselves. One critic wrote an essay titled "Ern Malley: 'The Greatest Writer that (N)ever Lived."[33] *The Penguin Book of Modern Australian Poetry* (1991) includes the entire sequence, though without its overarching title, and with the author's name, Ern Malley, in quotation marks.[34] The anthology's editors regard the poems "not as literary curiosities, but as an important work in their own right" and "as radical, intriguing challenges to traditional ways of writing and reading."[35]

Against this backdrop, it is not unimaginable that Helen Darville might have aimed to create a similar echo and win herself similar renown. Her ambitions were more complex in one respect, however, in that the target of her textual experiment included not only creative, but also critical and theoretical writing. The cultural scenario within which the Demidenko Affair took place was in many ways quite similar to that of the Ern Malley Affair: Without widespread skepticism about current literary fashion, neither event could have got off the ground. Whereas the Ern Malley poems attempted to expose what many contemporaries saw as the preposterous, factitious, and excessively hermetic style of poets like T. S. Eliot, Darville's novel lays bare what many believe to be the fraudulent nature of postmodern fiction and theory. Unlike the Ern Malley hoax, however, which brilliantly called modernism into question, the Helen Demidenko affair did not successfully pull the rug out from under postmodernism. Through its fundamental disconnection of author from text, intention from execution, postmodernism overtly and flamboyantly sets out to "fake it." To accuse it of being fake would thus seem redundant.

This is not to say, however, that the Demidenko Affair was meaningless. We need to reflect, at this point, on the reasons behind literary hoaxes of the Ern Malley variety. *The Darkening Ecliptic* differs from other famous hoaxes by its character as a deliberate experiment. Thomas Chatterton's medieval manuscripts and James Macpherson's *Poems of Ossian*, to name the two best known nineteenth-century examples, had other aims than McAuley and Stewart's Ern Malley poems. *The Darkening Ecliptic* was a hoax, Chatterton's medieval poetry and Macpherson's "Ossian" texts were frauds. Chatterton and Macpherson stood to profit from their alleged "discoveries," earning money and fame as editors of supposedly lost documents. They intended to deceive in quite a different way from the perpetrators of the Ern Malley poems. In today's critical climate—though more often within the academy than outside it[36]—as the Demidenko case testified—authorial intention is considered beyond the critic's bounds. In the 1940s, when the Ern Malley hoax was perpetrated, the academy was more divided about the issue of intention. Proust had already clearly declared that the author was not identical with the narrator, but many scholars still firmly believed in the concept of biographical criticism. Ern Malley, and his factitious sister Ethel, put biographical criticism severely to the test.[37] In certain respects, *The Darkening Ecliptic* bears similarity with the 1949 French hoax, *La Chasse Spirituelle*. Purporting to be a long-searched-for manuscript by Arthur Rimbaud, this text created headlines when it first appeared. A furor broke out when it was discovered that it had been written by two people closely familiar with Rimbaud's writing: two creative young members of the Parisian café culture. As one scholar wrote about the fake Rimbaud manuscript, the hoax "had important general implications for critical methodology and literary history."[38] Or, as another critic put it, "Here's a thing to tarnish the reputation of criticism for a long time to come !"[39] The Rimbaud case put to the test not just the aesthetic judgment of magazine editors and literary critics, as the Ern Malley Affair had done, but also claims about the scientific nature of textual editing practices. In their different ways, these two cases of the 1940s provoked a serious rethinking of literary value judgments and scholarly approaches to texts. The mischievous students who created the pseudo-Rimbaud and the irritated poets who invented Ern Malley shared a desire to expose these weaknesses of the culture and of the academic system. Both texts were themselves a form of critique, and in fact, the Ern Malley poems have been described as "the most decisive piece of literary criticism ever produced in Australia."[40]

Indeed, there is good reason to understand literary hoaxes in general as a kind of literary criticism. I would argue, in fact, that literary fraudulence of various kinds—ranging from actual forgery to pastiche and hoax—tends to proliferate in periods of cultural transition. Chatterton and Macpherson challenged the Romantic conception of original genius by exploiting the then fashionable obsession with collecting and editing ancient manuscripts. The ensuing debate threw the scholarly establishment into disarray precisely at a time of transition from a period where skillful, craftsmanlike imitation was valued to a period where original creativity was more highly prized. *The Darkening Ecliptic* and *La Chasse Spirituelle* challenged the modernist love of complex intertextual allusion at a time when frank literary borrowing was losing the stigma that Romanticism had given it, but when the Symbolist passion for obscurity and hermeticism was not yet completely discredited. *The Hand That Signed the Paper* alerts us to the transitional status of our own period, hovering between a desire for "authenticity" and an enthusiasm for pastiche forms. When Darville asked the advice of her university teacher, Con Castan, he told her that what made good fiction was "believeability—something that grabs you in and keeps you going."[41] But "believability" is not the same as "authenticity," a concept increasingly under attack today. In all three transitional periods—Romanticism, Modernism, and the postmodern era—discussions have turned in one sense or another on the place of "originality" in systems of literary values.

Helen Darville's novel presents an especially tricky case. By definition, postmodernism adheres to no clear standards of literary value. If she had had the ambition to become another Ern Malley, she was up against a difficult obstacle. Since hoaxes depend heavily on pastiche (in the sense of stylistic imitation), she had placed herself in the odd position of having to pastiche pastiche. As she wrote herself, in a 1995 newspaper article (still under the name Demidenko):

> For those who feel the need for ethical signposting, the fictional form I've employed clearly doesn't provide enough in the way of didacticism. I've always maintained that it is not the writer's task to do the reader's thinking for him. I don't provide a neat moral. Aside from being an insult to the reader's intelligence, authorial moralizing denies the reader space to draw his own conclusions.[42]

In many ways, Darville's novel exemplifies postmodernism's desire to eat its cake and have it too. Similarly, she herself boasted at different times in her life of Norman heritage, then of Czech decent, and finally of Ukrainian origins. She was able to be an active Young National, an Australian Democrat, and a campaigner for the Greens in rapid succession, just as she was happy to masquerade as a representative of multicultural Australia while also attacking political correctness. At one point, she quite ludicrously claimed that her mother was going to win the Nobel Prize for a new kind of potting mix she had invented.[43] In her chameleontic posing, she implicated what one newspaper article called "the whole apparatus of literary celebrity"[44]—and of celebrity in today's culture altogether. But of course, the chameleon is the quintessential image of the postmodern text and its author. Michael Heyward draws a crucial distinction between the Ern Malley hoax and the Helen Demidenko Affair:

> One big difference between what she's done and what Harold Stewart and James McAuley did is they very, very cunningly crafted the whole Ern Malley-Ethel Malley story. It's a brilliant story which they put together with tremendous panache. I think if we were to look at a lot of the fibs that Helen Darville has told about herself, we'd see that it probably doesn't cohere in the same way, that it's not nearly as cunningly worked out.[45]

Yes indeed: And yet it is precisely this incoherence that marks her fabricated self as a postmodern persona and her novel as a postmodern text.

In a radio interview at the height of the scandal, a talk show host asked Michael Heyward a leading question, "So it will go down in history as an unsuccessful hoax, do you think?"[46] He responded, "No, it will go down in history as a successful hoax."[47] Few of the other principals in the debate were inclined to see it this way, though there was a spate of stories in August 1995 "that Helen had plotted to deceive and make fools of the literary establishment."[48] Her ex-boyfriend, another of the nefarious cast of real characters in the public furor, said that Helen had hoped to win an award: "Oh, it was her mission, her fury. She was looking forward to the controversy, to stirring up an hornets' nest."[49] At one point in the debacle, Helen Darville claimed that she had planned to reveal her identity to her publisher, but tore up a draft of her letter when she received a reader's report objecting to antisemitic passages in the novel. It is impossible to judge, however, to what extent this story may have been a fabrication after the fact. Perhaps the most important element in a successful hoax is timing. After all, a hoax is designed to deceive only for a short while, in order to teach us a lesson we might otherwise be reluctant to accept. It is not always easy for hoaxers to decide the right moment to reveal the nature of the hoax. This may have been what happened to Helen Darville under the pressure of the strange unfolding of events surrounding her novel. But in the last analysis, the intricate, confusing, and contradictory nature of the Darville case is unlikely to provide a clear answer to this question even with the benefit of increasing hindsight.[50]

Perhaps the most problematic feature of *The Hand that Signed the Paper* was its attempt to exemplify the "death of the author" at the same time as it laid claim to the author's supposedly factual family heritage. Darville seems to have been caught in an irresolvable contradiction between postmodern skepticism about the possibility of coherent identity and multicultural identity politics. Despite its inability to negotiate this aporia, the novel effectively problematizes the concept of what it means to be Australian. It highlights a contemporary conflict between two conceptions of ethnicity, as an essentialist "real identity," on the one hand, and as what Benedict Anderson terms "imagined community," on the other.[51] One could even argue that Helen Darville's public displays of herself as Ukrainian involve the ultimate exposé, by means of an almost grotesque literalization, of "imagined community." Her novel also draws to its readers' attention specific aspects of national community that some would prefer not to include in their frame of vision: the fact that the Australian present includes not only what the nation officially considers to be its own past, but also the multifarious pasts of its present citizens, however inconsonant these may be with the myth of Australian national identity. Although the novel handles some of these conflicting interests remarkably well, there remain many unresolved problems. *The Hand that Signed the Paper* tells its story from the perspective of outsiders and underdogs, but unlike most "history from below," its narrators are not in the main sympathetic figures. Irresponsible and in some instances abhorrent figures function as lenses for large portions of the novel. While claiming to rely on personal experience and oral history, the novel also recasts less direct sources to give them a more personalized texture. Furthermore, it employs individualizing realistic techniques at the same time as it uses stereotype and cliché. All these aspects of the novel are undeniably part of its postmodern character. And their co-presence in the novel is what allowed it to appeal, for different reasons, to different segments of the public, while also alienating, for equally varied reasons, other segments of the public. But it was precisely these characteristically postmodern features that made the novel hard to identify as a critique of postmodernism. While it unmasks important contradictions in contemporary culture, it does not undermine postmodernism quite in the same way as *The Darkening Ecliptic* sabotaged modernism. This in itself says much about the different types of eclecticism practiced by the modernists, on the one hand, and the postmodernists, on the other. The heterogeneous character of postmodern texts is so extreme that most of the incongruities that may (if my reading is correct) have been clues to the novel's critical posture failed to leap out clearly enough from the clever pastiche of the contemporary novel that Darville had created. Perhaps in the last analysis, *The Hand that Signed the Paper*, though its imposture succeeded on many levels, should go down in history not as a fully-fledged hoax, but as a thought-provoking yet ultimately confused attempt by a young writer to explore the paradoxes of postmodern theory and the postmodern age. "Helen Demidenko" is dead, and Helen Darville—unlike James McAuley after the Ern Malley furor had subsided[52]—will probably not be able to publish under her own name in the near future.[53] There is an odd poetic justice in this strange new tale of the "death of the author."

Notes

1. See David Bevan, *A Case to Answer* (Kent Town, South Australia: Wakefield Press, 1994).
2. In the original manuscript, the narrator was called Fiona Demidenko.
3. Andrew Riemer, in *The Age*, September 24, 1994, reprinted in *The Demidenko File*, ed. John Jost, Gianna Totaro, and Christine Tyshing (Ringwood: Penguin Books Australia, 1996), p. 17.
4. The first prize won by *The Hand that Signed the Paper* was the Miles Franklin Award in 1995. But since this prize is given to a book which, by definition of the bequest, depicts "Australian life in any of its phases," the award did not seem to fit well with a novel in which most of the action occurs in Ukraine during the 1930s and 40s; as a result some members of the public felt that the award had been inappropriate. The other two prizes awarded were the Australian Literary Society's Gold Medal and the Vogel Literary Award, both also in 1995.
5. Natalie Jane Prior, *The Demidenko Diary* (Melbourne: Reed Books, 1996), pp. 149–150.
6. On the problem of plagiarism in literature, see Thomas Mallon, *Stolen Words: Forays into the Origins and Ravages of Plagiarism* (New York: Ticknor & Fields, 1989) and Susan Stewart, *Crimes of Writing: Problems in the Containment of Representation* (New York: Oxford University Press, 1991).
7. See, for example, David Marr's claim that she was entering the minds of her characters, *The Demidenko File*, pp. 117–118. Con Castan sees her as engaging in an "imaginative recreation of how certain Ukrainian peasants felt," *The Demidenko File*, p. 157.
8. Natalie Jane Prior depicts her as seriously unbalanced during the peak of the controversy (*The Demidenko Diary*, pp. 121–133). Andrew Riemer describes Helen Darville as "a talented though possibly deluded person" (*The Demidenko Debate* [St. Leonards: Allen and

Unwin, 1996], p. 217), and suggests that the possible existence of "exceptional circumstances which lie behind Darville's masquerade—circumstances that may require the competence of psychiatry to analyze and interpret" (p. 177).

9.   The first to point this out was Gerard Henderson. See *The Demidenko File*, p. 116.

10. Linda Hutcheon points out that Thomas's novel itself acknowledges its debts to Kuznetsov. "Literary Borrowing . . . and Stealing: Plagiarism, Sources, Influences, and Intertexts," *English Studies in Canada*, XII (1986), p. 230. Darville only acknowledges her debt to Kusnetzov in the second edition of her novel, published after her true identity had been revealed.

11. "Holocaust 'Abuse Excuse' Fails to Disguise Murder Most Foul," *The Australian Financial Review*, June 29, 1995, p. 16, reprinted in *The Demidenko File*, pp. 71–74.

12. Andrew Riemer, *The Demidenko Debate*, pp. 879, 146.

13. For this reason, I disagree with John Docker's argument that there are two Fionas, an earlier, less morally aware Fiona, and a later, more morally aware one. "Debating Ethnicity and History: From Enzensberger to Darville/Demidenko," in Gerhard Fischer, ed., *Debating Enzensberger: 'Great Migration' and 'Civil War'* (Tübingen: Stauffenberg Verlag, 1996), 213–224.

14. *The Demidenko Diary*, p. 165.

15. Patrick Hutchings, in *The Demidenko File*, p. 263.

16. Andrew Riemer, *The Demidenko Debate*, p. 196. He argues that, once Helen Darville's Demidenko role had been unmasked, the novel should have been "read and discussed as a work of fiction that employs literary techniques—principally irony and ambiguity—not inescapably as a treatise or disguised propaganda" (p. 175).

17. One critic pointed to other, even more extravagant experiments with unreliable narration, notably Martin Amis's novel, *The Information* (1995), which "is full of sly digs at the current craze for novels which offer a 'rotating crew of 16 unreliable narrators.'" (Richard Glover, in *The Demidenko File*, p. 135). Amis's novel speaks of "that miraculously sustained tour de force in which five unreliable narrators converse on crossed mobile phones while stuck in the same revolving door," *The Information* (New York: Vintage, 1995), p. 241.

18. See Robert Manne, *The Culture of Forgetting: Helen Demidenko and the Holocaust* (Melbourne: The Text Publishing Company, 1996), p. 172.

19. I cite here Stephen Heath's translation in *Image—Music—Text* (London, 1977, pp. 142–8).

20. *The Poems of Dylan Thomas*, ed. Daniel Jones (New York: New Directions, 1971), p. 66.

21. *Language, Counter-Memory, Practice*, trans. D. F. Bouchard and Sherry Simon (Ithaca: Cornell University Press, 1977), p. 116.

22. The manuscript version of *The Hand that Signed the Paper* used Demidenko as the surname for both the author and the narrator.

23. The judge, Jill Kitson, was referring to the way in which the novel worked creatively with what she then believed were its authors' family histories.

24. In both editions, she makes a point of thanking "friends and family who talked with me" (p. vi), thus implying a link between the novel and family oral histories.

25. Michael Heyward, *The Ern Malley Affair* (St. Lucia: University of Queensland Press, 1993).

26. See Michael Heyward, p. 137.

27. Heyward, p. 143.

28. Robert Hughes, "The Well-wrought Ern," introduction to Michael Heyward, *The Ern Malley Affair*, p. xvii.

29. There are similar effects in Darville's novel, first in the discussion about Heideggerian authenticity, and second in the passage about "lively peasant aubades" resounding on the killing fields.

30. Max Harris, "The Hoax," in *Ern Malley: Collected Poems* (Pymble: Angus and Robertson, 1993), p.16.

31. *Ern Malley's Journal*, vol. 1 (November, 1952), p. 6.

32. Composition board 122 x 122 cm., Art Gallery of South Australia.

33. Peter Anderson, in *Southern Review* 24 2 (1991), 121–131.

34. Ed. John Tranter and Philip Mead (Harmondsworth: Penguin, 1991), pp. 86–102.

35. Ibid., p. xxx.

36. A significant exception to the ban on consideration of authorial intention is the remark made by Helen Darville's teacher at the University of Queensland, Con Castan, that "those critics and theorists who want to dismiss authorial intention, should give themselves the experience of discussing, with a poet who can hold his or her own with you in critical dis-

cussion, poems by that poet" (*Dimitris Tsaloumas: Poet* [Melbourne: Elikia Books Publica-tions, 1990], p. x.

37. I adopt here Michael Heyward's astute observation (*The Ern Malley Affair*, p. 103).

38. Bruce Morrissette, *The Great Rimbaud Forgery: The Affair of "La Chasse Spirituelle"* (Washington, St. Louis: Washington University Press, 1956), p. 211.

39. "Voilà de quoi ternir pour longtemps la réputation de la critique!" Henri Pastoureau, cited in Morrisette, *The Great Rimbaud Forgery*, p. 151.

40. Heyward, p. 238.

41. Tanya Targett and Rory Callinan, "Author Lost the Plot, Says Tutor," *The Courier-Mail*, August 22, 1995, p. 6. Reprinted in *The Demidenko File*, p.128.

42. *The Sydney Morning Herald*, June 17, 1995, p. 11 (reprinted in *The Demidenko File*, p. 67).

43. Greg Roberts and Iris Makler, "A Fictional Life: the Fertile Mind of Helen Darville," *The Sydney Morning Herald*, August 26, 1995, p. 26 (reprinted in *The Demidenko File*, p. 214).

44. Gideon Haigh and Kate Legge, "Why the Whistle Was Finally Blown," *The Australian*, August 22, 1995, p. 11 (reprinted in *The Demidenko File*, p. 139).

45. Max Harris, "The Hoax," in *Ern Malley: Collected Poems* (Pymble: Angus and Robertson, 1993), p. 16. Interview between Patrick Condon and Michael Heyward, September 1, 1995.

46. Interview between Patrick Condon and Michael Heyward, September 1, 1995, *The Demidenko File*, p. 257.

47. *The Demidenko File*, p. 257.

48. Prior, p. 134.

49. *The Demidenko File*, p. 231.

50. See Adrian Mitchell, "After Demidenko: The Curling Papers," *Southerly* 56 (1996/7), p. 115.

51. The term is developed in Anderson's *Imagined Communities: Reflections on the Origins and Spread of Nationalism* (London: Verso, 1983).

52. His collaborator, Harold Stewart, emigrated to Japan, where he spent the rest of his life.

53. She has now entered law school with the plan of beginning a new career.

CHAPTER 10

Facts, Writing, and Problems of Memory in Memoir
*The Wilkomirski Case**

SUSAN RUBIN SULEIMAN

The French poet André Breton once wrote: "Life is other than what one writes."[1] He did not mean that writing is a lie, but rather, that writing is always one step behind or ahead of or next to the lived experience—all the more so when that experience took place decades ago. This essay will attempt to follow up on some of the theoretical implications of Breton's remark. What happens to the gap between facts and writing when the latter is concerned with issues of great collective significance such as the Holocaust? In what *kind* of writing do facts matter most, and why?

"Memory" and "memoir" are almost the same word in English, and are the same word in French: *mémoire*. But memory is a mental faculty, while memoir is a text. Although memoirs have no specific formal characteristics (other than those of autobiographical writing in general, which comes in many varieties), they all have at least one thing in common: A memoir relates "experiences that the writer has lived through."[2] Unlike a full-scale autobiography, a memoir can be confined to a single event or a single moment in a life. It need not be the work of an important person, nor does it have to be well written (though that helps). Its primary claim to our attention is not literariness, but

*This essay has been excerpted from a longer essay, "Problems of Memory and Factuality in Recent Holocaust Memoirs: Wilkomirski/Wiesel," in *Poetics Today*, volume 21, no. 3, pp. 543–559. Copyright 2000 by the Porter Institute for Poetics and Semiotics, Tel Aviv University. All rights reserved. Used by permission of the publisher.

factuality. In the novelist Anna Quindlen's words, "What really happened—that is the allure of memoir."[3] She adds almost immediately, however: "Fact is different from truth, and truth is different from insight . . . [W]ith few exceptions, . . . fiction tells the truth far better than personal experience does."

It may seem that Quindlen is suggesting fiction has no relation to personal experience, but her argument is just the opposite: Personal experience, when it is recounted in writing, veers almost inevitably toward fiction. The necessity for details that give the "feel of life" to narrated experience leads almost inevitably toward invention—which is why, as a former journalist who respects facts too much to invent them, Quindlen quips that she "will never write a memoir." In a more serious vein, she concludes: "I'm suspicious of memory itself . . . Memory is such a shapeshifter of a thing, so influenced by old photographs and old letters, self-image and self-doubt." Individual memories may merge with family mythologies, eventually taking on the feel of lived recollection. Quindlen's essay reminds us, in a pithy way, that the bedrock of factuality on which memoir rests (or is assumed to rest) is as fragile as memory itself.

Does that mean there are no significant differences between memoir and novel, between recollection and invention? No. Significant differences exist, but they are not so much textual as conventional or institutional.[4] Textually, a fiction can imitate any kind of speech act, including the act of imperfectly recollecting a personal past. We have a brilliant recent demonstration of it in W. G. Sebald's novel *The Emigrants*, whose narrator recalls fragments of his own past and seeks out the stories of dead relatives and acquaintances as they are recalled, incompletely and imperfectly, by those who knew them. Sebald even includes photographs in the book, a fascinating insertion of "the real" into a novel—but these photographs, apparently of real people long ago, highlight rather than efface the ontological difference between their historical subjects and the fictional characters whose stories they ostensibly illustrate.[5] In other words, novels can look and feel textually like memoirs. Is the opposite also true? One has but to look at the most successful memoir of the last few years, Frank McCourt's *Angela's Ashes*, to realize how close it is, *in its writing*, to a novel. Not only is McCourt's prose stylized, deploying a full range of rhetorical figures from anaphora to ellipsis to metaphor to onomatopoeia, but he also presents us with detailed dialogues that took place before his and even before his mother's birth! No reader can be unaware of such literary artifice and patterning—and yes, invention—in this work; yet *Angela's Ashes* is internationally recognized as a memoir, recounting events that really happened during the author's impoverished childhood in New York and Limerick.[6]

Textual traits, then, do not necessarily provide a criterion for distinguishing memoirs from novels written in the first person: the two genres look alike.[7] Yet the first question that any reader asks about a written narrative is: "Is it fiction or non-fiction?" And the way the work is read will largely be determined by the answer to that question. (Here as in some other domains, one finds parallels between genre and gender: despite psychological and biological demonstrations of the difficulty in drawing absolute lines between the sexes, the first question we still ask about a newborn child is: boy or girl?). There exists a conventional, institutional boundary between a work offered as memoir and a work offered as novel. Meir Sternberg, discussing the difference between fictional and historical narrative, puts it succinctly: "What kind of contract binds [writer and audience] together? What does the writer stand committed to? What is the audience supposed to assume?" In Sternberg's view (one he shares with many other theorists), the most important distinction between the two modes is that historical writing makes truth claims, whereas fictional writing is independent of such claims.[8] This distinction is conventional, not textual (many novels begin with a statement like: "I'm going to tell you my true story"). By conventional, I mean the set of implicit and explicit understandings that frame the publication and reception of any work, starting with the contract between author and publisher, proceeding with critical reception, and ending with the placing of the work on bookshelves of libraries and bookstores—and, in the case of a lucky few, in the columns of the *New York Times* bestseller list.

Memoirs resemble historical narratives insofar as they make truth claims—more exactly, claims to referentiality and verifiability—that put them on the other side of a boundary from novels. Interestingly, this conventional boundary becomes most apparent when it is violated, in cases of fraud or hoax. (Fraud or hoax does not refer to memoirs that "don't tell the whole truth"—few memoirs do; it refers, rather, to the work as a whole and its relation to the writer—this will become clearer in a moment.) Equally interestingly, the violation is felt as violation only in the direction from memoir to novel, not vice-versa. No one cares, particularly—except perhaps the author's friends and family—if a work billed as an "autobiographical novel" turns out to be straight autobiography. But if a memoir is shown to be fraudulent, because the person who claims to be recounting his or her experiences couldn't possibly have had those experiences or anything like them, then shock waves are created. All the more so if the experiences recounted are traumatic, whether in the framework of an individual life as in memoirs of sexual abuse, or in the framework of collective experience as in memoirs about war or genocide.

This brings me to the current, by now widely discussed case of Binjamin Wilkomirski and his book, *Fragments: Memories of a Wartime Childhood*.[9] Received with nearly universally hyperbolic praise when it first appeared in

Germany in 1995, and shortly thereafter in English and many other languages, *Fragments* presents itself as a memoir, specifically a Holocaust memoir written by a Jew who lived through horrendous experiences in extermination camps in Poland as a very young child. The memoir won several awards in the U.S. and abroad; its author, a Swiss musician and instrument maker whose first book this was, appeared in numerous official venues, and was the subject of documentaries and interviews as a Holocaust survivor. The story he tells in *Fragments* is that, the sole survivor of his family, he was smuggled out of a Krakow orphanage after the war and deposited in a children's home in Switzerland, from where he was adopted by a childless couple. Enjoined by all the adults around him to "forget the past," Wilkomirski explains in an Afterword that it took him many years to allow himself to speak or write about his memories. He likens himself to the hundreds of "children without identity" who survived the Holocaust "lacking any certain information about their origins, . . . furnished with false names and often with false papers too" (p. 154).

Fragments can be read as Wilkomirski's attempt to record the "shards of memory" that remained with him from his early childhood; and an attempt as well to show how those early memories continued to inflect his way of being in the world long after he had reached safety in Switzerland. Like *Angela's Ashes*, this is a highly stylized work: The decision to restrict the narrative perspective almost exclusively to the young boy allows for some very powerful effects. For example, when the boy first arrives in the Swiss home, he is left alone in the dining room, apparently just after the other children have had lunch. He is astonished to find that the tables have cloths and white plates, not the grey tin plates on bare wood that he is used to; when he goes closer, he is even more amazed: "The children hadn't eaten everything on their plates! They'd left bits in strips around the edges. These leftovers were all over everywhere, and apparently nobody was guarding them" (p. 21). He rushes to the table and begins to stuff the cheese rinds—for that is what they are—into his mouth and clothes:

> These stupid kids! I thought.
> How can anyone be dumb enough to leave food lying around unprotected? They don't seem to have a clue. Maybe they're new here, and they don't know yet that surviving means laying in supplies, finding a good hiding place, defending your food. Never ever leave food unguarded, that's what Jankl always told me. (p. 22).

When the workers at the home discover the child with his mouth full of garbage, they are disgusted: "Cheese rinds! He's eating cheese rinds! Monster!" (p. 23).

The clash of rules and world views between what the child had learned in order to survive in the camps and what he was expected to know in the

"normal" world afterward structures this memoir, and is rendere
what can only be called a masterful artistry.[10] Alternating between the
experiences during his first years in Switzerland and the earlier memo
they trigger (for example, the view of baskets heaped with fresh bread
the breakfast table triggers his one memory of his mother, who gave him
piece of dry bread on her deathbed in Majdanek), the narrative moves forward and back, producing new experiences and new memories but no new
understanding—until the final chapter, when the boy, already a senior in
high school, discovers that the war really is over. Watching a documentary
about the Nazi camps, he sees the liberation of Mauthausen by Allied
troops, and realizes that he is free and that he missed his own liberation.

Fragments is a powerful book, as most of its first readers agreed. But it
now appears certain that it is a fabrication, the work of a man who is not
who he says (and by all indications genuinely believes) he is; after more
than a year of doubt and controversy, the German and American publishers withdrew the book from the market.[11] As the story now stands,
Bruno Doesseker—for that was his legal name until he changed it to
Wilkomirski—was indeed an adopted child, but not one born in Latvia;
rather, he was the illegitimate son of a Swiss woman, Berthe Grosjean, who
gave him up for adoption but kept sufficiently in touch with him to leave
him a small inheritance when she died in 1981. Binjamin Wilkomirski is a
"found" name, chosen by Bruno Doesseker/Grosjean when he became
convinced of his "true identity" as a child survivor of the Holocaust. His
powerful memoir is based not on his experiences, but on his fantasies and
on the memories of others; before writing his book, Wilkomirski/
Doesseker/Grosjean had read thousands of testimonies and historical
works in his obsessive pursuit of a Holocaust identity.

This story, which reads like a psychological thriller, has already caused
much ink to flow and will probably continue to do so for some time.[12] It is
fascinating, existentially, historically, and in terms of narrative theory.
Here I will focus only on two questions, relating to problems of factuality
and of genre.

First, should we care whether Fragments is a memoir or a fabrication—
does it matter, finally, who Wilkomirski is and what the generic status of
his book is? I think it does matter, though perhaps not for the reasons that
may immediately come to mind. I am not overly worried, for example,
about the ammunition this book provides to the Holocaust deniers; the
deniers have already had their say, in an article circulated on the Internet
very soon after the story broke in 1998, "Des faussaires et des dupes" ("Of
frauds and of dupes") by Serge Thion, a well-known French negationist
and author of several negationist pamphlets.[13] Thion uses the familiar
negationist device of reasoning by synecdoche: If a single detail in a testimony is false, that renders the whole thing false; if a single testimony is a

nat renders all testimonies suspect. But we must resist such perni-
 reasoning by association: If Wilkomirski invented his memories, it
 s not follow that Elie Wiesel or Rudolf Vrba (both of whom Thion
 entions in his article) invented theirs.

Historians have never relied exclusively on survivor testimonies, and
even less so on a single testimony, in writing the history of the Holocaust.
This may seem obvious, but given the emotional stakes involved, it is
worth emphasizing. It does not mean that history has a privileged access to
"facts" whereas memoirs do not, merely that historians rely on multiple
sources and confront various kinds of documents in constructing their
versions of events. The constructedness of all narratives, including historical narratives, does not—as some people fear—undermine the historical
existence of past events. Ernst van Alphen, who espouses what can be
called a postmodernist view of Holocaust writing, including historiography (emphasizing the continuing reinterpretation and reframing of past
events in the present, as well as the inseparability of event from interpretive
framework even at the moment it is being experienced), insists, I think
rightly, that the *existence* of the Holocaust does not depend on individual
constructions: "If we are to make sense of the Holocaust, the ontological
question of the reality of the event—did it happen—must be firmly distinguished from the epistemological question of how we gain access to it."[14]
To admit the constructedness of all narratives, including histories and
memoirs, is not to renounce the distinction between invention and truth
claim. Memoirs, in their own way, make truth claims: "This is what happened, to the best of my recollection." But even if every memoir about the
Holocaust were to prove inaccurate in some details, that would still not
negate the Holocaust's historical existence.

Positivist historians sometimes fall into the trap of reasoning like the deniers: In an anecdote recounted by Dori Laub, a survivor witness of the attempted Auschwitz uprising (October 7, 1944), recalling her astonishment
at the event, mistakenly remembered seeing four chimneys burning when
in fact only one chimney had been on fire. According to Laub, the historians
at a conference who watched the videotaped testimony concluded that all of
it was unreliable: "Since the memory of the testifying woman turned out to
be, in this way, fallible, one could not accept—nor give credence to—her
whole account of the events. It was utterly important to remain accurate,
lest the revisionists in history discredit everything."[15] The historians were
no doubt right to insist on the documented facts about the uprising (which,
it should be noted, are based in large part on survivor testimonies, by
people who were more closely involved with the uprising[16]). However, the
value—and the particular truth—of this survivor's testimony was not necessarily diminished by the error in factual detail. A psychoanalyst at the

conference provided the interpretive frame: "The number [of chimneys set on fire] mattered less than the fact of the occurrence. The event itself [the uprising] was almost inconceivable. The woman testified to an event that broke the all compelling frame of Auschwitz . . . That was historical truth."[17] At this point, we might want to differentiate historical truth from factual detail, or introduce distinctions between various kinds of historical truth. In either case, the woman's account is not discredited as testimony to the *existence* of the Auschwitz uprising.

To return to our question, then—does the generic status of *Fragments* matter?—I believe it does, but not because the existence of the Holocaust is at stake.[18] Nor do I think that if *Fragments* were a genuine memoir, that would guarantee the factual accuracy of every memory recounted in the book. A memoir, whether it be a Holocaust memoir or any other kind, provides only a single mediated perspective on reality, not a direct, immediate apprehension of the "thing itself." Theorists of narrative as well as specialists in Holocaust writing have amply shown that no first-person narrative is "untouched by figuration and by shaping."[19] To believe in "the absolute authority given to first person testimony," writes Michael-André Bernstein, is to give credence to "one of the most pervasive myths of our era" (p. 47).

I agree with Bernstein on that point. It does not imply, however, that categorical distinctions don't matter. Contemporary thought is fascinated by borderlines, those areas where boundaries begin to blur; but boundary blurrings can exist only because categories do. And of all the categories in our lives, those of fact and fiction, with their various literary equivalents such as memoir or novel, remain—despite our theoretical sophistication about the constructed nature of representation, and even of perception—very strong.

Some contemporary writers play on those categories, mixing and twisting them in various ways; but such self-conscious playing does not do away with conventional designations—on the contrary, it maintains them. The French novelist Alain Robbe-Grillet includes in his autobiography a character named Henri de Corinthe, who is clearly fictional. The autobiography still functions as autobiography, however, with some novelistic "nuggets" in it.[20] A more interestingly ambiguous case is Georges Perec's *W ou le souvenir d'enfance* (*W or The Childhood Memory*), which consists of two parallel narratives told in alternating chapters: a science-fiction narrative about the island of W, which finally turns out to be an allegory of the Nazi death camps, and a memoir about Perec's childhood in wartime France. Although both narratives have first-person narrators, the fictional "I" and the autobiographical "I" are differentiated: The appearance of Perec's name is a clear textual indicator in the autobiographical sections, while the nonrealist mode of the science-fiction segments indicates fictional discourse. Since the book contains an equal number of chapters devoted to each, it could be said to be a hybrid. But I think it is more accurate to consider it a combination, with its component parts juxtaposed, rather than a hybrid that merges them. The overall effect of the work depends on this juxtaposition, with the reader constantly "shuttling" from one world to the other, and wondering what the relation between them is.

Unlike Perec's and Robbe-Grillet's, Wilkomirski's book does not *play* with categories—it obfuscates them, which is not the same thing. The problem with *Fragments*, as a text, is precisely that it does not recognize— or at any rate, does not admit—its own fictionality.

This leads to my second question: Is the solution to the problem simply to relabel the work, move it from "memoir" to "novel"? Or does it, rather, belong in another category, that of the discredited or false memoir? Given the highly crafted nature of this work, one can well argue for keeping it in print under a new label as fiction.[21] But if we take Wilkomirski's own affirmed commitment to referentiality seriously, we must hesitate to call his book a novel. In his Afterword (which, Elena Lappin reports, was included in the book because the German publisher had received a letter denouncing it and had asked Wilkomirski for an explanation), Wilkomirski states that the official identity papers he possesses have "nothing to do with either the history of this century or my personal history" (p. 154). In a newspaper interview given in September 1998, replying to Ganzfried's accusations, Wilkomirski suggested that the official document was forged by Swiss authorities after the war, just as in the case of other "children without identity."[22] According to the *New York Times*, even when confronted by the historian Stefan Mächler's report, which caused the German publisher to withdraw the book, the author "declared defiantly, 'I am Binjamin Wilkomirski.' "

Using the criterion of truth claim, therefore, we must call *Fragments* not a novel but a false—or better, a deluded—memoir. The question is, what happens to such works once they have been uncovered? Lappin mentions an earlier Holocaust memoir that was subsequently shown to be fiction, Martin Gray's *For Those I Loved*: Gray's book is now cited "only on revisionist websites."[23] It would seem that a false memoir does not, by virtue of its falsity, automatically convert into fiction. More often than not, it converts into oblivion.[24]

But there is a factor we have not sufficiently considered yet: Whatever else it might claim to be, *Fragments* is a work of literary art, powerful in its effect. Does it deserve to fall into oblivion? Tzvetan Todorov, in an essay aptly titled "Fictions and Truths," tells a story that bears an uncanny resemblance to Wilkomirski's, even though it happened almost three hundred years ago. A hugely popular book published in London in 1704 and immediately translated into French, *Description de l'île de Formose en Asie*, purportedly an eye-witness account by a native of the island who offered lurid descriptions of its cannibalistic religious practices (among other exotica), turned out to be a fake: "Today we know with certainty that the *Description* is a fraud, that Psalmanazar [the author] was never in China and that his real name wasn't even Psalmanazar"—this could be about Wilkomirski! But there is a major difference, which Todorov invokes in concluding his discussion of this work: "As a piece of historical writing, Psalmanazar's *Description* deserves no respect, because it is a fake. As a piece of fiction, it does not command admiration, because it does not present itself as a fiction and because its author lacks eloquence."[25]

Although Todorov lumps them together, self-designation and eloquence are independent categories. Wilkomirski's book, too, "does not present itself as a fiction," but its author does not lack eloquence. What then? Todorov answers this question by invoking a completely different oeuvre, written two hundred years before Psalmanazar's fake: Amerigo Vespucci's letters about his voyages to the New World, *Mundus novus* and *Quatuor navigatones*. Todorov shows that these accounts too had problems: They were clearly full of fabulation and may not even have been written by Vespucci—but they were artful and compelling, and earned their presumed author (who really did travel in the New World, at least that much is certain) "a continent" named after him! If they offered few truths about "American reality," they did offer truths, by their very artfulness, about the "European imagination" of the time. (Earlier, Todorov proposed a distinction between "vérité-adéquation," or truth corresponding to facts, and "vérité-dévoilement," truth that reveals or unveils—the latter being presumably a function of literary skill).

Might we salvage Wilkomirski's deluded memoir by treating it as a compelling piece of writing that "unveils" truths about the *effects* of the Holocaust on the contemporary imagination? Trauma, horror, a sense of absolute victimhood: It appears that the Holocaust has become, in today's Europe and America, the ultimate signifier of such torments, even for those who have no personal connection to that past event. James Young has written persuasively about Sylvia Plath's poetic identification with the "Holocaust Jew," and the ethical and interpretive problems it poses. Plath was criticized, by Irving Howe and other Jewish critics, for her use of the Holocaust as a metaphor for personal suffering; the incommensurability of the two terms was, they argued, a trivialization of that collective event. Young, while recognizing and even sharing that criticism, nevertheless concluded that "to remove the Holocaust from the realm of the imagination . . . is to risk excluding it altogether from public consciousness. . . . Better abused memory in this case, which might then be critically qualified, than no memory at all."[26] Wilkomirski's book presents an extreme version of this problem, a literalization of Plath's metaphors as well as of her self-identification as a "Holocaust Jew." Being an extreme case, *Fragments* poses certain questions starkly: Where does literature end (or begin) and psychopathology begin (or end)? Where should the line be drawn— should the line be drawn—between personal memory and imagined or "borrowed" memory? To whom does the memory of the Holocaust belong? The fact that *Fragments* raises these questions, powerfully, may be reason enough for its continued presence in our literary landscape—if not as a memoir (it is not that), and not as a novel (it is not that either, at least not yet), then at least as a "case."

Notes

1. André Breton, *Nadja*, trans. Richard Howard (New York: Grove Press, 1960), p. 71.
2. This is the main definition given in *The American Heritage Dictionary of the English Language*.
3. Anna Quindlen, "How Dark? How Stormy? I Can't Recall," *The New York Times Book Review*, May 11, 1997, p. 35. All subsequent quotes from this article refer to this page.
4. The question of fictional versus historical narrative is one of the oldest in literary theory, discussed both by Plato and Aristotle and by hundreds of theorists since then. For a concise and thorough recent overview of the various meanings attributed to the term "fiction," see Dorrit Cohn, *The Distinction of Fiction* (Baltimore: Johns Hopkins University Press, 1999), ch. 1. Cohn's definition of fiction (following Paul Ricoeur's in his magisterial study *Temps et récit*) as "nonreferential narrative" is one I subscribe to, on the whole. I do not agree with Cohn, however, that fictional narrative is "ruled by formal patterns that are ruled out in all other orders of discourse" (p. vii).
5. W. G. Sebald, *The Emigrants*, trans. Michael Hulse (New York: New Directions, 1996).
6. McCourt has recounted in recent interviews that travel tours are being organized to visit the sites in Limerick immortalized in his memoir. This bears out the referential appeal of his book—but just to complicate matters, in St. Petersburg, tourists can visit both the house where Dostoevsky wrote *Crime and Punishment* and, in the same neighborhood, the house where his fictional creation Raskolnikov killed the old pawnbroker . . . (One interview where McCourt describes the Limerick tours appeared in a Swiss paper, *Sonntagszeitung*, September 9, 1998).
7. Narratologists, following the lead of Philippe Lejeune's classic work on autobiography, *Le pacte autobiographique* (Paris: Seuil, 1975), propose a single decisive textual criterion: If the proper name of the narrator-protagonist is identical with that of the author on the book's cover, the work is autobiography, not fiction. But many works do not tell us the narrator's name, and some contemporary writers have taken pleasure in playing with the criterion itself—whence the genre that Serge Doubrovsky has dubbed "autofiction," where the narrator-hero's name is identical to the author's but the work is presented as a novel. A highly autobiographical novel, to be sure—see, for example, Doubrovsky, *Le livre brisé* (Paris: Grasset, 1989).
8. Meir Sternberg, *The Poetics of Biblical Narrative* (Bloomington: Indiana University Press, 1985), p. 26. This view (expressed in varying terminologies) is shared by Cohn, Ricoeur, and others. Christopher Ricks, going one step further, argues that even in novels, factual accuracy about historical events, places, or people is important to the reading experience. Here one might want to invoke Sternberg's distinction between truth-claim and truth-value, the latter referring to factual *accuracy* (as opposed to "commitment"). For Ricks, factual inaccuracies mar the reader's experience even of a novel, especially a realist novel— assuming, of course, that the reader "catches" the inaccuracy. (See Christopher Ricks, "Literature and the Matter of Fact," University Lecture, Boston University, October 30, 1990, p. 22. I thank John Silber for informing me about this essay).
9. Binjamin Wilkomirski, *Fragments: Memories of a Wartime Childhood*, trans. Carol Brown Janeway (New York: Schocken Books), 1996.

10. Although some of the first reviewers (such as Robert Hanks in *The Independent*, Dec. 8, 1996, p. 31) mentioned the book's self-conscious artistry, others (e.g., Susannah Heschel in *Tikkun*, March 13, 1997, p. 73) praised its absence of "artifice" and its "unpretentious recounting of a child's inner life." Jonathan Kozol, while aware of the book's "stunning and austerely written" quality, considered it "free from literary artifice of any kind at all" (*The Nation*, Oct. 28, 1996). The equation of "lack of artifice" with authenticity—and, conversely, of "artifice" with inauthenticity—is symptomatic of the factual appeal of memoir. "Artifice" in this context appears to mean "tampering with the facts" in order to achieve literary effects.

11. See Doreen Carjaval, "Disputed Holocaust Memoir Withdrawn," *New York Times*, October 14, 1999; and "Publisher Drops Holocaust Book," *New York Times*, Nov. 3, 1999). The book was published by Suhrkamp Verlag in Germany and by Schocken Books in the U.S. The first published accusation against Wilkomirski appeared in August, 1998, in an article by the Swiss journalist Bruno Ganzfried, based on documents as well as interviews with people who had known Wilkomirski as a child ("Die Geliehene Holocaust-Biographie," *Weltwoche*, August 27, 1998). After replies by Wilkomirski and others, Ganzfried wrote two more articles in the same newspaper, repeating his charges: "Fakten gegen Erinnerung," September 3, 1998, and "Bruchstücke und Scherbenhaufen," September 24, 1998. The matter was complicated by the fact that Ganzfried himself had published, in 1995, a Holocaust novel based on his father's experiences that did not have anywhere near the success of *Fragments*. Wilkomirski continued vehemently to deny the charges; his publishers, as well as some specialists who had worked with child survivors or who had met Wilkomirski in person, continued to defend the status of his work as a memoir. Others, however—including the distinguished historian of the Holocaust Raoul Hilberg—claimed that from the start they had doubted the work's authenticity. The document that provoked the book's withdrawal was the report prepared by a historian, Stefan Mächler, who had been charged by Wilkomirski's literary agent with investigating the matter. See Mächler, *The Wilkomirski Affair: A Study in Biographical Truth*, translated from the German by John E. Woods (New York: Schocken, 2001).

12. Aside from many articles in the European and American press, the most thorough version of Wilkomirski/Doesseker's story to date is by Elena Lappin, "The Man with Two Heads," *Granta* 66 (1999), pp. 9–65. Another compelling version, which arrives at similar conclusions, is Philip Gourevitch's "The Memory Thief," *The New Yorker*, June 14, 1999, pp. 48–68.

13. The sender of this Internet article (message dated October 10, 1998), gives its name as "Le Temps Irréparable," with the e-mail address: tempus@flash.net.

14. Ernst van Alphen, *Caught by History: Holocaust Effects in Contemporary Art, Literature, and Theory* (Stanford: Stanford University Press, 1997), p. 64.

15. Dori Laub, "Bearing Witness or The Vicissitudes of Listening," in Shoshana Felman and Dori Laub, *Testimony: Crises of Witnessing in Literature, Psychoanalysis, and History* (New York: Routledge, 1992), pp. 59–60.

16. For a detailed historical account, see Martin Gilbert, *The Holocaust: A History of the Jews of Europe during the Second World War* (New York: Henry Holt & Co., 1985), chap. 38. For indications of other sources besides survivor testimonies, see Danuta Czech, *Auschwitz Chronicle 1939–1945. From the Archives of the Auschwitz Memorial and the German Federal Archives* (New York: Henry Holt, 1990).

17. Laub, "Bearing Witness," p. 60.

18. Obviously, subjects of huge collective importance magnify problems of factuality as well as of genre; it is because *Fragments* purports to be a Holocaust memoir that it has elicited so much attention—but its inauthenticity does not undermine the existence of the Holocaust, as some commentators have argued. For a further discussion about facts in memoir, concerning the Aubrac "affair" in France, see my "Reflections on Memory at the Millennium," Presidential Address of the American Comparative Literature Association, *Comparative Literature*, 51:3 (Summer 1999).

19. Michael-André Bernstein, *Foregone Conclusions: Again Apocalyptic History* (Berkeley: University of California Press), 1994), p. 47. See also Sidra Ezrahi, "Representing Auschwitz," *History and Memory*, 7:2 (Fall 1996), pp. 121–164; James Young, *Writing and Rewriting the Holocaust: Narratives and the Consequences of Interpretation* (Bloomington: Indiana University Press, 1988); and, more generally, Paul John Eakin, *Fictions in Autobiography: Studies in the Art of Self-Invention* (Princeton: Princeton University Press, 1985).

20. A. Robbe-Grillet, *Le miroir qui revient* (Paris: Eds. de Minuit, 1984). In the subsequent volumes of what became an autobiographical trilogy, *Angélique ou l'enchantement* (Paris: Eds. de Minuit, 1987) and especially *Les derniers jours de Corinthe* (Paris: Eds. de Minuit, 1994), the fictional element became ever stronger and the mixing of genres more self-consciously explicit and thematized.

21. Arthur Samuelson, the American publisher at Schocken, told Elena Lappin in early 1999: "It's only a fraud if you call it non-fiction. I would then reissue it, in the fiction category" (Lappin, "The Man with Two Heads," p. 49). In November 1999, however, when the book was withdrawn from the market, there was no mention of reissuing it as fiction—but the American edition is now back in print.

22. "Niemand muss mir Glauben schenken," *Tages Anzeiger*, Sept. 1, 1998, p. 51.

23. Lappin, p. 49. The quote here is actually from a statement by Gary Mokotoff, a member of the board of the Jewish Book Council in the U.S., which awarded *Fragments* its nonfiction prize in 1995. Mokotoff states that he knew from the start the book was "historical fiction," and "would never have won in the Holocaust category." Presumably, he was not on the jury that awarded the prize.

24. Wilkomirski's case bears striking similarities to a *cause célèbre* of about a decade ago, *The Education of Little Tree*, which was purportedly an autobiography by a Native American and was praised for its authenticity—but turned out instead to have been the work of a white supremacist. Henry Louis Gates, Jr., reflecting on the *Little Tree* case, cites other examples of fraudulent autobiographies, notably some nineteenth-century slave narratives, which proved to be an embarrassment to their first publishers and promoters. Gates argues that "authenticity" is a category easy to fake, and suggests that the difference between factual and fictional writing may be ultimately imposssible to maintain. Even if all that is granted, I believe the categories continue to function. (See Gates, " 'Authenticity,' or the Lesson of Little Tree," *New York Times Book Review*, November 14, 1991.)

25. Todorov, "Fictions et vérités," in *Les morales de l'histoire* (Paris: Grasset & Fasquelle, 1991), p. 141; my translation. Like Wilkomirski's book, Psalmanazar's *Description* was challenged even before it was published: Members of the Royal Academy suspected him of fraud, but the book was published anyway and enjoyed several years of notoriety. The issue of Psalmanazar's identity was finally laid to rest by the author himself, in his *Memoirs* published after his death (1764). Of course, one may wonder about the reliability of this work as well.

26. James E. Young, *Writing and Rewriting the Holocaust: Narrative and the Consequences of Interpretation* (Bloomington: Indiana University Press, 1988), p. 133.

CHAPTER 11

The Fascination of a Fake
The Hitler Diaries

ERIC RENTSCHLER

When Adolf Hitler appeared "live," what did the German masses see and hear? Now that Hitler is no longer alive, what is left of him? I want to reconsider the often noted fascination of his presence as well as the lasting presence of his fascination. Hitler remains, in historian H. R. Trevor-Roper's words, "a frightening mystery."[1] To speak of Hitler, I wish to suggest, is above all to speak about an entity that, in crucial regards, was never all there. Let us explore the problematic continuing fascination of Hitler, a fascination, that is—and indeed in large measure was—the fascination of a fake.

Scenes from a Debacle

During the course of 1982, Richard Hugo's novel, *The Hitler Diaries*, arrived in American bookstores. In this thriller the secret journals of Hitler's valet suddenly surface in New York. They contain lurid details about the dictator's sex life, accounts of clandestine meetings and confidential dealings. A second diary appears; it is from 1942 and allegedly in Hitler's own hand. Publisher Magruder and his partner, Hirsch, contemplate whether they should publish this document even though they suspect its provenance to be dubious:

"You could try finding out whether it's authentic."

"I think I know the answer to that one. It may be more interesting to discover just how good a fake it is. But then what? . . . It still beats every book on record I ever heard of."

"Let's say we can persuade people the diaries are genuine: then what do we have?" He thought for a minute and then said, "You know, if I had to think of a book that everybody in the world would want to read, then this would be it."[2]

Hugo's pulp fiction was, for all its bad taste and commercial sensationalism, bizarrely prescient; it soon found itself in competition with the breaking developments of a strikingly similar news story.

On April 22, a press release from the prominent West German weekly magazine, *Stern*, caused an international sensation. The magazine announced that one of its reporters had discovered Hitler's diaries, precisely those pages, in Hugo's words, "that everybody in the world would want to read." On April 28, the cover of *Stern*, proclaimed "Hitler's Diaries Discovered" ("Hitlers Tagebücher entdeckt"). The headline appeared in large red letters over an image of black volumes, the top one of which bore the initials "FH." These materials, the subsequent text triumphantly declared, promised extraordinary revelations about a host of matters, including Hess's wartime flight to Scotland, Hitler's attitude toward Ernst Röhm and Neville Chamberlain, his private thoughts about the Kristallnacht and the Holocaust, and his relations with Eva Braun. After the publication of the diaries, boasted *Stern*, "the biography of the dictator, and with it the history of the Nazi state, would have to be in large part written anew." It was, as the *Daily Mail* put it, a *coup de théâtre*, as if "Hitler had suddenly thrust an arm out of the grave."[3]

Intrepid ace reporter Gerd Heidemann was responsible for the remarkable discovery of some sixty volumes whose pages allegedly contained extensive entries in Hitler's hand from June 22, 1932 to mid–April 1945. Heidemann, it must be noted, was known by his colleagues to be an odd personage, indeed something of a loose cannon. He was an ardent collector of Third Reich memorabilia and an enthusiastic camp follower of Nazi luminaries. Two SS generals had officiated at his wedding; he had spent his honeymoon looking for war criminals in South America. He maintained that he possessed a recent photograph of Martin Bormann and averred that he could prove that there had been secret wartime negotiations between Churchill and Mussolini. During his investigations, Heidemann claimed to have been offered a veritable archive of sensational materials, including a handwritten third volume of *Mein Kampf*, Hitler's written plan for the "Final Solution," a book detailing the dictator's experiences with women, the leader's notes from the final days in the bunker, documents about his supposed French son, books on Frederick the Great and King Ludwig II as well as an opera, *Wieland the Blacksmith*, which the young Hitler had supposedly co-authored (Harris, 245–246).

Stern officials repeatedly assured the public that the diaries had under gone extensive verification by handwriting experts; no one less than the highly regarded British historian Trevor-Roper had enthusiastically confirmed their authenticity. To be sure, Trevor-Roper would quickly take back his words. The examinations of the diaries, it soon became apparent, had been at best cursory. Responses that called the documents into question had either been disregarded or overruled by the *Stern* editors. A full and careful laboratory test had in fact not taken place prior to the immodest public announcement. A forensic scientist could have easily and quickly established that the diaries were patently false.

The media circus after the initial announcement soon escalated into a grand-scale travesty. On May 6, a long-anticipated report from the West German Federal Archive was presented to grim *Stern* lawyers. The findings were devastating. Chemical tests in Wiesbaden and Berlin revealed that the paper used for the diaries was from the 1950s. The binding, glue, and thread, likewise, contained chemicals of postwar origin. Beyond these material insufficiencies, both the quantity and the actual substance of these documents were judged to be altogether meager. Each of the sixty volumes ran an average of only one thousand words. Konrad Kujau, the fabricator of the Hitler diaries and an energetic confidence man of long standing, had not taken even rudimentary precautions. Working out of his home office in Waiblingen, he wrote the diaries in ordinary school notebooks. The initials used for the diary covers were purchased in Hong Kong.

Subsequent scrutiny made it all the more apparent just how crude, clumsy, and transparent Kujau's acts of counterfeit had been. To create headed stationery he used Letraset; to age documents he poured tea over them. His spelling and grammar were faulty (Harris, 112) and the texts abounded with factual errors. What Kujau lacked in precision, however, he made up in energy and boldness. Writing with an unfailingly certain hand, he could complete an entire diary in about four and a half hours. His privileged source was a two-volume edition of Hitler's speeches and proclamations, a daily compilation of the leader's activities from 1932 to 1945 published in 1962 by the German historian, Max Domarus.[4] Laboring under pressure and with the incentive of escalating payments for each new novel, Kujau, as Robert Harris reports, "resorted to wholesale plagiarism, copying out page after page from Domarus. The Hitler Diaries—the object of one of the most extravagant 'hypes' in the history of journalism—were for the most part nothing more interesting than a tedious recital of official engagements and Nazi party announcements" (Harris, 167). There were, to be sure, a few private observations as well. A sample passage from June 1941 reads: "On Eva's wishes, I am thoroughly examined by my doctors. Because of the new pills, I have violent flatulence, and—says Eva—bad reath." For entries like this, Harris estimates, *Stern* paid the equivalent of fifty pounds a word (Harris, 169).

Stern had invested several years and over nine million marks in the Hitler diaries. In what can only be described as a demonstration of group psychosis (Harris, 138), the members of the staff had let themselves be seduced by the prospect that they had privileged access to the inner workings of Hitler's mind. Their poor judgment was, without a doubt, a consequence of a credulity fueled by greed and ambition. Extensive plans for publication throughout the world had been hammered out; intensive negotiations with a host of international media agencies had taken place; and, to be sure, enormous profits had been expected. At a certain point no one at *Stern* or at its publisher Gruner und Jahr wanted to consider—or dared to acknowledge—that the diaries were not the real thing. The entire affair caused the magazine great embarrassment and a significant loss of prestige and circulation. Most of the main players in the scandal were forced to resign.

The debacle unfolded in the shadow of the 50th anniversary of the Nazi rise to power. It was an extension of a new *Hitlerwelle*, a widespread renascence of interest in the leader, the Third Reich, period regalia, and Nazi images. The "Hitler Wave" spanned a variety of sites, from television series to pornographic movies and arthouse films, from glossy magazine spreads to scholarly endeavors, from far-fetched novels to serious dramas. The Hitler diaries thus were no anomaly; they were simply the most conspicuous products of a world-wide apparatus that sustained still resonant wishes to behold the German leader. Ever since reports of his death in a Berlin bunker, Hitler has remained the continuing object of imaginative conjecture and popular lore. Take, for instance, the inventory of often-posed questions enumerated by the American historian Alvin Rosenfeld: "Did he really die in the bunker? Is it true that he left behind a son? Are there surviving letters or diaries that will at last unlock the secret nature of the man and his ambition? Was he cruel or gentle with Eva Braun? Are his followers today planning to establish a Fourth Reich to rule the world according to his ideas?"[5] Enthusiasts fixated on the Hitler diaries with a fetishistic abandon, thinking that these entries might bring them closer to the Nazi leader. These ostensible secret documents were, if anything, both a creation of and an answer to public desires.

Hitler's Diaries—The Film

The *Stern* debacle of 1983 was dramatized almost a decade later by director Helmut Dietl in *Schtonk*, the most expensive German production since Wolfgang Petersen's *Das Boot*. (Schtonk is the pet phrase of Chaplin's Great Dictator; it is a variation on the German "Schtunk" which comes from Yiddish and means a terrible mess ["eine riesengroße Sauerei"]). The film received numerous State Film Prizes; it was also nominated for Golden Globe and American Academy awards as the Best Foreign Film of 1992. Featuring an ensemble of well-known German actors (including Götz George, Heiner Lauterbach, Uwe Ochsenknecht, Rolf Hoppe, Harald Juhnke, Christine Hörbiger, and Veronica Ferres), it presented a fictional reenactment of the affair. The narrative divided its attentions between a shameless picaro forger and a frenzied mercenary reporter, a fraud and a dupe who become collaborators, indeed an odd couple. Dietl's scenario (which he co-authored with Ulrich Limmer) had an acerbic tone and a satirical resolve. He meant to chronicle a comedy of errors and to disclose the collective loss of reality which had made the bizarre fiasco possible. Much of what happened during the scandal, claimed Dietl, was "so absurd and grotesque" that it seemed like the function of a poorly written screenplay.[6]

Dietl's film begins with a flashback to Berlin during the closing hours of World War II. As is so often the case in retrospective visions of the Third Reich, we see an obligatory inventory of period signifiers. The credits flash by in an echo chamber from the past. We listen to the fanfare that preceded special reports (*Sondermeldungen*) followed by a station identification and the announcement, "Hitler is once again in our midst, the Führer will now speak." A swift montage from a sonic archive ensues: marching boots, a Wagnerian flourish, party marches, Hitler speeches, and the voices of other political luminaries. As ever, our sense of the Nazi past is mediated by Nazi representations. We gain access to the Berlin of April 1945 by means of Nazi sights and sounds.

The soundtrack segues seamlessly to a song by the famous diva, Zarah Leander, "Davon geht die Welt nicht unter" ("That Won't Bring the World Down"), the signature tune from the box-office hit of 1942, *Die große Liebe* (*The Great Love*). The song accompanies documentary images from Berlin, April 1945, shots of tumbling bombs and shattered buildings, of anti-aircraft guns catapulting fireballs into the night. One might be tempted to see ironic intention behind this mixture of aerial warfare and aural distraction. This blend both mimics and reiterates Nazi Germany's own instrumentalization of mass culture for the purposes of mass mobilization. Songs like Zarah Leander's performed a double duty: They diverted German audiences from the war while heightening the war experience. "Davon geht die Welt nicht unter" and *Die große Liebe* became integral parts of a larger German combat spectacle, both cushioning and intensifying the collective experience of danger. The scene also provides images that aestheticize the ordeal of armed conflict, choreographing it as an impressive phantasmagoria through expressive contrasts between dark silhouettes in profile and bright search lights in the background. Repeatedly a bursting bomb will give way to an empty image, creating a *tabula rasa* in which the visual pyrotechnics of the battleground become one with the projective space of the cinema.

We move from the wartime footage to a studio simulation in a smooth and seamless cut. Figures scurrying across the frame to the right taken from a newsreel camera spill into a perfectly matched shot filmed in the Bavaria Studio, a transition edited so skillfully that the viewer easily overlooks the leap of registers. This film about an act of forgery thus begins with its own act of forgery in which Nazi footage is extended and prosthetically enhanced. These newsreels were of course instruments of war shot by propaganda companies and functionalized as sources of public misinformation. The reenactment of 1992 replicates images whose truth status was manifestly specious, foregrounding the act of forgery before our very eyes in the invisible cut between an image caught by a Nazi newsreel camera and a shot staged in a postwar studio.

The opening sequence concludes with yet further instances of forgery. We behold Hitler's dead body and cannot help but be reminded of the Chaplin figure from *The Great Dictator* (1940). Dietl's deceased Führer is more and less than an illusion. As a body double, he is a double body, a stand-in at once for Germany's Hitler and Hollywood's Herr Hynkel.[7] The leader appears as a prop from a slapstick movie, dragged from the bunker by two soldiers, put into a bomb crater so that he can be incinerated. But this puppet resists easy disposal. A match is lit, but Hitler's body refuses to ignite. "He won't burn, Colonel," reports a desparate minion. "Who?" "The Führer. And Frau Braun. She won't burn either." "Douse them with petrol," screams the officer, "they'll burn then." Petrol is tossed over the two bodies, another match is lit, and a grand explosion ensues. The image once again goes blank and gives way to what appears to be grainy footage. In a subsequent mock biography of the film's master forger, a take-off on the "News on the March" sequence from *Citizen Kane*, we see scratches on the image, further attempts to simulate material of older vintage, quite in keeping with the character's subsequent artificial endeavors to date his forged diaries. The opening sequence of *Schtonk* offers a quite appropriate preview of coming attractions: Its point of departure involves multiple cinematic feats of forgery.

The History of a Mediated Presence

Like the Stern affair, *Schtonk* derives from and depicts a world that, for all its avowed critical distance from the Third Reich, literally buys and sells swastikas and openly relishes the Nazi past. Hitler and the whole era, a character in Don DeLillo's *Running Dog* observes, are "endlessly fascinating . . . People can't get enough."[8] The enterprising reporter of *Schtonk*, like his historical counterpart, refurbishes Göring's yacht, proudly donning the minister's bathrobe and bedding the Reichmarschall's niece. One elaborately choreographed sequence (clearly deferent to Roman Polanski's *The Fearless Vampire Killers*) shows old Nazi dignitaries and their sympathizers celebrating Hitler's birthday in an ornate castle.

Schtonk sought to intervene against the contemporary Hitler industry in the form of a screwball comedy. Some of it was witty and amusing; much of it was, as German critics have argued, inappropriate and in questionable taste. *Schtonk* nonetheless acutely recognizes that Hitler comes to us above all as a function of the media (the film's first words are "Here is the Radio of Greater Germany"). His legacy constitutes a site of curiosity and desire and, as such, abides as the continuing object of wide attention and commercial speculation. The forger Knobel (the film's counterpart for Kujau) is nothing less than the embodiment of a free market economy that supplies consumer demand for Führer-related artifacts.[9]

Hitler's afterlife is a thorny province of discussion and debate, in Ron Rosenbaum's assessment, "a terra incognita of ambiguity and incertitude where armies of scholars clash in evidentiary darkness over the spectral shadows of Hitler's past and the maddening obscurities of his psyche."[10] An often repeated concern of these exchanges involves the mass-mediation and mass-marketing of Hitler. In the mind of Alvin Rosenfeld, Hitler has evolved into a fiction and a phantasm divorced from historical fact. What dominates our attention today (above and beyond scholarly debates), he avers, is a mythological Hitler, a fantasy figure who has become synonymous with power, pornography, and madness. Hitler, he notes, "has become a kind of silly putty in the hands of postwar fictioneers, who stretch him this way and that, devising as many shapes from his memory as the motive for metaphor will allow."[11]

Popularized and commodified, representations of Hitler abound in postmodern mass culture. Nazi icons circulate as floating signifiers and mythical entities in countless postwar images, plays, stories, songs, and films. These acts of recoding are for Rosenfeld primarily a function of fascination, "fascination that is relentlessly unhistorical and hence an easy trigger for fantasies of the most extreme kind."[12] Such transformations are dangerous for they diminish and destroy the integrity of memory. Indeed, a pornography of the Third Reich may well undermine history lessons about National Socialism and the Holocaust.

Saul Friedländer shares Rosenfeld's moral concern. Initially, claims Friedländer, the Nazi past was indicted and castigated. By the end of the 1960s, images of that past underwent a dramatic change throughout the Western world. Attention shifted from memories of Hitler's horror and violence to visions of his banality and everydayness, of his love of sweets, dogs, and dirndls. In books like Albert Speer's *Spandauer Tagebücher* (*Inside the Third Reich*, 1975), films such as Joachim Fest's *Hitler, eine Karriere*

(*Hitler—A Career*, 1977) and Hans Jürgen Syberberg's tetralogy, *Hitler, ein Film aus Deutschland* (*Our Hitler*, 1978), the German leader bears a double aspect. He is both a petit bourgeois and a superhuman force, the object of sympathy and terror, a function of kitsch and death.[13] "Thus," submits Friedländer,

> We are here confronted with the two sides of Hitler: that of yesterday and that of today: with the facts and with their reinterpretation; with reality and with its aestheticization. On the one hand, the approachable human being, Mr. Everyman enveloped in kitsch; on the other, that blind force launched into nothingness. Each side did attract, and, for some, as I try to show, the attraction continues to operate today. The coexistence of these two aspects, their juxtaposition, their simultaneous and alternating presence is, it seems to me, the true source of this spell."[14]

Reflections on National Socialism, even serious and scholarly ones, unwittingly become reflections of National Socialism—a fascination recreated. This for Friedländer is the troubling mark of a New Discourse about Hitler and the Third Reich. "What is uncanny about the new fascination with Hitler," submits Rosenfeld, "is its resemblance—often recognizable in impulse, idiom, tone, and direction—to the fascination of the 1930s and 1940s."[15]

Susan Sontag had articulated a similar uneasiness in her famous essay, "Fascinating Fascism." Here, as we recall, she scrutinized the celebration of Nazi aesthetics by contemporary appropriators, by formalists or camp enthusiasts. People are drawn to the beauty of the images Leni Riefenstahl created in *Der Triumph des Willen* (*The Triumph of the Will*) and *Olympia*, but they do not adequately reflect on the human and historical consequences of these films. "Without a historical perspective, such connoisseurship prepares the way for a curiously absentminded acceptance of propaganda for all sorts of destructive feelings—feelings whose implications people are refusing to take seriously."[16]

Rosenfeld's, Friedländer's, and Sontag's critiques are, without question, accurate and well warranted. In my mind, however, their interventions, no matter how incisive, remain in a crucial regard shortsighted. Hitler did not suddenly become dehistoricized in the course of the postwar era. He in fact arose from the Weimar era as a distraction and a special effect; his privileged space was a mediated performance that seized the moment and freely disposed over the past in accordance with the needs of the present. For this reason, we might rethink Susan Sontag's notion of "fascinating fascism." What is fascinating—as well as seductive and dangerous—about representations like *Triumph of the Will* are their patent falseness. A rather unimposing and unattractive man became transformed by modern machinery into a captivating leader and a mass celebrity.

At first Hitler employed the live speech as his essential means of propaganda. *The Völkischer Beobachter* succeeded in gaining him multi-regional exposure, using boulevard press techniques for the purposes of political agitation. The National Socialists went on to diversify their appeal in more specialized organs such as the radical and elitist *Schwarze Korps* and the crude and pornographic *Der Stürmer*. Radio brought the crucial breakthrough for Hitler, however. The medium carried his voice in the factories, in bars, and on the streets. " 'The Führer will now speak,' it was said and the nation listened to the radio. During the war the people were electrified by special announcements that were introduced with a popular fanfare." By 1941 65% of German households owned a "people's receiver" (*Volksempfänger*).[17]

After Hitler's rise to power, Joseph Goebbels, his Minister of Propaganda and Public Enlightenment, relied on film as the key instrument of political persuasion. Leni Riefenstahl's chronicle of the 1934 NSDAP Rally at Nuremberg, *Triumph of the Will*, is a singular artifact in the history of audio-visual mass communications. Adolf Hitler is the only politician of the twentieth century who would play the lead role in a feature-length film devoted to the creation of his own political legend. The Hitler who won over Germany, however, was not just the larger-than-life subject of monumental spectacle and newsreel footage. Equally important for the promulgation of his myth were smaller scale posters and photographs (e.g., the cards sold in cigarette packages and collected in photo albums). Indeed, there was a functional relation between large and small images, between overwhelming presentations and mass-produced images of stylized intimacy, shots where Hitler mingles with his people and he stands with normal citizens in everyday situations. Hitler's iconography sought to engender equal measures of awe and identification.[18] "While appearing as a superman," T. W. Adorno notes, "the leader must at the same time work the miracle of appearing as an average person, just as Hitler posed as a composite of King Kong and the suburban barber."[19]

Triumph of the Will is National Socialism's ultimate self-advertisement, the celebration of a new order staged for almost five dozen cameras (30 cinematographers plus an additional 29 newsreel cameras charged to capture additional footage). The party convention offered a grand photo opportunity in which politics and showmanship became indistinguishable. It was a proto-media event, a simulation, a spectacle choreographed and performed for cameras, produced to be shown to mass audiences throughout Germany and throughout the world. The Nazis carefully stage-managed Hitler's voice and image. No actor was allowed to play him and no feature film dramatized his life's story. In that sense his calculated absence was a crucial part of his captivating presence. The first full sentence of Riefenstahl's film articulates a mass demand to experience their leader from a close-up perspective: "We want to see our Führer!"

Hitler emanated as the extension of state-of-the-art technology and audio-visual instrumentation, similar to MGM's Great Oz (*The Wizard of Oz*, 1939), albeit a malevolent variation. Hitler is neither a monster nor an Everyman; his evil is neither metaphysical nor banal. His renown was—and is—that of a media star and a modern anti-hero. In that sense, he is very much a man of our times.

Imagining Hitler/Imaginary Hitler

In my final section, let me return to *Schtonk* and the Hitler diaries and make three concluding points.

1. The Hitler diaries were a casebook example of forgery as Monroe C. Beardsley defines the term, an instance of "passing off one's own work as another's."[20] (Given Kujau's reliance on Domarus, the diaries also consisted of an equal measure of plagiarism.) The homemade concoctions, however unremarkable, appealed to mass fantasies about the leader's private life. They represented forgeries for which there was no original, for we know that Hitler did not like to write and did not keep a journal. Indeed, he was a person loath to leaving tracks, be they personal notes or letters. As Koch-Hillebrecht points out, Hitler "did not wish to commit himself in writing and expressly prohibited that graphologists might look at lengthier samples of articles bearing his longhand."[21] Despite Hitler's immodesty, John Lukacs relates, the leader

> did not wish to see an adulatory biography of himself published during his lifetime in Germany; in fact, except for a few odd earlier biographies, photographic albums, and collections of his speeches, there were none . . . From his various remarks, it also seems that—unlike Churchill or de Gaulle, or even Napoleon at St. Helena—in the event of his retirement, Hitler would have had little inclination to write or dictate his memoirs.[22]

When we speak of the historical figure Hitler, it is difficult to pin down the object under discussion. In a crucial way he remains to this day an imaginary signifier, a sign with an uncertain referent.

Postwar documentaries about the Third Reich would be unthinkable without Riefenstahl's stylizations which themselves were acts of aggrandizement and inflation meant to bolster the Nazi cause. Lacking counterimages and counterstrategies, critical approaches to Nazi visual culture customarily seek refuge in distanced verbal commentaries, paring off words against far more powerful images, as in Joachim Fest's *Hitler—A Career*. "This film," maintains Wim Wenders, "is so fascinated by its object, by its importance, in which it takes part ('He [Hitler] gave truth to the phrase that history on occasion loves to take shape in a SINGLE person'), that this object again and again takes control of the film, becoming its secret narrator." Fest, claims Wenders, is woefully mistaken in believing that his voice-over narration can compete with the language of demagogic images.[23] To this day very few filmmakers have succeeded in finding a visual or discursive distance from Nazi images.

In looking back at the Third Reich, we always seem to be partaking of Nazi simulations, experiencing the world through their eyes, participating in their fictions and sharing their fantasies, no matter how offensive or horrific we consider them to be. Hitler has no grave or memorial. The site where we recall him and where he continues to live is above all the mass media.

2. If Hitler's image appears to be unreal and mythical, this is not solely the result of postwar distortion, but equally a consequence of his own fradulent legacy. To speak of a "real Hitler" is difficult—unless, as Rosenbaum argues, one seeks it "in his slippery, conniving falseness."[24] How can we distinguish a private person from the public presence given Hitler's incessant posing and performativity? Even statements made to intimate circles in his own quarters late at night indicated how the leader remained "on" during his downtime.[25] Hitler's prime achievement, according to J. P. Stern, was

> to introduce a conception of personal authenticity into the public sphere and proclaim it as the chief value and sanction of politics. What he does is to translate the notions of genuineness and sincerity and living experience . . . from the private and poetic sphere into the sphere of public affairs; and to validate this move by the claim that he, the exceptional individual with his intimate personal experience of 'the little man's weal and woe,' is the Nation's representative by virtue of the genuineness of that experience.[26]

The element of deception (*Betrug*) was essential for Hitler; he wrote about it candidly and at length in *Mein Kampf*. According to Alan Bullock, Hitler initially only pretended to be a true believer. He would come, however, to believe sincerely in his own dissimulation. He was an actor inextricably bound to his own act, a man whose identity inhered in a duplicity and fakery so intense that it took over his person. In Bullock's explanation, the leader's dynamic "begins with what seems like a cynical, opportunistic calculation: What is most important is not to believe but to be *seen* to believe; that is, the acting of belief is more important than the sincerity. But if there is calculation behind the act initially . . . , what follows is 'a remarkable process' in which the actor-deceiver becomes carried away, possessed, overcome by his own act, a believer in his own deception. Possessed by himself."[27]

This notion of an identity that knows no real person finds a hyperbolic extension in Don DeLillo's *Running Dog*. Numerous groups of people search for footage of Hitler in the bunker, hoping that it will reveal the true leader during his final hours. When the film finally unreels, it proves to be an altogether murky and inconclusive artifact. We see what appears to be

Hitler doing an imitation of Chaplin's Great Dictator, i.e., a simulation of a simulation. The *mise-en-abyme* effect of the image increases, however, with the subsequent information that the onscreen figure may himself be merely Hitler's double.

Hitler, the great imposter and master plier of authenticity, represents a radical extension of the Weimar Republic's culture of cynicism. Paraphrasing Erich Wulffen's treatise of 1923, *Die Psychologie des Hochstaplers* (*The Psychology of the Imposter*), Peter Sloterdijk explains how the deceiver enacts collective dreams in a compelling performance which becomes a practiced piece of art. "Swindle, like poetry and dramaturgy, is dominated by the pleasure principle. It obeys the magical spell of great roles, the pleasure in playing games, the need for self-aggrandizement, the sense of improvisation. The great impostors build up nothing more than the stages for their roles."[28] Hitler was a deceiver who was carried away, overcome by a belief in his own deception, a man whose very being was a show and a sham.

Authenticity mediated by lights, cameras, and microphones served as this charlatan's enabling act. Modern fascist leaders, as Horkheimer and Adorno point out, are not so much supermen as the creations of propaganda machines, the focal points at which mass fantasies come together. These individuals, like movie stars, "are powerless in themselves but deputize for all the other powerless individuals, and embody the fullness of power for them, without themselves being anything other than the vacant spaces taken up accidentally by power."[29] Hitler is above all the nothingness of a projective space, a container for strong fantasies and immense yearnings, the embodiment of great hates and fierce desires.[30]

3. In the *Stern* debacle a transparent forgery and a poorly written fiction assumed the status of valuable properties and lucrative commodities. *Schtonk* dramatizes the loss of reality that gave rise to the affair (a condition shared by trickster and dupes alike) not so much as a pathology as an everyday state of affairs, a consequence of free market enterprise and untrammeled avarice. The film's picaresque drama discloses the frenetic workings of the culture industry, an apparatus inextricably bound to the buying and selling of allure and illusion. And the scenario demonstrates the continuing appeal of Hitler's Reich of fakery for our contemporary society of spectacle. Hitler and the Nazis were consummate cynics and impressive showmen. As I have suggested elsewhere, they might well be seen as postmodernity's secret sharers.[31] The film is not only about an act of forgery; it foregrounds its own workings as a film that shamelessly exhibits its own acts of forgery in representing this forgery which itself is in fact an extension of a bogus legacy.

Much of this mass market movie's indictment of the culture industry takes place in the top floor of a publishing house whose majority owner was Bertelsmann, the largest German media concern. At a crucial point the editorial staff beholds the secret diaries and agrees they should be published. "It would be a sensation." But the obvious question poses itself: Are they genuine? Why, someone asks, do the letters on the cover read "FH" rather than "AH"? After all, the man's name wasn't Fritz Hitler. Consternation ensues as the figures try to account for the discrepancy. No denying it, what they all see is FH. How to explain it? The sound F slides off the reporter's tongue and expands into the phrase "Führer Hitler."

> "That's it!"
> "Nonsense!"
> "Flag on high, maybe" [Fahne hoch].
> "Baloney!"
> "Führer . . . Führer . . . Führer's Heil, Führer's hound."
> "Führer's hound . . ." [One editor sneers.]
> "Führer's . . . hand . . . Führer's head . . . quarters. Führer's headquarters!"

That's it. The figures in the room nod in agreement. Yes, it would seem, they have found the answer: "Führer's headquarters."

Or perhaps not. What do these letters really stand for? There is, I believe, an obvious, but unspoken conclusion. The "F" is a purloined letter, a letter there for all to see, but a letter that no one manages to read correctly. This letter, the evidence of a bungled forgery, makes it apparent that the legacy that is the Führer's is a fake (*Fälschung*), a fake that people want and need to believe in. Fälschung Hitler. Faszination Hitler. Fantasie Hitler. Fake Hitler. The scandal around the Hitler diaries attests to the lasting power and continuing fascination of that fakery.

Notes

1. Quoted in Ron Rosenbaum, *Explaining Hitler: The Search for the Origins of His Evil* (New York: Random House, 1998), p. 68.
2. Richard Hugo, *The Hitler Diaries* (New York: Morrow, 1982), p. 32.
3. Quoted in Robert Harris, *Selling Hitler* (New York: Penguin, 1986), p. 321. I have relied on this invaluable study for the particulars of the *Stern* scandal. All subsequent references from this source will be cited in the main text.
4. Translated in English as Adolf Hitler, *Speeches and Proclamations, 1932–1945: The Chronicle of a Dictatorship*, ed. Max Domarus, trans. Mary Fran Gilbert (London: Tauris, 1990).
5. Alvin Rosenfeld, *Imagining Hitler* (Bloomington: Indiana University Press, 1985), p. 44.
6. See Peter Körte, "Ernst dämonisiert, dann banalisiert: Helmut Dietl über seine Hitler-Tagebuch-Fälschungs-Film *Schtonk*," *Frankfurter Rundschau* 12 March 1992.
7. For an incisive discussion of the problematic role of film actors as body doubles in representations of history, see Jean-Louis Comolli, "Historical Fiction: A Body Too Much," *Screen* 19.2 (Summer 1978): 41–53.
8. Don DeLillo, *Running Dog* (New York: Vintage, 1989 [1978]), p. 52.
9. H. G. Pflaum, "Der ganz finale Wahnsinn: Helmut Dietls Film-Komödie *Schtonk*," *Süddeutsche Zeitung* 12 March 1992.
10. Rosenbaum, p. xii.
11. Rosenfeld, p. 4.

12. Rosenfeld, p. xvi.
13. Saul Friedländer, *Reflections of Nazism: An Essay on Kitsch and Death*, trans. Thomas Weyr (New York: Harper & Row, 1984), pp. 59–60.
14. Friedländer, p. 72.
15. Rosenfeld, p. xviii. "What is uncanny about the new fascination with Hitler is its resemblance—often recognizable in impulse, idiom, tone, and direction—to the fascination of the 1930s and 1940s."
16. Susan Sontag, "Fascinating Fascism," in *Under the Sign of Saturn* (New York: Vintage, 1981), p. 97.
17. Manfred Koch-Hillebrecht, *Homo Hitler: Psychogramm des deutschen Diktators* (Munich: Goldmann, 1999), p. 57.
18. See Eike Hennig, "Hitler-Porträts abseits des Regierungsalltags. Einer von uns und für uns?" in *Führerbilder: Hitler, Mussolini, Roosevelt, Stalin in Fotografie und Film*, ed. Martin Loiperdinger, Rudolf Herz, and Ulrich Pohlmann (Munich: Piper, 1995), pp. 27–50.
19. T. W. Adorno, "Freudian Theory and the Pattern of Fascist Propaganda," in *The Essential Frankfurt School Reader*, ed. Andrew Arato and Eike Gebhardt (New York: Urizen, 1978), p. 127.
20. Quoted in Sándor Radnóti, *The Fake: Forgery and Its Place in Art*, trans. Ervin Dunai (Lanham: Rowman & Littlefield, 1999), p. 11.
21. *Homus Hitler*, p. 35. See Lukacs, p. 49: "One of the problems of the historiography of Hitler is the scarcity of written documents he left behind."
22. Lukacs, p. 3.
23. Wim Wenders, "That's Entertainment: Hitler (1977)," in *West German Filmmakers on Film: Visions and Voices*, trans. and ed. Eric Rentschler (New York: Holmes & Meier, 1988), p. 130.
24. Rosenbaum, p. 73.
25. Cf. Lukacs, p. 157: "'Private' may not always be a useful term, since so many of his statements to his private circle were meant to impress them."
26. J. P. Stern, *Hitler: The Führer and the People* (Berkeley/Los Angeles: University of California Press, 1975), p. 24.
27. Rosenbaum, p. 88.
28. Peter Sloterdijk, *Critique of Cynical Reason*, trans. Michael Eldred (Minneapolis: University of Minnesota Press, 1987), p. 486.
29. Max Horkheimer and Theodor W. Adorno, *Dialectic of Enlightenment*, trans. John Cumming (New York: Seabury, 1972), p. 236.
30. Cf. Max Picard, *Hitler in Our Selves*, trans. Heinrich Hauser (Hinsdale, Illinois: Regnery, 1947), p. 79.
31. Eric Rentschler, *The Ministry of Illusion: Nazi Cinema and Its Afterlife* (Cambridge: Harvard University Press, 1996), p. 223.

Contributors

Reinhold Brinkmann is James Edward Ditson Professor Emeritus at Harvard University. He has written extensively on the history and aesthetics of music from the eighteenth through the twentieth centuries. He was awarded the Humboldt Prize in 1998 and the Ernst von Siemens Musikpreis in 2001. His most recent publications include: *Musik nachdenken: Reinhold Brinkmann und Wolfgang Rohm im Gespräch* (2001); *Late Idyll: The Second Symphony of Johannes Brahms* (1995, pb. 1997); *Schumann und Eichendorff: Studien zum Liederkreis op. 39* (1977); *Arnold Schönberg und der Engel der Geschichte* (Wiener Vorlesungen 82); and, coedited with Christoph Wolff, *Music of My Future: The Schoenberg Quartets and Trio* (2000) and *Driven into Paradise: The Musical Migration from Nazi Germany to the United States* (1999).

Julie A. Buckler is Harris K. Weston Associate Professor of Slavic Languages and Literatures at Harvard. She works on imperial Russian literary and social culture, with an emphasis on performing arts and urban environment. She is the author of *The Literary Lorgnette: Attending Opera in Imperial Russia* (2000) and *Mapping St. Petersburg: Urban Text and Topography in Imperial Russia* (forthcoming, 2004).

Brad Epps is Professor of Romance Languages and Literatures at Harvard University. He has published over fifty articles on modern literature, film, art, and architecture from Spain, Latin America, Catalonia, and France and is the author of *Significant Violence: Oppression and Resistance in the Narratives of Juan Goytisolo*. He is currently preparing two books: *Daring to*

Write, on gay and lesbian issues in Latin America, Spain, and Latino cultures in the United States, and *Barcelona and Beyond*, on the city and modern Catalan culture.

Ewa Lajer-Burcharth is Professor of History of Art and Architecture at Harvard University. In addition to numerous articles, she has published *Necklines: The Art of Jacques-Louis David after the Terror* (1999) and *Pompadour's Touch: The Other Eighteenth Century* (forthcoming). Her research interests include the cultural history of the self, with an emphasis on the eighteenth century, and questions of subjectivity, sexuality, and modernity. She has also published on the role of video and the new media in contemporary art.

John E. Malmstad is Samuel Hazzard Cross Professor of Slavic Languages and Literatures at Harvard University. He is the author of many studies of modernist Russian literature, among them a biography of Mikhail Kuzmin, and the editor of several Russian-language editions of the works of modernist authors such as Andrei Bely, Kuzmin, and Khodasevich. He is presently at work on a critical biography of Andrei Bely and a two-volume edition of the poetry of Bely for the Poet's Library (in Russian).

Derek Pearsall is the Gurney Professor of English Language and Literature Emeritus of Harvard University, as well as Honorary Research Professor at the University of York. Published work includes a monograph on John Lydgate (1970), a study of *Landscapes and Seasons of the Medieval World* (with Elizabeth Salter, 1973), a history of Old English and Middle English Poetry (1977), editions of the C-Text of *Piers Plowman* (1978) and of Chaucer's *Nun's Priest's Tale* (for the Variorum Chaucer, 1983), a critical study of *The Canterbury Tales* (1985), a critical biography of Chaucer, *The Life of Geoffrey Chaucer* (1992), an anthology of English writings from 1375 to 1575 titled *Chaucer to Spenser* (1999), and a monograph on Gothic Europe (2001).

Eric Rentschler is Professor of German languages and Literature at Harvard University. His publications have concentrated on German film history, theory, and criticism, with particular emphasis on cinema during the Weimar Republic, the Third Reich, and the post-1945 era. He is the author of numerous articles and books, including *West German Film in the Course of Time* (1984), *German Film and Literature* (1986), *West German Filmmakers on Film* (1988), *Augenzeugen* (1988), *The Films of G. W. Pabst* (1990), and *The Ministry of Illusion* (1996). His current project bears the working title "Courses in Time: Film in the Federal Republic of Germany, 1949–1989."

Judith Ryan is the Robert K. and Dale J. Weary Professor of German and Comparative Literature at Harvard University. She is the author of *Umschlag und Verwandlung* (on Rilke's poetry; 1972); *The Uncompleted Past: Postwar German Novels and the Third Reich* (1983); *The Vanishing Subject: Early Psychology and Literary Modernism* (1991); and *Rilke, Modernism and Poetic Tradition* (1999). She has also written articles on such authors as Franz Kafka, Paul Celan, Christa Wolf, and Günter Grass. She is currently at work on a book about the relation of the contemporary novel to literary theory.

Susan Rubin Suleiman is the C. Douglas Dillon Professor of the Civilization of France and Professor of Comparative Literature at Harvard. Her books include *Authoritarian Fictions: The Ideological Novel as a Literary Genre* (1983); *Subversive Intent: Gender, Politics, and the Avant-Garde* (1990), *Risking Who One Is: Encounters with Contemporary Art and Literature* (1994), *Budapest Diary: In Search of the Motherbook* (1996); and the edited volume *Exile and Creativity: Signposts, Travelers, Outsiders, Backward Glances* (1998). She is coeditor of the forthcoming anthology *Contemporary Jewish Writing in Hungary* (2003). Her current project is a book on "crises of memory" and the Second World War.

Sarolta A. Takács, Associate Professor of Classics at Rutgers University. Professor Takács received her Ph.D. in history from the University of California at Los Angeles. Her research focuses on two ancient cultures: pagan Rome and its Christian successor, Byzantium. She is the author of *Isis and Sarapis in the Roman World* (1995) and numerous articles on Roman religion and history as well as subject matters dealing with Byzantium. Professor Takács has also edited a number of books on Roman and Byzantine topics.

Alfred Thomas is Professor of Slavic and Baltic Languages and Literatures at the University of Illinois at Chicago and Head of Department. From 1996 to 2002, he was John L. Loeb Associate Professor of the Humanities at Harvard University. He is the author of four books, the most recent of which are *Anne's Bohemia: Czech Literature and Society, 1310–1420* (1998) and *Embodying Bohemia: Questions of Gender and Sexuality in Modern Czech Culture* (2004).

Index